THE DEVIL'S DISCUS

RAYNE KRUGER

To confuse truth with lies or good with evil is to
mistake the Devil's lethal discus for the Buddha's lotus.
Siamese saying

DMP
Publications

Rayne Kruger
THE DEVIL'S DISCUS: The Death of Ananda, King of Siam

First published London 1964
Second edition 2009

DMP Publications
Hong Kong

Cover image: Funeral pavilion of King Ananda. See also images facing pp. 146, 147.

ISBN: 978-988-97752-5-4

CONTENTS

ILLUSTRATIONS

vii

viii

ACKNOWLEDGEMENTS

Many people helped me with this book and I am deeply grateful to each of them.

The pleasure of naming those who are in any way connected with the subject matter must be denied me, either for reasons which they will know or because for me to mention some and not others would be invidious.

The ballistics department of a leading police force gave me invaluable, if unofficial, guidance and test-chamber facilities. In London, the renowned forensic authority Dr Francis Camps was good enough to check the MS, as a result of which he concurred in my conclusions on the facts here presented.

I also thank Sir Geoffrey Thompson (and Hutchinson & Co. (Publishers) Ltd.), Dr David Stafford-Clark (and Penguin Books Ltd), and Dr P. M. Yap for their kind permission for me to quote from their published works.

Before

In the summer of 1946 the London *Times* carried an Associated Press despatch from Bangkok datelined 9 June:

The young King of Siam, Ananda Mahidol, was found dead in a bedroom at the Barompiman Palace today with a bullet wound in his head. The discovery was made by a servant shortly before noon. The Chief of Police and the directors of the Chulalongkorn Hospital, who were called immediately to the palace, said afterwards that the death was accidental . . . Great crowds have gathered in silent grief outside the palace. Most of them were unaware of the death of the King until news was broadcast by the Government radio at seven o'clock.

AP's correspondent erred in detail. But to extract hard fact out of Siam—Thailand—is not easy. He did well to get the core of the matter right: twenty-year-old King Ananda was dead, shot through the head.

No killing has ever taken place in such illimitable splendour. The Barompiman Hall is part of the Grand Palace, which shines with a tinsel glory unlike anything in this world.

Beyond the room where the slight figure of the dead youth lay flanked by blocks of ice in the loneliness of his double bed, the other buildings of the Palace keep wondrous company. Their telescoped roofs are of glazed tile, their gables a jewelled intricacy of designs and figures in relief, and their ridges and eaves decorated with serpentine dragons whose scales of fragmented glass seem to split light into an iridescence of purple, saffron, green, and sapphire. Pinnacles of gold and coloured brilliance rise into the ever-blue sky. There are frescoed cloisters; pillars and pavilions of porcelain mosaic; great doors inlaid with pearl; sculptured demi-animals; and a pair of gaudy giants which are said to fall on anybody who walks between them with evil in his heart—so the killer never passed this way, that's for sure.

Among these glowing wonders none challenges credulity more than the Temple of the Emerald Buddha. It is named after the image within, that supremely sacred, supreme symbol of hope and happiness for all Siamese. The image, so huge in importance yet scarcely a metre high, sits aloft on folded legs and with hands in lap, eyes fixed upon eternity. It is not as slender as most Siamese images of the Buddha, nor half so fat as the Chinese. On the morning of Ananda's death, 9 June, being in the hot season, the Emerald Buddha would have been dressed in fewer gems than during the other two seasons (the wet and the so-called cold), but even this garb is beyond price—though of utterly incalculable value is the stone itself, of jade not emerald, carved by an artist left in India by Alexander the Great.[1]*

For all the closeness of the Temple of the Emerald Buddha to the King's quarters in the Barompiman Hall, the sacred image was remote and impersonal, bathed in a white glacial light. Friendlier and more personal was the image separated from the corpse on the bed by only a dozen paces and a curtain. Like his subjects, Ananda kept his household image of the Buddha. Like theirs it was in the upper storey of his dwelling, since respect demands of a Siamese that his head should be below that of a superior. Ananda's bedroom was also on the upper storey, and the Buddha room formed a kind of large recess off it.

Before getting into bed the previous night the King had gone, as on all his nights since infancy, to make obeisance and pray in front of his household Buddha. He lit candles, offered flowers, and performed that most affecting of gestures, the *wei*, which a Siamese also does instead of a handshake, by placing his fingers and palms together before his face (or at stomach level if acknowledging the *wei* of an inferior). But on the morning of 9 June neither Ananda's household image of the Buddha, nor the most sacred one gazing out over all his kingdom from the nearby Temple of the Emerald Buddha, availed to save him when a single bullet spun from the muzzle of a ·45 American Army pistol and in one-thousandth of a second travelled through his head.

A blob of metal, a thousandth of a second: and round the dead king gathered a mystery as extraordinary as any in modern times. To this day it spreads a hush upon the East. Round it have turned the lives of men in the anguish of the death cell or exile. The consequences for a nation of twenty-three million people have been, and still are, immeasurable. And peace in South-East Asia, precious to the peace

* References listed on page 247.

of the world, is precarious while the voices that cry for revenge, or merely for justice, remain unsilenced.

The basic question is simple enough: Who killed King Ananda? The answer, if you accept it, is likewise brief. But between question and answer little is simple and nothing brief.

Before he can reach the tangled heart of the mystery, the investigator finds he has become a detective on a vast scale. I had to try to understand a nation which consists of a unique aristocracy, a marvellously charming peasantry, and between them a middle class half Chinese and half Siamese, unsure in its idealism and its corruption of where hope begins and resignation ends. I had to travel Europe as well as Asia in order to scour history, the pedigree of families, the depths of private lives, and the complexities of politics, because none had been completely or objectively recorded. All are inextricably related to Ananda's death, therefore all must be comprehended*.

This could only be attempted by endless interrogation of innumerable people. Many had to be tracked down in secret; few would speak openly. Siam is a police state, and royalty has the ambience of divinity, so that fear and reverence alike explain their reluctance to talk; even more, to talk the truth. In the end they did talk. But in return for their trust I pledged myself to conceal their identity in order to protect them from danger to their life, liberty, employment or social position.

It would add piquancy to this book if I were to describe the hazards and shifts to which our bargain committed them and me; but if I were to do so, or even to name people not endangered by speaking freely to me, I would provide clues as revealing to the knowledgeable as a direct betrayal of identity. And really what we are after are the facts, not how I got them or from whom. Nevertheless, if the reader has to rely on my integrity without benefit of defined sources, he is entitled to two assurances. The first is that I have accepted no information as valid unless it has been fully checked, so that—let this be noted in Bangkok—no single informant is responsible for any single detail. The second assurance is that my approach entirely lacked bias or preconceptions, for the simple reason that I started by knowing nothing and nobody, that I toe no political line, and that I reached no conclusion until all the data had been gathered.

* For the reader's benefit, a short list of the principal figures appearing in this book has been printed on pages 245-6

3

It is not necessary to start as far back as I am about to describe. Yet it is an advantage because in Siam the present is so impregnated by the past that the processes behind Ananda's life and death belong to both. And both provide a guide as rewarding to curiosity as the sequel.

Some authorities say that the Siamese came from Outer Mongolia. This summons up a picture of rugged men in turbulent deserts, very different from the petite and graceful people I met from the teak forests of their hinterland which spreads down from immense mountains; or the shores of the mild green Gulf on their southern borders; or the rich ricefields of their central plain dominated by the city of Bangkok where factory stack, radio mast and demi-skyscraper seem as uncouth by the side of their shapely pagodas as the Westerner's limbs and features appear gross compared with their own. At all events they were immigrants to Siam, for by 3000 BC they were certainly in Southern China—before the Chinese, who then harassed them into trekking further south. On the way, they met tribes enslaved by overlords, unlike themselves who were *thais*, free men, though not until 1939 did they officially call themselves by this name, and their country Thailand, instead of Siamese and Siam—names whose origin is wrapped in controversy.

For the greater part of their history the Siamese have been free men in their external status. The gall of colonialism has scarcely been suffered, permitting them to cultivate their superiority like any Englishman. Indeed, when an Englishman and a Siamese sit down together it is hard to tell whose cheerful condescension is the greater. But though they have in common this quality, and a strong attachment to tradition, it is a fact very material to our story that the Siamese knew nothing of individual freedom—democracy—until the beginning of the twentieth century.

Their trek took them down the valleys of the rivers by which the Himalayan snows give life to tropical south-east Asia, itself reaching like a forceps into the Indian Ocean and the Yellow Sea: the lands today called Burma, the Malayan peninsula, Thailand, Laos, Cambodia and the Vietnams. When Marco Polo was bringing back noodles from Cathay to found the spaghetti industry of his native country, the sub-continent was called Lesser India. He wrote of brazil wood and gold and elephants, though 'it is such a savage place that few people go there'. The Siamese themselves were probably still much

4

further north, keeping but a tenuous claim to freedom as their tribes paid tribute to the stronger peoples in possession. The greatest of these were the Khmers, whose weird and mighty capital of Angkor—even in ruin a wonder of the world—they helped build with tributes of labour and water. In return they acquired notions of art and religion which prevailed when they formed their first sovereign state, called The Kingdom of the Dawn of Happiness, in the thirteenth century.

Its most famous king was Rama the Valiant, who may be reckoned founder of the throne Ananda was to ascend. His court bore Hindu (Brahminic) influences transmitted to the Khmers and lasting to this day, but deep in the soul of his race he implanted the southern form of Buddhism, also brought from India via the Khmers. The complications of religion do not end with this blending of Hinduism and Buddhism: outside almost every Siamese house stands a structure like a dovecote, the abode of the spirit of that house, perpetuating the animism which the Siamese brought with them from China. The Siamese have no difficulty reconciling these various beliefs, to which they often add a liberal dash of astrology. Their borrowings in religion and art were repeated in their adoption of a written language, though likewise transmuted into an expression wholly Siamese. Here is the earliest known specimen, belonging to Rama the Valiant's rule:

This Kingdom of the Dawn of Happiness is good. In the water there is fish, in the field there is rice. The King takes no advantage of the people. Who wants to trade, trades. The faces of the people shine bright with happiness.

In spite of the long face and longer hand of the West, and in spite of the grim events to be related, you have there still the true prospectus of a nation.

Rama the Valiant's line faded. His state merged into a larger kingdom with its capital established (1350) about fifty miles north of present-day Bangkok and on the same broad river. It was called the Divine Blessed City of Ayudhya (pr. eye-youth-ee-ya). The Kings of Ayudhya ruled to the confines of almost all modern Siam. They avenged themselves on the Khmers who retreated, calling their country Cambodia and leaving sacked Angkor to the jungle for six hundred years.

When the first Europeans arrived in about 1500—Portuguese in the

wake of Vasco de Gama's voyage round the Cape of Good Hope—
they found Ayudhya to be a city of a million people and hundreds of
wats, monasteries. In the latter were schools, libraries and temples with
huge images of the Buddha, one nearly fifty feet high and covered in
eight hundred pounds' weight of gold.

Siamese life from that day to this has been extraordinarily un-
changing. If it is imagined as three concentric rings with the King-
Government at the centre and the family at the periphery, the
monastery occupies the middle ring. A Siamese first goes there in his
supplicant mother's womb. He toils there over his schoolbooks, and
kneels there to have the top-knot of his hair cut off at puberty. He
attends festivals there with his parents to eye prospective brides and to
make merit by bringing gifts for the monks. He retires there himself
to serve in the priesthood for a season before his marriage (one enters
or leaves the Order at will). He goes there for services, or to have his
fortune told, or for intellectual discussion. And in due course his body
is carried there for cremation. Peasant or king, his life has been threaded
into the monastery as intimately as strands of silk through a loom.
This is substantially so even today when he also goes to the monastery
to watch television if he has no set of his own.

The continuity of ancient ways has its apotheosis in the jet aeroplane
carrying the present King, Ananda's brother, on his travels abroad.
Members of his entourage in their Paris dresses or Savile Row suits
crawl up the aisle on their knees when they approach their monarch to
give him the benefit of their Cambridge- or Harvard-trained minds.
(In the houses of the more conservative aristocracy in Bangkok one is
apt to see a servant, intent on keeping his head below his superior's,
moving in the same way while carrying a tray of cocktails. The
Siamese's smallness and supple grace make the spectacle less absurd
than you might think. And its motive of respect is very touching to
the Westerner who is prone to put scorn before reverence.)

The royalist attitude exemplified at thirty thousand feet in an
airliner stems from the Ayudhyan kingdom when people gave liege
not to a country but a king. His rule was absolute because he was—is
still in the eyes of millions—divine. Such sacred blood could never be
spilt: treacherous relatives were never decapitated but tied in a silken
sack and beaten to death by a scented sandal-wood club. He had many
relations because he was polygamous. His chief wife ranked as queen

and her eldest son usually succeeded. A whole complex of titles was created according to relationship with the king, though to prevent the aristocracy eventually outnumbering commoners no title could nor can continue through more than five generations, the title of each being a rung lower than its predecessor.

A long way below the aristocracy (and the few commoners who reached high office) was the peasant. Except for occasional conscription for war or public works he was left alone to cultivate his basic freeholding of ten acres. He still is, usually, a freeholder. Much of the land is so fertile that rice springs up at a touch of the sun. The absence of starvation, over-population, or landlordism has long kept him impervious to the political ideas of East or West. Nor has he felt the need to work more than he must in that torrid climate. Commerce has been left to the immigrant Chinese, whose energy has enriched the country and their blood Ananda's line; but they present the acute problems of a large unassimilable minority.

After the Portuguese arrived in Ayudhya the Dutch, English and French followed. All were well received, given trading facilities, and the King himself contributed to their first church. Tolerance is an integral part of Buddhism which holds that every man's search for salvation should be conducted in the chapel of his own mind. But the Enlightened One also taught gentleness; and though I do not know a more gentle race than the Siamese (except when they kick each other in their peculiar form of boxing), violence was no stranger to the upper hierarchy of the kingdom. Murderous intrigue often surrounded the throne: on one occasion a king took the precaution of murdering seven of his sons lest any gave way to premature ambition. And there were wars. Besides Christianity the Portuguese brought from the West the art of gun-casting; but the elephant, used like the modern tank, was the chief tactical weapon in campaigns against neighbouring states. The Siamese usually won, except against their greatest rival, Burma, who had the edge of a long and bitter struggle.

The trouble started over a Burmese king's request for a white elephant. The Siamese have long revered these animals—albinos, more pink than white—as sacred harbingers of regal joy. A belief lingers that being appendages of majesty, as they still are, though kept at the zoo instead of their great stables in the Grand Palace, they are fed in infancy by young women lined up with breasts bared to their ravening trunks.

7

Certainly they have always been excessively pampered, the king feeding them with the first shoots of sugar cane and bestowing royal names and titles on them. The king to whom the Burmese made their request had no fewer than seven white elephants, a remarkably auspicious number.

Rejection of the Burmese request started three hundred years of intermittent warfare, creating as many legendary heroes and villains as the wars between England and France, until the British conquest of Burma ended the constant threat of invasion from the Three Pagoda pass beyond the River Kwai. But before then, on a night in 1767, the Burmese entered the city of Ayudhya to loot, sack and destroy it utterly, butchering the king along with so many of his subjects that counting those they removed as slaves they left only ten thousand people where a million had lived. In the four centuries of the Kingdom of Ayudhya's existence thirty-three kings ruled it, of whom a third were murdered or murdered their rivals. The murderers included *state officials, brothers, a mother*; so that when Ananda died, and persons of each description were closely concerned, suspicion had plenty of precedent to draw on.

The Ayudhya destroyed by the Burmese had become one of the great trading centres of the East. The safe broad river flowing past it made this possible, and the animistic Siamese gave it the high title of Duke, *Chao Phaya*, though Westerners persist in calling it the Menam, the Siamese word for river. Its use for trade was stimulated by the kings, especially one who operated through a Greek named Constantine Phaulkon. He arrived as a humble sailor in a British East Indiaman, rose to bear the august title of Lord of Cool Knowledge, and was hacked to pieces in 1688 because he aroused fears of Western aggrandizement. A stockade was thereupon built round Siam against the West. It stayed up for a century and a half, until Ananda's great-grandfather pulled it down—and sowed the seeds of Ananda's tragedy.

For it was from the ruins of Ayudhya that the Chakris arose, the line of kings to which Ananda belonged. A general named Taksin escaped from the city, led a resistance movement that ousted the Burmese, established a new capital, and proclaimed himself King. To the post of commander-in-chief he appointed the son of an old palace official and his Chinese wife. Up to a few decades ago the name of an office of state became the name of its incumbent, who abandoned his birth-name. Hence Taksin's *chakri*—commander-in-chief—acquired this title as his own name. While Chakri was on campaign a revolt broke out against Taksin who had gone mad and was fasting and praying to enable himself to fly. The rebel leader offered the throne to Chakri. It was accepted on 6 April, 1782. The new King had Taksin executed—with a scented sandalwood club—and then the rebel leader, lest rebellion became a habit.

Chakri is called Rama I. On the Menam about twenty miles from the sea he built a new capital out of the village of the Wild Plum—*Bangkok*—renaming it the Jewelled Abode of the God Indra, which name Westerners ignore. It burgeoned into monasteries and palaces amid a maze of canals. Its heart then as now was the Grand Palace. Every visitor knows the high white crenellated wall surrounding this miniature city within a city—temples, mansions, pavilions, audience chambers, pleasure gardens, theatres, and that forbidden zone called the Inside, the quarter of the royal wives and their children.

The Inside typified the status of women which still obtains. The idea of companionship or partnership between man and wife grows but slowly through the few women educated in the West. A woman thinks it enough to look beautiful, to love with surpassing tenderness, to inhabit a mental wonderland between the crystalline reason of the Buddha and the dark mysteries of her horoscope, to smile upon perplexing life even while tears fill her rich black eyes, to hoard pretty jewels, to spoil her sons, to punish her daughters by pressing back their fingers and thereby giving them the flexibility of her own, to have food ready by dawn when monks pass by with their bowls, to sit quietly at one side in her house until her husband's visitors should choose to address her: so she lives like the moon, taking her glory from man the sun, but also like the moon she is not without a secret power that can direct the tides.

This power invariably comes up against another, the tradition which enables a man to take more than one wife. Even if modern laws only allow the first wife to be registered, society accepts without question any number of wives, or their children. A man may have a town house and a country villa, a fast car and a sedate limousine, but material possessions are limited in their variety whereas every new wife is a vision of unexplored bliss; alternatively, a poor man acquires an additional earner. There are also often business or diplomatic reasons

9

for polygamy. For instance, that first Chakri, Rama I, had twenty-nine wives, but many were the daughters of noblemen desirous of making an expedient gift which he expediently accepted.

The royal wives lived in and never could leave the Inside, with their forty-two children and thousands of retainers, who were all women including the police, since no man but the king could enter. Chakri's family attentions were in fact fitful. He was too busy campaigning or reconstructing Siam by codifying the laws, overhauling the scriptures, encouraging the arts, and establishing both a government and a splendid capital city. Right down to the present monarch, Bhoomipol, brother of Ananda, the Chakris have been singular people and often extraordinarily able. When Rama I was crowned, the ceremony—repeated for all his successors except Ananda who was thwarted by death—derived from the Hindu belief that after the earth had cooled down from its pristine state of a fireball, aromatic vapours attracted the gods to it: there they became humans and their leader the progenitor of all kings. Today even the most sophisticated Siamese cannot quite shake off a belief in the king's quasi-divinity. Outstanding achievement has given some justification for this belief and for the monarchy's thunderous titles, notably *Lord of Life*.

There was an attempted usurpation of the Chakri throne in Rama I's last days; and again in the first days of his son Rama II's accession, when the son of Taksin was moved to thoughts of revenge by his father's ghost. This troubled start to Rama II's reign doubtless owed something to his possession of a mere two white elephants, one of which was defective because its original owner had hoped to keep it by cutting off its tail. Later, however, three perfect new specimens were acquired, and all was well.

Rama II reformed many laws, including that which still permits divorce by mutual consent (failing consent, a wife's adultery enables her husband to divorce her, but not *vice versa*). Notable for his leniency he nevertheless prescribed severe penalties in an attempt to stop opium addiction, though it still goes on even though everyone in Siam knows that the worst punishment comes with death, when the addict turns into a horrible demented spook. Still, like Britain, he profited from opium exports, even if unlike her he did not go to war over Peking's obstinacy in refusing to import the stuff. British expansionism was now in full spate, doing him the service of overwhelming Burma but, with France's entry into Cochin-China, placing Siam uneasily between the two Powers. The West was pushing against the stockade put up after Phaulkon the Greek's death. Rama II haughtily paid little heed. He thought more of composing poetry, magnanimously conferring on his leading rival in the art the noble title of Sir Beautiful Speech.

But among his seventy-three children was a son of awkward and lovable genius who saw over· the anti-Western stockade and was destined to start pulling it dowm. This was Ananda's great-grandfather Mongkut, best publicized of Siamese kings because of Anna Leonowens' journals and the entertainment ˉbased on it, like *The King and I*.

He was serving in the priesthood when Rama II died, but though he was the eldest Celestial Prince—the title given to sons of the Queen —an elder and more ambitious half-brother got himself made Rama III. Mongkut stayed in his monastery, acting upon a Siamese principle that discretion is the better part of valour. It is a principle which makes them adroit diplomatists. Even when pushed too far they continue to give way: only, they come back promptly when opportunity offers, as though the inner spring of national being can infinitely be repressed without losing its torque.

Rama III worked so hard that he could not wake up in the mornings. No one could touch a royal personage. The penalty was death. This most powerful of palace taboos—to have its macabre exemplar when Ananda died—confined Rama III's page to stating the time, over and over for an hour, until his master stirred. Then Rama was all activity. The long religious ceremonies in court routine did not hamper his activity since he freely gave audience to his ministers against the background of monkish liturgy. The tolerance of the Buddhist church is very relaxing. Once when the present King returned to Bangkok from prolonged state visits abroad, I happened to go into a leading temple where eighty life-size models of monks sit in timeless immobility as if listening to the towering image of the Buddha, and nearby I saw three or four live monks sitting on the marble floor. They were sipping cups of tea, smoking, and listening to a transistor radio giving out a commentary on King Bhoomipol's arrival. (Cigarettes and unsweetened tea keep hunger at bay between a day's last meal at noon and the next day's first meal at dawn. You see no fat priests in Siam.) The temple was cool and beautiful. How agreeable to sit there listening to the radio, thought I, leaving with renewed respect for so unpompous an orthodoxy. True, you are expected to take off your shoes, but so are you on entering a private house—out of respect for your host and to keep the fine teak floors clean.

The tolerance of Buddhism helps explain the total failure of Western missionaries to turn the Siamese to Christianity. A century and a half's devoted work has produced a mere handful of converts, despite the help freely given by the kings themselves at all times—except once. That was when Rama III, trying to ward off one of the periodic epidemics of disease which afflicted Bangkok, ordered a period of piety. As an example he bought up animals awaiting slaughter and freed them. Such acts of merit are performed by the Siamese on their birthday or important occasions when they buy up a few trussed chickens or live fish in the market-place and free them. Some of the missionaries declared the practice mere superstition, arousing Rama III to the blind rage the Chakris have often suffered from, until a bishop soothed him with a gift of ducks and geese for setting free. More to the purpose, Dr Bradley, the most notable of the American missionaries then starting their work, proved the advantages of vaccination. Rama III had him teach the method to Siamese doctors, and so the West made its first effective penetration at the point of a hypodermic needle.

But the points of its bayonets were moving closer also. Mindful of Burma and Malaya's fate, and even of China that had been obliged to buy England off with Hong Kong, Rama III signed a treaty in which 'The English and Siamese engage in friendship, love and affection with mutual trust, sincerity and candour. . . .' At least the friendship, love and affection have endured. A few years later a similar treaty was signed with the United States of America which was represented by 'Edwin Rabad, a nobleman from America', namely Edmond Roberts, envoy from President Andrew Jackson.

Promoting trade, adding to the beauties of Bangkok, dredging the river, digging canals, slaughtering three thousand of the Chinese immigrants who had formed themselves into criminal secret societies, capturing his rebellious vassal the King of Laos and publicly exhibiting him in a cage—Rama III's reign of twenty-seven years did not lack energy. And all this time Mongkut quietly remained a monk. At the age of thirty-three he was appointed abbot of the monastery of the

Excellent Abode in Bangkok, where he introduced a purified form of Buddhism.

He also learnt English, becoming the first of his nation to speak and write it, often of a wondrous kind, for it is hard for a Siamese whose words have different meanings according to which of five tones is used. Besides, his words have only single syllables and therefore he strings them together like beads on a Chinaman's abacus: a worker is son-of-hire; a thumb, mother-of-hand; electricity, heaven-fire; matches, wood-strikes-fire; river, mother-of-water. Having no plural he adds the word body: table-three-body means three tables. The language also lacks tenses but he gets on well enough by saying, 'I go to Bangkok yesterday.' Nor has it gender, so that in a moment of faulty English he may warmly introduce his brother to you as his sister, the word for either being the same in Siamese. Anditiswritten-withoutspacingthewords whilepunctuationisachievedbyspacesbe-tweengroupsofwords likethis. Also, he has a separate royal language when he talks to—and often about—the king: the names for parts of the king's body are different, and for his actions like eating, sleeping, walking, and for delicate subjects or 'unclean' animals like pigs, and so forth. However, before the Westerner learns anything of language he runs into almost unmanageable confusion of nomenclature. Not only have the Siamese and Westerner different names for the country, its capital and its principal river, but nobody's name is pronounced as spelt: the Siamese are a race of Cholmondeleys.

Mongkut also learnt Latin and read the Bible in it; but English enabled him to gaze upon the uplands of Western knowledge. This became vastly important after Rama III died and he could himself at last leave the priesthood to become King. When England's envoy visited him in 1855 he found him enthroned in the moonlight wearing a jewelled headdress; offering the Englishman a cigar, Mongkut then took him to his study crammed with a collection of clocks, barometers and other instruments, to which a model train from Queen Victoria was presently added. It typified a mind shaking off barbarism and with eager rapture entering the nineteenth century. And he was resolved his country should follow him.

Previously the populace had been obliged to avert their gaze from the sacred person of the king, under pain of having their eyes blackened by darts fired by his guards. In future, he decreed, they could look at him. Previously, too, men and women went about with only the lower half of their bodies covered: their torsoes, he said in a decree explaining why they must henceforth dress more fully, *might be blemished by skin marks or they might be heavily perspiring: in both cases it is utterly disgusting*. In over five hundred decrees he sought to modernize Siam. Each began with his numerous titles and the words *By royal command reverberating like the roar of a lion*. They ranged from permitting religious freedom to forbidding the *inelegant practice of throwing dead animals into the waterways*.

While continuing his forbears' work of beautifying Bangkok, he was the first to build roads by land as well as water, and he drove about in a two-horse buggy to superintend these operations. He proudly sailed the Gulf in his paddle steamer, both for pleasure and to review his steam-propelled merchant fleet which he formed under English captains. He encouraged the missionaries' introduction of Western medicine and hospitals, built a printing press with Dr Bradley's help, established a mint to make coins in place of lumps of metal, and organized his army under English officers and wearing English scarlet (his brother was so keen on artillery that even his gardeners and cooks had to be trained gunners). But Mongkut's most potent action was the importation of Western advisers to reform and help run his government. Behind all this was more than a passion for modernity: he was determined to give no Western Power an excuse for 'intervention'. To this end also he made treaty concessions without parting with sovereignty, and he liberalized trade, stimulating rice production which has ever since been the mainstay of the economy.

As his family provided the bulk of the nation's leaders he ensured their progressiveness by using Western teachers for his children. He had in fact eighty-two children by his thirty-five wives, a Siamese record and the more remarkable because being already once married and having two children when he entered the priesthood at the age of twenty, he observed strict abstinence until his emergence as King at the age of forty-seven; and he died when he was sixty-four. The most important of his sons was Chulalongkorn, his successor and Ananda's grandfather. It was to educate Chulalongkorn and his brothers and sisters that Mongkut imported the Englishwoman Anna Leonowens, whose mis-reports have not been improved by Hollywood's distorting lenses. Yet a residual truth remains: Mongkut had great sweetness of character despite irascible outbursts, and with his bounding intellectual curiosity he remains the most attractive of all Siamese kings.

He once wrote a book about white elephants, noting among their finer points a beautiful snore, though he conceded that as in judging a woman individual tastes vary. But science remained his passion. Especially astronomy. While out riding he always took a reading of the sun to fix his latitude and longitude, and he correctly calculated the time for the total eclipse of the sun in 1868, refuting his people's belief that the phenomenon was due to a colossal snake's gurgitation of the sun. He invited foreign scientists to view the eclipse with him from a vantage point some distance from Bangkok. But there he contracted malaria. Dying, like the Buddha, on his birthday, he turned —as the Buddha had also done—onto his right side, murmuring calmly, and instructively as ever, 'This is the correct way to die.'

And so to the throne came his son Chulalongkorn (pr. Choo-le-long-corn), to escort Siam into the twentieth century with the same ebullient gallantry the ladies of Europe were to know on his state visits. He was the first Siamese king to go so far abroad. His father stood half in the shadows of the past: he himself strode round-bellied and confident into the present.

He had learnt well from Mongkut, importing Britons to advise on finance, Americans on foreign affairs, Frenchmen on law; and Danes, Germans and a notable Belgian on other departments. Through this government he established educational facilities from bottom to top. A police force. Post and telegraph services, and railways. Hospitals, a mental asylum, a medical school, an organization for Public Health. A law school, a criminal code, a reformed judiciary and penal system. Title-deeds for ownership of land, much of which he bought up himself to found the wealth of his successors. And, in short, as if at a rub of his magic lamp—lo! a Twentieth Century state.

What could have been more appropriate of one whose favourite reading was *The Arabian Nights*? Chulalongkorn seems himself like a creation of the story-teller who beguiled a thousand and one dawns. Observe him, potentate of potentates, going on picnics with two, three, four *thousand* people in his retinue, all travelling in countless exotic craft propelled by standing oarsmen dressed in scarlet and stopping-over in bamboo pavilions built only for a night, yet covered with flower-petals stitched together in sheets of colour. Or observe him teaching the more fortunate of his seventy-seven children as he sits among them. Or again, Lord of Life, rising at noon to work until four in the morning and the whole administration by compulsion with him, breaking off to drive round the city in his open yellow electric car or to eat meals prepared by Chinese and Indian cooks. Such was his liking for food, he wrote a book of Western recipes, including fourteen for sandwiches. It was a liking unhelpful to a physique afflicted in later life by diabetes and other maladies.

Though he died (in 1910) aged only fifty-seven, his reign lasted forty-two years, since he had succeeded Mongkut in his teens. During his minority he had a regent who bore the same name as a regent who murdered one of the Ayudhyan kings. Though this precedent was not followed a worse was created, of powerful princes (i.e. royal relations) who headed departments of state ably, but being answerable only to a busy king became the nodes round which everyone else, and especially the increasing number of products of the educational programme, had to cluster for work, advancement and wealth. The palaces of these barons became minor courts where favourites could fawn and officials had to flatter. Here, precisely, is the origin of Siam's twentieth century political struggle.

Of importance also to the tragedy of Ananda was the scattering of seed by the royal loins. Many of Chulalongkorn's ninety-two wives never shared his bed. Among his personal apartments in the Inside was one called the Yellow Room where unfavoured wives waited hopefully each evening, through all the years, as he passed by without even glancing at them. Three women never waited there. These favourites were three sisters who, being the daughters of one of his father's favourite wives, were also his own half-sisters. Incestuous royal marriages were nothing new, but subsequent events do not suggest that the Chakri line was thereby strengthened. Less scientifically verifiable yet equally important to the sequel was the personality of the leading wives. But for it Ananda might not have died, and he would certainly not have been born.

At the age of twenty-one one of the three sisters fell into the river when her boat capsized. Because of the taboo against touching a royal personage, neither she nor her two small children could be saved from drowning. Chulalongkorn turned for solace to the two surviving sisters. Both were queens but the younger he entitled Supreme Queen.

Hers was the power behind the throne. Appointed regent during his travels abroad, she sent him an hour-by-hour record of her feelings, her food and drink, and the state of her bowels and bladder. Upon her diminutive person he showered titles and jewels, including a £100,000 pearl necklace, as well as property producing £90,000 per annum.

She followed royal tradition in making her court a school where girls learnt the domestic sciences, good manners and self-discipline. She built and endowed girls' schools, and gave scholarships for girls to study abroad. She founded the Siamese Red Cross Society, and sent girls to learn nursing in England. She also had mid-wives trained to reduce a mortality rate made calamitous by the traditional method of giving birth (a woman in labour squatted on an unhygienic floor, and then the newborn infant was put beside a blazing fire). After Chulalongkorn's death she was entitled Queen With Ten Thousand Years and continued in internal command of the Chakri family, maintaining her husband's highly inconvenient hours (she began with breakfast at ten-thirty at *night*) and her own passion for motor-cars. From the catalogue of the London Motor Show she each year selected three or four models as gifts for her relations.

Her elder sister, named Queen Sawang, was only a degree less lavishly endowed by the King. Though she was as insatiable a gambler as most of her countrymen—at the age of fifty-seven she once played poker for twenty-four hours on end—in most other respects she followed her sister's service to the state. The importance of this to our story is that to her court too came young girls for instruction, and she paid for many to study abroad. Thus it came about that one of these girls, the very last anybody would have thought, was to marry one of her sons. And if this was something which nobody could remotely have foreseen, still less to have been guessed at was how by an even more extravagant fling of chance the girl's own two sons would both become kings.

The first was Ananda. The other, his brother Bhoomipol: after Ananda's death.

How this happened brings us squarely before the mystery, the strangeness and the tragedies of that death—more than a single tragedy since, as will be seen, killing can be contagious.

As contagious were the rumours and suspicion which fastened on Ananda's brother, his mother, the two foremost men in modern Siam

17

and other individuals who will appear as the story unfolds. Nor has speculation confined itself to the identity of the murderer: the manner of Ananda's death itself, whether by assassination, accident or suicide, is still disputed. Despite a regicide trial as extraordinary as any in the history of murder cases, the confusion still persists, recoiling at every contradiction.

The purpose of this book is to end the confusion and place a clear verdict before posterity.

The Life and Death of Ananda

I

THE events decisive to Ananda's life and death often happened nowhere near his native land. His own birth took place at Heidelberg in Germany. The year was 1925, and at the same time some of his young countrymen temporarily in near-by Paris were committed to a destiny inseparable from his.

No one could have thought so then. They were merely students, mostly living on graduate scholarships. Wearing ordinary Western suits they excited no particular attention, for students enough from the Orient wandered the Paris of the 'twenties. Besides, who cared in that ethos of exuberant self-indulgence. When people tossed back their cocktails saying, Here's mud in your eye, they did not mean the mud of Flanders. That was forgotten in the universal necessary forgetting.

The Siamese' natural gaiety matched the mood of the hour. But beneath it was anxiety and hard thinking by those sensitive to the welfare of their country. The name of one of the students will recur to the end. Pridi Banomyong.

Pridi (*pr.* pree-dee) was a well built, almost chunky young man with hair cut short, *en brosse.* His looks were not notable except for deep brown eyes of even greater brilliance than usual in his countrymen. He smiled as readily as they, laughed if anything more, but he had a kind of impenetrable reserve, a mask over his soul, that his qualities of warmth, kindliness and patience made unexpected.

He was the son of a rice merchant in a small village near the former ancient capital of Ayudhya north of Bangkok, and he is said to have inherited some Chinese blood. Since a great number of Siamese from the King down are similarly enriched this is not unlikely. He started with the frailest claim to life. At his birth on 5 May 1900 his mother was so ill, nobody thought he could possibly survive, and all attention was given to her until someone chanced to notice that the child lived. After attending a near-by state primary school he was sent to the torrid capital where his name today arouses such emotion. Of that there could have been no hint when the shy respectful little boy arrived, the poor relation of a senior official who took him into his house while he continued his education at a monastery school. He liked playing football, but a highly gifted mind found less difficulty than delight in study, and he easily matriculated to the Law School. This institution had had a brief but significant history.

In the Introduction I have described how the twentieth century was ushered in for Siam by a brilliant and ebullient potentate, King Chulalongkorn. He begat seventy-seven children and a great many reforms: the former governed, the latter modernized, his country. But between these offspring was an inherent conflict. The reforms produced educated commoners who could find work only in the government departments headed by despotic princes. Yet, ironically it was a prince who provided a direction, an ideal, for the protesting new intelligentsia. At the Law School founded by Chulalongkorn he lectured on a novel, confusing and inflammatory idea called democracy. It started little fires all over the place. When a cavalry officer was punished for brawling in a tavern with a man who went unpunished because he enjoyed the patronage of Chulalongkorn's senior son, the Crown Prince, the soldier's comrades marched out with drawn swords and a riot was narrowly averted. Other unprecedented incidents in the state service implied a similar challenge to the immemorial concept of royal absolutism. In fact a petition was got up for Chulalongkorn urging him to grant the country a constitution. He replied that the country was not ready, though one suspects he really meant what Wellington concluded upon another matter: *That which we require now is, not to lose the enjoyment of what we have got.* Soon afterwards he died and his son the Crown Prince succeeded him. A plump melodious-voiced man this, who had been educated at Sandhurst and Oxford and withdrawn himself exclusively into the society of his male courtiers—through whom he ran the whole government. In World War I a small expeditionary force went to France, arriving too late to suffer serious molestation but vastly stimulating patriotic idealism, which seethed over into post-war discontent at the King's unabated favouritism.

It was in this post-war period that young Pridi attended the Law School, the font of liberalism in Siam. He drank deep. The law he studied was not enough: it had little worth unless made by free men freely consenting: all men: democracy. Reason and compassion for the people he had been born among combined in this conviction. If it was not already strong within him it became so soon after he graduated and won a scholarship which took him to the Paris of the 'twenties.

He and his fellow students lived in various centres but they had a watchdog, the Ambassador. He was a half-deaf prince, and he was irascible, despotic and impossible. A visitor to lunch in the Embassy, a small house at number eight in the Rue Greuze near the Trocadéro, recalls that the Ambassador's son told an anecdote which made everyone laugh except his father, who peremptorily ordered him to repeat it, not once but a second and a third time, and then thundered, 'I haven't heard a word. Go and write it out.'

At first the daily tyrannizing of this petty monster over the young intellectual élite of Siam meant little to Pridi. He enrolled at both the Law School and l'Ecole Science et Politique, read avidly, ranged new realms. With his friends he did not neglect dancing, billiards, the Moulin Rouge and similar pleasures of Parisian life. But you would have seen them also in long and earnest political discussions at the Café Siefe in the Latin Quarter, or turning up at political meetings of all kinds, sniffing the air of radicalism upon which the Parisian intellect flowers. His own bounding intellect made him foremost among his friends. They learnt from him and nicknamed him Mentor or Teacher, which a whole generation of his people would call him.

From time to time the Paris students met a young prince very different from the despotic Ambassador. This man, of immense kindness and idealism, was rather an oddity in the Chakri royal family to which, being a half-brother of the King, he belonged. They enjoyed his visits to Europe and were delighted by the news from Heidelberg in the autumn of 1925 that he had been blessed with his first son, named Ananda. For Pridi the news brought no premonition; no finger pointed to the heavens where all unknown his star and that of the newborn infant gleamed in tragic conjunction.

It seemed, in fact, of no consequence, and certainly irrelevant to the absorbing question of who would succeed to the throne. For His favourite-loving Majesty lay in earthly dissolution, having spent the last of his strength on sudden erratic jousts in the matrimonial arena. In the result, his belated wives produced between them one mere girl,

23

leaving the throne open for his full brother, a soldier named Prajadhipok (*pr.* pra-jod-ee-pok).

The Paris students were pleased. Least eccentric of the entire Chakri line, the new King was incidentally the first to restrict himself to one wife. A man of liberal impulses; of honour; of no selfish ambition: he would have been content to live out the military career for which he had trained at Woolwich in England. They could justifiably believe that his accession marked the end of privilege and despotism. And so Prajadhipok himself believed.

But the advancing world depression quickly turned his reign into a nightmare. England's departure from the Gold Standard priced Siamese rice out of the sterling market. Prajadhipok entrusted the government to an executive of princes who, though ably selected, imposed unpopular economies. These bred discontent that began to smell ominously like despair when the King's intention of admitting outstanding commoners to his executive came to nothing because of the opposition of his powerful relatives.

The reaction these gloomy tidings from home provoked in Pridi is crucial to everything that has happened since—to Siam, to the still infant and unregarded Ananda, to himself—who was unregarded also, being only a poor scholarship lad talking a lot of hot air from the garrulous heights of Montmartre to the steamed-up café windows on the Boulevard St Germain. He wore a hat and smoked Gauloises, appearing as removed in spirit from Siam as his physical being was by its presence in Paris. Yet there could be moments when Siam seemed less remote: standing, say, on the Pont Alexandre III at sunset, gazing beyond the pinions of its lofty statuary, one's eye could be carried across banks of gilded cloud from the dome of the Invalides to the slender eminence of the Eiffel Tower; and then the fantasies of Bangkok's own silhouettes seemed not so far away. Nor was Pridi's heart or mind ever far away. He was resolved upon serving his people. And perhaps saving them.

To his friends, the Mentor urgently propounded a solution to Siam's problems. The monarchy must be limited to the British parliamentary system. And the economy could only be salved by all-out planning, for Pridi was true to his generation in responding ardently to the generous hopes of socialism.

Unregarded he might be by the world, even by that tiny segment which comprised his own country, but his influence had a germinal force. It already disturbed the old guard. His fellow students scattered through Europe elected him president of their association. They came to him with their money troubles, girl troubles, parent troubles: staunchly he stood between them and the furies that persecute the young. On occasion he championed them in conflicts with authority. The half-deaf Ambassador did not like him for that, any more than for the hints His Excellency had gathered of too much ill-bred interest in radical politics. Inevitably there came an explosion.

It happened that Pridi and others were invited to a gathering of Siamese students in London. The Ambassador point-blank refused permission. In the angry aftermath he composed a letter to the King himself, complaining of a bunch of Bolsheviks with Pridi their commissar. The students politely produced a counter-charge: the Ambassador had embezzled royal funds, seduced another man's wife, and disgraced Siam at the League of Nations! Such things said of a prince deserved a wholesale chopping off of heads, but upon investigation the fair-minded King Prajadhipok said the bunch of Bolsheviks must complete their studies.

Pridi rubbed salt into the Ambassador's wounds by gaining a *très bien* in his doctorate. But the despot was not done yet. He decreed that Pridi must travel home third-class, wearing a workman's brown suit. The other students promptly clubbed together to buy him a first-class berth and an appropriate wardrobe. More than that: they exchanged vows to live and labour for democracy.

In due course all of them returned home. They got jobs in government departments, and many of them married, set up home, started families. So six years passed. Their vow seemed smothered under the cosy down of normality. Pridi himself married a daughter of the official who had taken him into his house when he first went to school in Bangkok. He was no bumpkin up from the provinces now. In the Ministry of Justice they gave him increasingly important assignments. And he returned to his old Law School as a lecturer.

There, it is true, the intelligentsia flocked to hear the expositions of democracy with which he laced his teaching of the law, but the authorities could comfortably regard this nascent liberal movement as mere academic froth. They had enough to do trying to cope with the Great Depression that by now threatened to strangle the life out of the country. It was creating unemployment and suffering everywhere, even in the army whose officers were retired in droves. Thus there came into being a faction of civilians, the ideas-men, and a faction of soldiers, the action-men; and when these two were brought together, the mind and body of revolution were joined.

The man who joined them was a young artillery officer named Pibul Songgram. His parents give him the nickname of Plaek, meaning odd, because his eyes were above the level of his ears, but since he was to become a Field-Marshal he may more easily be remembered as FM Pibul (*pr.* pee-búhn). His family were fruit growers outside Bangkok where he was born on 14 July, 1898. They say he was a tearful baby and a delicate child, always falling into ditches, which made him take early to reading, though he grew up as energetic as he was amiable. It is worth not forgetting: FM Pibul was an amiable man. He loved wearing uniforms and duly went to the Royal Cadet school. Soon after graduating as a second lieutenant he encountered a girl who did not belie her name, La-iat (very fine, delicate). Previously he had shyly run away from the many girls attracted by his good looks, but now he approached saying, 'Little sister, stop and talk to me.' La-iat, who was thirteen years old, showed him her fist and ran. But he composed love poems to her, assiduously plied his suit, and in a couple of years married her. The episode may seem a frivolous introduction to so portentous a life as FM Pibul's: but that silky approach, that dulcet wooing, and that certain accomplishment of his purpose, are all of a piece with a man who will seldom be absent from these pages.

He gained his full commission after a course at the Staff College, where too he won a scholarship to the Artillery School at Fontainebleau outside Paris. When he arrived in 1924 he was soon aware that his birthday coincided with Bastille Day. No Siamese can shrug off the astrological significance of his birthday, though how it would be manifested could scarcely have been foretold of the young man who took his place among the Siamese students in the Paris of the 'twenties, listened attentively to the arguments of the brilliant Pridi, and joined in the vow they all exchanged to work for democracy on their return home.

Subsequent transfer and promotions chanced to bring FM Pibul— Major Pibul at the time—in close proximity with some of the leading officers disaffected by the iron-fisted princely executive. And it was he who carried his friend Pridi's ideas to them, offering a clear ideology and programme in place of formless protest.

Democracy, expressed in a draft constitution Pridi wrote out for them, was the magic formula they seized on without bothering themselves about his economic proposals which they did not much understand anyway. They formed an alliance with his civilian followers, calling it the People's Party. Within this People's Party of about two hundred people was an even more hush-hush band of fifty-seven who were to be called the Promoters, headed by four colonels known as the Four Tigers. In deep and desperate secret they plotted to overthrow the power of the Chakri family.

All this time, unknown to them, there was actually a member of the Chakri family as anxious as they to liberalize the régime. King Prajadhipok himself. He might groan to his family, 'I'm only a soldier. How can I understand such things as the Gold Standard?' but he did understand what led to the recent eclipse of the Czars of Russia and the Emperors of China, and he had no wish to be party to the injustice that denied his people some say in the government that avoidably or not was imposing great hardship on them. Therefore he urged his princely executive to grant a constitution. Supported by the American adviser on foreign affairs they insisted that the time was not yet ripe. Prajadhipok then decided to push through a constitution under threat of his abdication, and turning this idea over in his mind he took a short holiday at his seaside palace which was called Far From Worries.

One morning while he played golf—*one morning*, but a morning that burns in Siamese memory: 24 June, 1932—a prince rushed on to the links with ashen face and fantastic news. Amplified by the details which came in the anguished hours that followed, it makes a considerable saga, but a brief résumé must here suffice.

Among the public works in Bangkok which Chulalongkorn had inspected from his yellow electric car was a ceremonial highway called Rajdamnoen Avenue, inspired by London's Mall and the Champs-Elysées: it extends for a mile or two from the Grand Palace to a square in front of the domed Dusit Palace used for high Government occasions. Shortly after dawn that morning the bulk of the Bangkok garrison had marched to the square thinking they were about to see an anti-aircraft demonstration. This was a ruse by the Promoters to make sure they came unarmed while the tank corps, of which the Promoters had

27

command, trained its guns on them. By such means either the co-operation or neutrality of the army was secured. At the same time the ministries and public communications were being quietly and swiftly taken over. But the crux was the dawn arrest in their great mansions of all the leading princes. To their utter incredulity they found them-selves, many still in their pyjamas, herded together in the marble throne hall of the Dusit Palace: the god-like privilege of centuries was suddenly shrunk to a gallery of unshaven faces.

The public had little notion of these staggering events. Their indifference to political struggles will be a recurring theme, and in the remarkable absence of any violence (total casualties: one policeman shot) they scarcely reacted one way or the other to the manifesto put about by the Promoters. This rather unfairly blamed the economic depression on the King, and rather more fairly charged him with filling posts with relatives who 'were left to do as they wished in their own aristocratic ways, satisfying their greed', while the people were denied any voice 'because they, the people, were regarded as fools'. The revolution, said the manifesto, aimed at a limited monarchy; and an ultimatum had been sent to the King.

At his palace, Far From Worries, he pondered this fateful climax to a day that had started so innocently with a game of golf. He could call up his provincial garrisons and plunge the country into civil war besides risking the lives of the royal hostages. Instead, he chose to give way. Whatever his misgivings, he turned with relief from the in-flexibility of his powerful relatives; and full of hope he faced the challenge of democracy.

For the next six months he worked gladly with Pridi and others to evolve a constitution. He signed it, written on palm leaf, on 10 December, 1932, abandoning the absolute power of a thousand years. Said the Promoters: 'We take this opportunity before Your Majesty to make a solemn declaration that we shall be faithful to Your Majesty for ever.'

A new cabinet went to work, and since the constitution barred princes from politics it consisted entirely of commoners—some Pridi's civilian followers, some soldiers—under the premiership of a former Chief Judge. Pending an election, an Assembly was formed of People's Party members. So was the fruition reached of the glorious 1932 Revolution, and to publicize the marvellous new era of freedom and democracy, copies of the constitution were ceremoniously carried to remote country districts. On being told of its imminent arrival puzzled villagers asked, 'Whose son is this Mr Constitution?'

Mr Constitution flourished—for four months.

Pridi, appointed Minister of Finance to resolve the financial crisis, presented a sweeping Economic Plan. The fat of his socialist ideas was fairly in the political fire, for he wanted to nationalize all agriculture and commerce. The cabinet split. Pridi resigned. The Premier suspended the constitution, prorogued the Assembly, and reshuffled the cabinet to exclude Pridi's followers. Pridi himself he sent into exile in France because, the ex-Chief Judge announced to reporters, he was a communist—a point rammed home with an emphatic forefinger: 'Now I expect you to print my statement as it is, without any of your silly additions or subtractions.'

It sounded very like the voice of despotism again, and indeed there was talk of a royalist comeback by aristocrats and others hankering for a return to the past. It alarmed the former Promoters of the revolution who feared vengeance if not a betrayal of such idealism as survived the disillusioning reality of politics. The punctured unity between civilians and soldiers was patched up, and the army sprang a *coup* which sent the finger-jabbing ex-Chief Judge packing and put a bluff patriot named Colonel Bahol in the premiership. Pridi returned from exile to face an inquiry into his alleged communism. An independent, international commission exonerated him completely; and becoming Minister of the Interior soon after, he introduced a law banning communism from Siam.

The threat to the régime, however, lay elsewhere—in the royalists flexing their numbed muscles, army officers disappointed in their expectations, and even moderates suspicious of the Promoters' sincerity.

In October 1933 an impetuous and unbalanced prince gathered some of the disaffected together and with outlying army units marched on Bangkok. After four days' fighting the affair, known as the Royalist Insurrection, petered out in a wave of arrests. In the ensuing trials six men were sentenced to death and about three hundred to imprisonment. These were the first of the Political Prisoners who will frequently appear in the story. Of more immediate consequence, the King misconstrued his constitutional function during the Royalist

Insurrection by remaining neutral. Instead of standing by his government he fled to the borders of Malaya, helped on his way by a friendly British merchantman. His return when the issue had already been decided created incorrigible suspicion among the Promoters who mistakenly saw his hand behind the insurrection.

The following month Siam's first general election revealed an electoral apathy which has scarcely altered since. The government continued unchanged under the premiership of Colonel Bahol. But there *was* change hidden from the eye: the true repository of power had proved to be not the people of this so-called democracy but whoever had the backing of the army. If Colonel Bahol had that backing for the moment, close behind him stood one whose fortunes were suddenly in the ascendant.

FM Pibul, though the vital go-between for the 1932 Revolution, had little personal gain to show from that event, nor from the ex-Chief Judge's sacking of Pridi. I suspect that it was at this stage of his life that he began to identify the national welfare with his own. He kept a copy of Malaparita's *Technique du Coup d'état* but seems to have been no less tutored by Iago. Using a voice and manner persuasive enough for people to call him golden-tongued, he it was who, professing friendship here and sowing suspicion there, manipulated the tortuous events behind the *coup* which brought Colonel Bahol to power and incidentally restored Pridi. And rewarded with the command of the Bangkok garrison, he it was who boldly quelled the Royalist Insurrection.

As for King Prajadhipok—poor man, he had staked the past glory of the Chakris upon their future vital rôle in an enlightened democracy. Instead, he found himself isolated by suspicion and watching an increasing scramble for individual advantage. He seized the excuse of medical necessity to sail for England. From there he negotiated with his government. He did not wish to sign the death warrants of the condemned Political Prisoners and he wanted his people to have greater freedom of speech, more democracy. The Promoters, fearing for the stability of the new State and their own safety, would not agree. On 5 March, 1935 he abdicated. In a letter of sad dignity to his people he adjured them not to rise in his name. He wanted now only the peace of the green pastures of Virginia Water outside London, where he was to die six years later.

He had no children. The succession therefore passed to his half-brother, or rather to the line of his half-brother—that same prince whose visits had been so welcomed by the students in Paris—for he had died a few years ago. Thus there came to be enacted, at a luxury flat on the Avenue Tissot in the Swiss city of Lausanne, a curious scene. A delicately built young Siamese woman of shy but resolute character went to her ten-year-old boy who was in bed with a slight cold: 'Nand'—that was her abbreviation of his name—'there are three high emissaries here from the government. They have come to ask if you will be King.'

The boy had a serious, thoughtful nature. He said: 'I want to do whatever you say is right, Mama.'

'It is for you to decide.' She paused. 'You have your duty.'

'Then I must.'

She nodded and smiled; and if in the aftermath she wished ten thousand times over she had said, *No you must not!* at that moment she felt only the bewilderment and wonder of having a son who was King of Siam. King Ananda.

II

In England when a man succeeds to the throne he is said to be King *by the grace of God*. The phrase is not used in Siam but Ananda's succession could scarcely have been contrived without some supernatural disregard of the odds. His grandfather King Chulalongkorn had two queens, sisters. The senior bore five sons, of whom two died young and one dropped out by marrying a foreigner. The elder of the remaining two succeeded as the King whose rule through male favourites caused such discontent. His death without an heir had no precedent in the Chakri dynasty and only one in all Siamese history, so that when his brother Prajadhipok succeeded—aged thirty-two and not long married to a healthy young woman—any repetition of this break with the tradition of fecundity seemed improbable. Yet Prajadhipok abdicated without issue. The line of succession therefore moved over to Chulalongkorn's sons by his junior queen. Now she had eight children, but of the boys only one survived into adulthood—himself to die before Prajadhipok's abdication. However, he had fathered three children, first a girl and only then two boys, upon the elder of whom the succession devolved like the spinning ball in a roulette wheel coming finally to rest: Ananda (*pr*. on-on-dah).

In the whole history of kings the odds against a particular succession could never have been greater. Yet there he was at the age of ten: Lord of Life.

His father's name was Prince Mahidol (*pr*. mah-ee-don). Born 1892. Educated at Harrow, England. His life and character are worth more than a glance for what they contributed to Ananda's.

Chulalongkorn, sending his sons to different Western countries for diplomatic and educational reasons alike, enlisted Mahidol in the Kaiser's fleet. However, after receiving his commission he served only briefly in the Siamese navy: Europe had opened his eyes to the country's need for Public Health experts and he decided to become one.

For this purpose he was in the US, at the Massachusetts Institute of Technology, when Siam entered the war. He wrote to a relation:

Although having been educated in Germany and still being thankful and true to those friends of mine in that country, I nevertheless rejoice at the King's decisive policy. My country and my people first, then afterwards my own feelings. . . . We are sending troops to France. We send the sons of our peasants to fight and be killed by the Germans, but we have not sent the sons of our rulers to share their hardship.

He was refused permission to go himself, but a powerful desire to serve others never left him. By living simply he was able to endow scholarships for study abroad, making it his business to meet every Siamese student arriving in the US and to help him. At this remove it is difficult to appreciate the extent of his break with sacred tradition when he, a prince entitled celestial and a possible heir to the throne, aspired to be but a man. A student who stayed a few days at the Prince's Boston apartment after travelling via England, where he had learnt to put his shoes out for polishing overnight, has never got over finding this service quietly being done for him by his host himself, since he kept no servants.

His crowning act of unorthodoxy was to get himself engaged to a commoner. This was in 1919, and his fiancée was a pretty, vivacious Siamese student nurse at Simmons College, Boston. We are now meeting someone as important as any in this story, and many times in the course of my investigation I took up the strands of her life for where they might lead me. Her birth is a subject wrapped in some obscurity, though the truth in the belief that her origins were humble is important not because of its unexpectedness about one who would contribute two kings to the House of Chakri, but because of its possible effects on attitudes and relationships.

She was eight years younger than Prince Mahidol, whom she must first have seen at the court of his mother, Chulalongkorn's junior queen: having been orphaned before she reached her teens she was introduced into that multitudinous court through connections of her father, a minor official. The girl was miserable—everything so formal, so snobbish. When she had a slight accident and went to the Queen's surgeon-general for treatment she found the atmosphere in his house

33

and the friendship of his little daughter more to her liking, and the Queen yielded to her pleas to stay on there.

Siamese family ties seem to me both more and less close than the West's. People will hold a ceremony at the *wat* to mark, say, the anniversary of their grandfather's death; a prince passing a public statue to a forebear raises his hat in respect; and when a girl marries she is often set up in a house in her father's grounds, looking to him rather than her husband as head of the family. On the other hand, people readily give their offspring away: a woman might allow one or two children to be brought up by an otherwise lonely grandmother, or if she is poor she might present one of her boys to a monk as his servant and pupil.

So the girl was farmed out to the doctor and his wife, who enjoyed her high spirits and companionship with their own daughter. They sent both girls to a good state high school and then to study nursing at the principal hospital, a cluster of modern three-storeyed buildings across the river near the Temple of the Dawn. The orphan girl was bright. She gained a scholarship endowed by none other than the Queen whose court she had once attended. And the Queen's son, Prince Mahidol, she saw again upon being presented to him when she passed through Boston to start her studies in the US.

She went to the Emerson School at Berkley, and later to the North-West School at Hartford, Connecticut, in both places living with American families. Occasionally Prince Mahidol visited or was visited by her as the patron prince of Siamese students in America. Love made a remarkable leap across the huge chasm separating their rank. When he announced that he wanted to marry her the news created a sensation and a scandal in Bangkok.

Prince Mahidol in fact chose well. Princess Mahidol, as she became by their marriage late in 1920, matched him in qualities of mind and heart. When I met her, in the simple three-roomed flat she occupies in Switzerland as a retreat from the protocol and heat of Siam, she was over sixty and had endured the terrible experiences presently to be related. I was aware of an unaffected, graceful person who spoke fluently in a light voice with little accent. Her features were mobile, her smiles frequent but fleeting as though hiding shyness and sadness and a deeply pensive spirit. Yet not all the gaiety which animated her as a young woman had been extinguished, though she was grown very thin and her fingers were nervously unstill. I was aware too of a mind open to the world at large—or space for that matter, since she said she hoped she would live to visit the moon. It was a wish which also reflected her love of travel, shared by her husband, and indeed they spent their honeymoon travelling all over Europe, so seeing Lausanne for the first time.

Prince Mahidol decided that his Public Health course limited his usefulness. He must learn medicine. He enrolled at Harvard, graduating *cum laude*, though this was not until 1928 because he often went home on official business and also attended special courses in Europe. The pleasure he gave Pridi and his fellow students in Paris has been mentioned, but here is a revealing recollection by a nephew going to school in England when the Mahidols came on a Christmas visit:

We were taken to many theatres and cinemas as well as to museums, Uncle Mahidol being a perfect guide with his vast and varied knowledge, and he was emphatic that wherever one went one must go to museums, otherwise one was uncivilized. Although immensely rich, Prince Mahidol was economical, and in this was supported by his charming young wife . . . so we stayed at a cheap apartment house in Cromwell Road.[2]

It was in London during 1923 that their first child was born, a girl. Then in 1925 they were spending four months in Heidelberg, Germany, for the Prince to undergo treatment for dysentery; the Princess was confined at the general hospital where Ananda arrived on 20 September. Two years later the birth of their third and last child took place at Boston, Massachusetts—Bhoomipol (*pr.* póom-ee-pone), who is the present King of Siam and incidentally the only monarch ever to have been born in the US. A significant feature of these births is that the German doctors, unlike the British and Americans, refused to administer analgesias, disregarding the Princess's pleas for relief from her intense suffering which lasted for two weeks. So Ananda, most considerate of people, arrived amid pain as he was to depart amid anguish.

The births in three countries of their Serene Highnesses—as the Siamese addressed the Mahidol children—reflected the peregrinations of their parents throughout the 'twenties. But Boston was almost more their real home than Bangkok. They had an apartment first on Longwood Avenue and then on Brookline Avenue. Both addresses were unpretentious four- or five-roomers. They employed no servants except a nanny, one of the Princess's former fellow-students in Bangkok who in a girlish exchange of friendship vows had promised to help her in motherhood. As the Royal Nanny she will appear in the story for one swift tragic moment and then scarcely be heard of again.

Bostonians meeting His Royal Highness the Celestial Prince Mahidol knew him merely as Mr Songkla, derived from one of his titles. Though he dedicated his life to the service of his beloved country, America had none of the stifling ceremonial surrounding royalty in Bangkok. And his wife was in the country where origins mattered least.

So they were happy. They had their three babies and the inevitable array of books on how to bring them up, their apartment, the Nanny, and a modest Ford Whippet. Neither drank nor smoked (though I noticed the Princess smokes now). She was cook and usually he helped wash up. Siamese students were always dropping by for long conversations with them, mostly about the improvement of medical conditions in Siam. Occasionally they went to the theatre but rarely anywhere else. Though both their boys were to be very musical, curiously little music was heard in those Boston days. Prince Mahidol had an intensely serious nature. This was still a long way from Western gravity, and he could be a highly amusing story-teller, but most of the fun was supplied by the Princess.

All this time the Prince was still studying medicine at Harvard. And then in 1928 he got his MD, they returned to Bangkok, and the Princess's long journey through the shadows began.

For the usual one-year's internship which a newly-qualified doctor has to serve, Prince Mahidol wanted to work in Bangkok's principal hospital, the Siriraj. He was asking for something vastly more difficult than you might think. Here is how another prince who qualified as a doctor described his experience on returning to Bangkok: 'It was almost impossible for me to practise. When a patient came to me I had to ask, "Which part of your body is sick? Because I'm a prince and can only treat your head." If it was the King, of course, I could only treat his feet.'

The explanation for this extraordinary demarcation is that a Siamese attaches prime importance to his head and despises his feet. How social behaviour is affected has been mentioned in the Introduction—you must keep your head below the level of a superior's. Furthermore, you should avoid ever actually touching anyone's head, though if he is an inferior and you have to touch him at all touch only his head as the least contemptible part of him. This is not class consciousness gone mad: for all the Siamese' awareness of rank they respect each other. It has its origins in superstition and taboo—the belief, for example, that the head harbours the soul. Hence you should not wake anyone suddenly lest his soul has gone wandering and not had time to return to his head. Hence also, any breach of the rules is not only considered bad manners: *it brings bad luck*. For a long time whenever Westerners affectionately patted the head of a Siamese child they were startled by the menacing reaction, but now this extraordinary uncouthness of the visitor is accepted as unharmful. The corollary to the importance of the head is the lowly status of the feet. Hence, to point with your feet threatens the people around you with bad luck. The first time I called on a Siamese in Bangkok I was accompanied by a local friend whose agitated nudges were eventually explained by a whispered plea for me to uncross my legs, since my raised foot inevitably appeared to be pointing at someone.

The appalling importance of all this will presently be seen, but its immediate relevance is that Prince Mahidol was obliged to give up any hope of working at the Siriraj Hospital. The British and American doctors who ran it advised the King that taboo and etiquette made the presence of a prince on the staff quite impracticable. The hospital was on the farther bank of the Menam River and in visiting it by ordinary hire-craft instead of crossing with traditional princely ceremony Prince Mahidol had already strained the King's tolerance. There was to be no unfitting behaviour again, no internship at the Siriraj. Thereupon he went far up north to Chiengmai where the McCormick Hospital established by American Presbyterian missionaries was being run by Dr Cort. Though not strong he threw himself with ardour into his work. Soon alarming reports reached royal circles that he was even bathing his peasant patients.

He left his family in the care of his mother, the old poker-playing former junior Queen. They lived at the Mahidol palace called the Srapatum. It stands only a mile or two from the Grand Palace, well within the noisy and heat-laden confines of the city, but its large grounds look like an untidy rural estate. Not that there was anything untidy about that rigidly ordered household with its one hundred servants and hangers-on ruled by Princess Mahidol's former patron. During this time the young Princess suffered severely from headaches, perhaps not unconnected with the strain of life far removed from the simplicity and independence of Brookline Avenue, Boston. Besides, her husband was away from her for the first time, and that in the north where he risked all the hazards of tropical disease and did not hesitate to help even the lepers.

On a morning in 1929, three months after his departure for Chiengmai, he was observed alighting from a boat at the Siriraj Hospital in Bangkok. He was dressed merely in shorts, open shirt and sun helmet like any Westernized commoner, and like any busy doctor he carried a bottle with the specimen of a patient's intestine he wanted tested. But he had some personal business also. He consulted Dr Noble, English Professor of Surgery at the Medical School, about his own health. Noble sent him straight home to bed; then with William Perkins, American Professor of Medicine, struggled for three months to save his life. He had an amoebic abscess in his liver. They could not save him. He showed great courage and unfailing gentleness to the moment of his death. He was thirty-seven—best, most loved of Chakri princes.

Grief was intense among forward-looking young Siamese, not only those he had directly helped but others like Pridi and his friends recently returned from Paris where they had rejoiced in his visits. For Princess Mahidol the blow was too great for her ever to have entirely recovered from it. Henceforward her children were to be her entire life. At the time Ananda was four, his sister six, his brother two.

A year or two later Ananda began his schooling at the Mater Dei convent. It stands opposite the handsome colonial-classical British Embassy on the tree- and canal-lined main avenue through the fashionable area of Bangkapi, and like it belongs to an age of acacias and shiny carriage wheels. Beyond lawns and tropical trees the long double-storeyed wooden building stands aloft on thick posts: the style is only partly Siamese and indeed the place was built by an Indian to house his harem, which is scarcely the pedigree for a convent. However, its black-habited Ursuline nuns, true to its motto *Serviam*, turned it into a much sought-after academy for girls and for boys up to ten.

The Roman Catholicism of the international staff has never bothered parents, mostly Buddhist like Princess Mahidol.

Ananda went into the kindergarten held in a corner at ground level among the pillars. Dressed in the school uniform of white shirt buttoned to his navy blue shorts he was daily taken there and fetched, often by his mother as the other children were; but unlike them he ate his own noon meal which his nurse brought. He was already very serious, though a fuller account of him may be found among the back numbers of the school magazine *Inviolata*. Despite its soggy adulation the following extract, written a few years afterwards, will be found valuable in the final analysis.

He was very interested in his lessons, but he was always ready for some fun too and loved to make his little friends laugh. His Royal Highness not being very strong was not allowed to come to school as early as the other children—his arrival a little later was always a signal for some excitement in the class, and eager little voices called out to the mistress, 'Mother, Mother, Ananda is coming.' Prince Ananda entered with a jump, ran to the mistress saluting her gaily with 'Good morning, Mother,' then taking his place amongst the others he was soon busy making up for lost time.... Whenever a new toy was given to him the next day it was triumphantly displayed in school. On those days his excitement was so great the 'Good morning' was nearly forgotten in his anxiety to display his new treasure—a mechanical boat, an aeroplane which could be illuminated or some other equally fascinating object. It was possible on these occasions that the lessons would be slightly re-arranged to admit of showing off the beauties of the pretty toy. Prince Ananda's toys were always pretty for His Royal Highness had a good eye for colour and rejected anything which did not please his taste. He was obedient and listened readily to the advice and instruction of his teacher. If pain or suffering was brought to his notice he was invariably touched and even expressed his compassion in words. Handwork was Prince Ananda's favourite lesson, and he excelled in it . . . he showed initiative and seldom required his mistress to help him.

After about a year at the Mater Dei he went to the Bepsirind School for Boys near the Central Railway Station in the heart of the city. It is the closest approach in Bangkok to an English public school. A pair of double-storeyed brick buildings confront each other across a lawn, and a mild ochrous wash of pink and yellow does not dispel its some-what dispiriting Gothicism. Ananda went there in March 1932.

Three months later the Revolution came.

To the seven-year-old boy the events let loose upon Siam in the dawn of 6 June were exciting yet incomprehensibly fearful. He would remember but did not understand his mother's anxiety over the incredible news that the most powerful princes were cooped up in the Dusit Palace. These were bitter hours for royalty, and bitter years followed when the new constitution's ban on the princes reduced them politically to below the common people. Though a few accepted the ban as a means of helping to achieve the democracy they themselves desired, many conceived an undying hatred for the Promoters and an unquenchable suspicion of Pridi, the brain and ideological passion behind the Four Tigers. Such was the context in which Ananda probably first heard his name.

His mother was moved by mixed emotions. Her origins, her husband, her years abroad, had all fostered her democratic inclination. She had no blood ties with the people concussed almost into paralysis by their abrupt humbling, but so long as King Prajadhipok remained childless her son was heir to the throne. Like Prajadhipok himself she might have seen the blessings disguised in a Revolution which relieved the King of blame for the misdeeds of the government: Great Britain's constitutional monarchy keeps the throne safer than any absolute monarchy ever could. Calm political judgement was hardly likely, however, amid the convulsive emotions of her husband's relatives. And if she told herself that her only concern was bringing up her children, there was a strain here too in the formidable presence of these same relatives: their outlook on such matters as child-care was very different from the authorities the Princess studied in her Western books.

Any hope of the 1932 Revolution producing a Utopian democracy foundered on the uproar over Pridi's Economic Plan. Then there was his exile to France until he was brought back into the new government set up by Colonel Bahol with FM Pibul's assistance. These eruptions presented Princess Mahidol with an opportunity for escape. She insisted to me that the official explanation of her departure from Bangkok was correct—that is, for the sake of her children's health and education. But much has happened to dim her memory and I fancy she was glad of an opportunity to bring up her children in greater freedom and safety. The King could be persuaded because if he had no son Ananda would be the possible heir to the throne and should therefore be kept from harm.

Prajadhipok consented to her leaving in May 1933 and himself suggested Switzerland. Remembering Lausanne which she had seen on her honeymoon, the Princess selected it in preference to the damper Geneva.

At first she put up at the small Windsor Hotel. The Government thought this damaging to Siamese prestige so she moved to a big luxury flat in the Avenue Tissot. She did not much like it, but at least it seemed remote from the struggle for power in Bangkok.

Yet scarcely had the family moved in than the boulder cast by the Royalist Insurrection began to send its ripples to the shore of Lake Geneva. The death sentence passed on six of the Political Prisoners precipitated the final crisis of King Prajadhipok's abdication. Thus it was to the Avenue Tissot that the three high officials arrived with the gift of a throne for a ten-year-old boy with a cold.

From this moment the life of Siam, and of men like Pridi and FM Pibul, and of Ananda, were all related, conjoined, counterpoised. For long, however, Ananda and they continued upon separate planes as distinct as the two continents they occupied, since Ananda would stay in Switzerland until his majority while a Council of Regency exercised his royal functions in Bangkok.

Some old-fashioned folk brooded on the absence of an essential omen of auspicious majesty. Never before had a Chakri become King without owning a single white elephant. But surely this was the twentieth century, and a third of the way through it at that?

III

PRINCESS MAHIDOL, the ex-nurse of humble origin, found herself elevated to the rank of 'Her Royal Highness the Princess Mother' and entrusted with the upbringing of a most unordinary child. He had suddenly stepped into the forefront of his country's several thousand years' history, and he was hallowed by twenty million people as a living fragment of divinity.

To provide surroundings more appropriate than an apartment, the Government rented a villa in Pully. Quiet lanes, meandering walls, and the leafy gardens of comfortable chalets which with shuttered sobriety overlook the lake below, make Pully seem a village; yet it is a suburb only ten minutes from the centre of Lausanne, that sleek plump adornment of the Canton of Vaud. Ananda grew up in the villa named by his mother—diplomatically choosing one of her mother-in-law's names—*Watana*, meaning rays of light.

It was built into a hillslope above the shore of the lake. Though the grounds are now smaller the house remains: two storeys high, with garrets above and semi-cellars below, and white walls and a red scallop-tiled roof. It seems what it is, a home built by a Swiss professional family, though the dullness of this impression was relieved by the two acres of ground bordered by fir trees and chestnuts. Lawn and shrubberies rolling down from the house ended at a small orchard; and to one side was a vegetable garden, for the Princess Mother was fastidious about her family's diet.

She furnished the interior of the Villa Watana with a mixture of European and Siamese objects. It was unusual in having open fires, since the family who built it had caught a liking for them in England. A Swiss woman kept house, with two Siamese maids. An old man and a couple of assistants tended the garden. Well-bred ladies-in-waiting, officials, tutors, a chauffeur, guards and other people periodically swelled the royal entourage. The twelve-roomed house was much too

The Paris students, photographed in the Place de Trocadéro after a visit to the Embassy in 1927. Pridi is sitting fourth from the left and FM Pibul on the extreme right, while Kuang stands

King Prajodhipok handing down the Constitution, written on palm leaf, after the 1932 Revolution

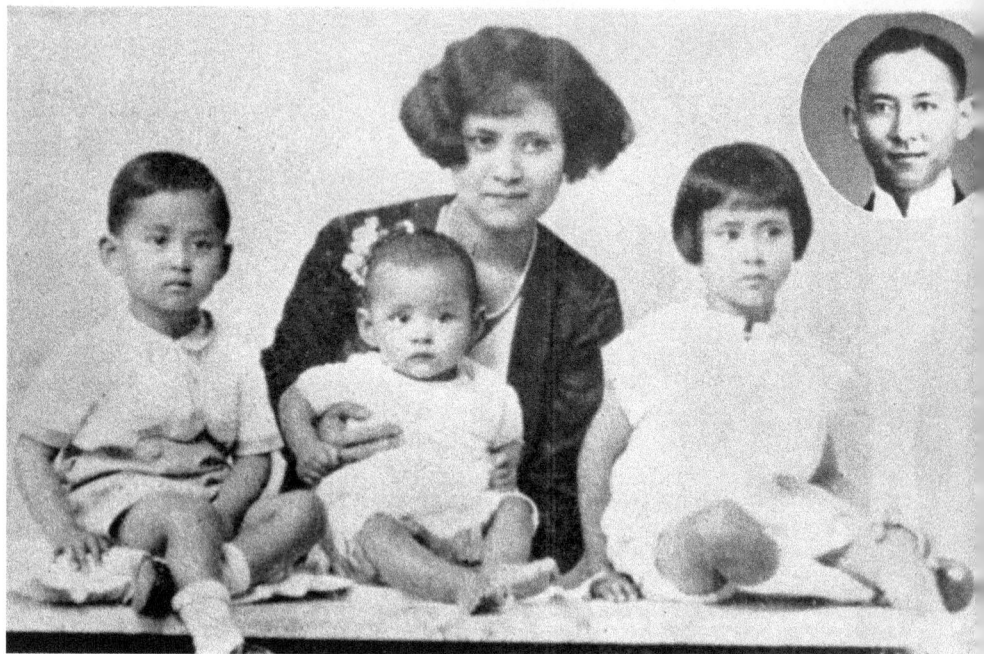

Princess Mahidol, the Princess Mother, with her three children—Ananda, Bhoomipol, and Gayani. *Inset:* Prince Mahidol

Ananda (standing in the middle) with his class at the Mater Dei Convent in Bangkok, his first school.

Ananda during his first visit as King to Bangkok in 1938. Behind him walk
his brother and sister

King Ananda, followed
by Prince Bhoomipol, on
their arrival in Bangkok,
December 1945

The Barompiman Hall from the south-west, overlooking the Tortoise Garden. The upper floor of the projection on the right (the East Wing) contained Ananda's bathroom, which opened off his dressing-room. See the sketch-plan on page 76.

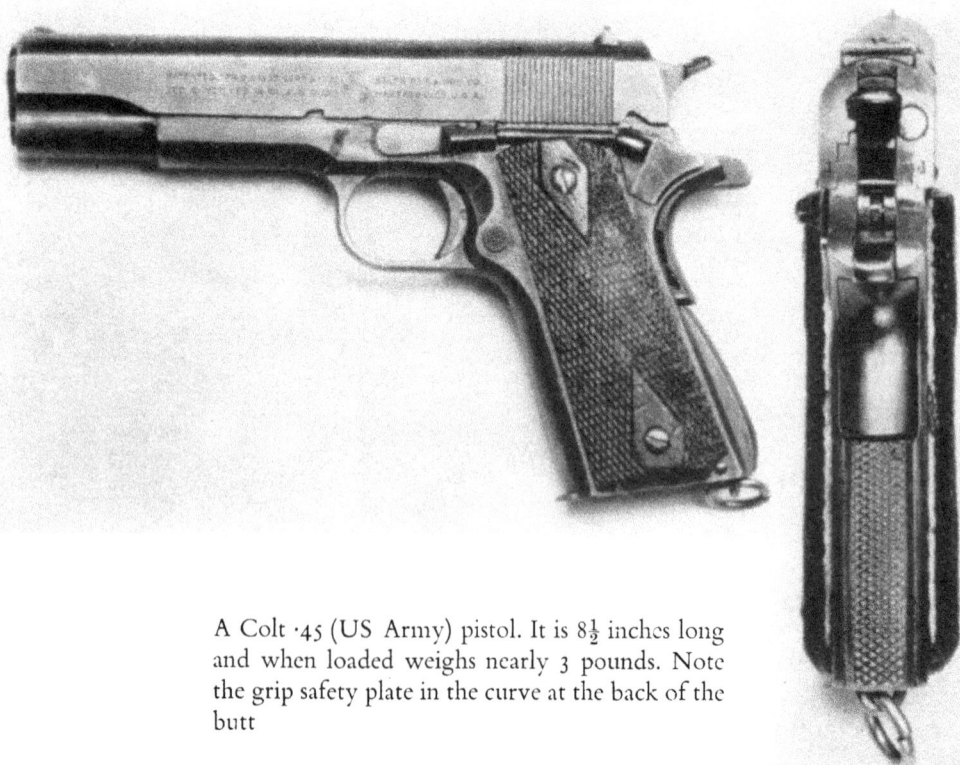

A Colt ·45 (US Army) pistol. It is 8½ inches long and when loaded weighs nearly 3 pounds. Note the grip safety plate in the curve at the back of the butt

small for them all and a house across the road had also to be rented. The Princess Mother dealt with the unwonted burden of her drastically altered domestic circumstances as best she could, at the same time keeping the inner core of her family life singularly little touched. The family images of the Buddha were kept in a room where she could go for contemplation, the outcome of which was her decision to continue bringing up her son as normally as possible. That is, she clung to what was immediate and real—her duties as housewife-mother like any Swiss châtelaine round about.

But unlike most of them she did not have haphazard notions about bringing up her children. The writings of Jean Jacques Rousseau had much influenced her, leading to the ideas of Maria Montessori: through understanding and not fear a child could learn self-discipline in an atmosphere of freedom limited only by consideration for others. This did not exclude the learning of good habits: the three royal children had to tidy their rooms (the boys shared a room), and perhaps Ananda was the first monarch in history to make his own bed in his own home.

The Princess Mother learnt French, chiefly in order to help the children whom she sent to an infants' school soon after their arrival in Lausanne. They were daily taken and fetched in a French Samson, later a Mercedes, driven by the French-Swiss chauffeur—a very acceptable authority on motor-cars, for which Ananda and his brother had a craze, no doubt inherited from their great-aunt. In the year they moved to the Villa Watana, 1935, Ananda started at the Ecole Nouvelle. (Bhoomipol also went there, and their sister to a convent school.)

His first sight of the Ecole Nouvelle, which he would attend for eight years, was a couple of large prosaic houses girt by straggling grounds on the hilly environs of the city centre. This impression of barrenness was quickly forgotten in the relaxed yet purposeful atmosphere of the place. *We consider it our solemn duty . . . to prepare our pupils both for the trials of present-day life and at the same time for their examinations. That life at the School should be a school of life is our motto.* On these principles a staff drawn from several countries nurtured the minds of their one hundred and fifty boys and girls, local and foreign. The practical meaning for Ananda was that he had a busy programme of secondary education, games and handwork.

43

The latter including cultivating a vegetable plot. By selling its products he augmented his pocket money of two and a half francs. He never got more while at school since his mother adhered to his father's economical habits.

His teachers found their new pupil keen, intelligent, obedient, courteous, quiet. He formed friendships easily but he had a reserved manner which prevented familiarities. This was fundamentally due not to awareness of his difference from them, of history and the call to destiny, but to his own nature. He was not boisterous. His thoughts were tender: a few years before, he was heard commiserating with a horse because it had to work and so was not free to play like himself. He disliked violence: a boy about to tackle him during a friendly free-for-all at his new school was stopped in his tracks by Ananda's hand raised in imperial veto.

By 1938, securely settled in at the Villa Watana and the Ecole Nouvelle, he was emerging from small-boyhood into the larger adventures of youth. The year is important: it marked his first official visit to Siam. The time had come for the thirteen-year-old King to meet his subjects.

With his mother, brother and sister he went aboard the SS *Meonia* at Marseilles on 17 October. His entourage included a certain Mr Pepys, engaged as his English tutor. During the ensuing month-long voyage, the captain reported, 'His Majesty the King proved a good sailor, enjoying all available sports and games on board, never once feeling seasick in spite of the heavy weather encountered in the Indian Ocean.' But there was heavier weather to be encountered in Bangkok where he had a memorable introduction to the political clime.

Nearly four years had passed since King Prajadhipok's abdication, itself the product of revolution, *coups* and the abortive Royalist Insurrection. After so much upheaval the country had tackled the business of recovering from the depression and creating a democracy. Or rather, a small group at the top had, since the masses thought little and cared less.

It may be recalled that the Prime Minister was the bluff soldier Colonel Bahol. In the name of King Ananda his administration had placed both the central and local government on a more democratic footing and carried out reforms in many spheres like education, fiscal policy, penal methods. Behind them all glints the mind of Pridi. His own direct responsibility was first the Ministry of the Interior and then Foreign Affairs. Helped by his American adviser he persuaded the Western Powers to renounce the last vestige of extra-territorial rights which they had screwed out of Siam as the price of her independence. The new treaties made her completely free and improved her finances. They also restored to her relationship with the West the cordiality which had been chilled by the Revolution. This was specially important at a time when Japan was beginning to stir up the East with the gospel of Co-Prosperity. Pridi had reopened a lifeline.

Though a busy cabinet minister he continued to be the Mentor, and he continued to teach at what had been the Law School but which he transformed into a university devoted to the skills and knowledge needed for a democracy. A man has grown too old to whom morality and politics are not indivisible; and Pridi, without ever having been young, has never been old. So he called his new institution the University of Moral and Political Sciences ('UMPS'). Students filled the lecture halls to hear him. Yet though he stood in such close proximity before them—slightly bigger-built and paler than most Siamese, with his cropped hair, fine sparkling eyes and a ready if shy smile—there was something inaccessible, enigmatic about him. This did not temper their passionate regard for their Mentor. Besides lecturing he wrote books on law and one called *An Outline for Boys and Girls and Their Parents*, which explained democracy with a liberal-socialist flavour. But it was repressed. For all the country's progress, there was a sinister undercurrent.

Its effects could be seen in the growing number of curious official appointments. Men became governors of provinces without any more qualification than a commission in the army. Or again, army appointments in the government resulted in misuses of public funds and contracts for public works that put private gain before standards of construction. It was a government which did more than any royalist régime to encourage the craft of the 'squeeze', the 'percentage', 'tea money', or as the Siamese say, 'lubrication'.

This state of affairs was largely the result of one man's manoeuvres for power. FM Pibul had gained hugely from helping the *coup* which gave Colonel Bahol the premiership, and from squashing the Royalist Insurrection. Made Minister of Defence and deputy Commander-in-

Chief he set about building up a preponderant following in the army by means of judicious promotions within it and government appointments outside it. Pridi's civilian followers were thereby denied or elbowed from office. From their resentment and alarm at the prospect of a military dictatorship flowed intrigue and a bitter struggle behind the scenes.

Colonel Bahol's influence over the army was still paramount and he did his utmost to keep faith with the fraternity of civilians and soldiers which had achieved the Revolution, so that his sole function as Premier became that of a catalyst and emollient to prevent either faction ousting the other. But such was the strength FM Pibul acquired that as the time of Ananda's first official visit drew near, Pridi's civilian members of the administration were merely tolerated as a sop to satisfy the Colonel.

FM Pibul's horoscope was once shown anonymously to an astrologer who opined that the subject had a 'rare ability to see wrong as right'. The youth who ran away from girls had developed somewhat fleshy good looks enhanced by his soldierly bearing and smiling self-confidence. His clothes were impeccable to the point of dandyism— he was addicted to beautiful shark-skin suits—and he comported himself with no less beautiful manners. He had immense magnetism. His fine voice was one asset, his apparently open and candid manner another, and he neglected no trick of persuasion. I like a newspaper report on his handling of a fractious delegation of politicians: with tears pouring down his face he begged them to remember Buddhist principles and reject anger. No one could forget those principles and affect that anger quicker than himself if he chose, and if all else failed to persuade he exerted the hidden sinews of his power.

In his acquisition of that power his staunch companion was the woman who as a little girl had been wooed by his love poems. Mother of his six children, she was to become Siam's first woman member of parliament, and when they had been married twenty-six years he wrote a magazine article about her. 'I am not,' he wrote, 'a man who likes to spoil a woman but I like to make her as happy as I can.' So if he did not mention that she had difficulty in collecting the jewellery which every Siamese woman regards as her entitlement, he stressed that he helped her with the poetry she was fond of writing, and he described her as the perfect wife—beautiful, clever, loyal—from whom he had never been separated 'except when duty called'. His reputation suggests that duty often called him to arms more eager to caress than kill. A book in the National Library in Bangkok entitled *Pibul's Love Life* does not however support the legend of a rampant Casanova. Covering thirty years of his public life, it mentions only a singer from the Government Publicity Department's band that played at official receptions; a dancer from the Fine Arts Department; and a beauty queen contestant (the modesty of Siamese women is oddly at variance with the national passion for beauty queen contests), who bore him a son. A romantic embroilment was the cause of the permanent scar on his cheek: he was getting into his car after presenting trophies at a football match when a hired gunman fired at him. Whatever the truth of his amours, their immediate relevance is to point another contrast with Pridi whose name has never been linked with any woman except his wife. In Siam where such matters raise no eyebrows this difference was less one of morality than due to Pridi's asceticism.

Despite the bitterness of the struggle between the two men's followers they themselves remained, outwardly at least, the friends of their Paris student days. Pridi in fact kept aloof from the intrigue and corruption. His self-interest and his idealism came together in his hope that democratic sentiment and responsibility would grow fast enough to frustrate the army's dominance.

His most potent source of confidence lay in the National Assembly, the parliament set up by the 1932 Revolution. Under the constitution half its members were those nominated by the defunct People's Party of the revolutionary Promoters and were predominantly of the military faction; but the other half, returned in the first general election (1933), were mostly either moderate conservatives or Pridi's liberals. Despite lingering suspicion of Pridi's 'communism' these two groups were drawing together to give voice to the aspirations of Siam's dawning democracy.

But in 1937 came brutal disillusionment.

Much of King Prajadhipok's property had been seized as state land, and rumours leaked out that the Regency Council had let many of the Promoters, excluding Pridi but including FM Pibul, buy parcels of this land at low prices on easy instalments. In the National Assembly the reaction of informed public opinion was so outraged that the Regency Council and Colonel Bahol's cabinet felt obliged to resign. By this unequivocal act of governmental obedience to the will of the people democracy seemed fully established at last. But in the next instant FM Pibul destroyed it.

He surrounded the Assembly with tanks and threatened a *coup d'état* if the deputies did not 'behave'. The Regents and the Government resumed office, but clearly it was FM Pibul who held the key to power which only Colonel Bahol's restraining influence prevented him from using—yet.

Much unrest followed. Certain sympathizers of the Political Prisoners who had been in gaol since the abortive Royalist Insurrection of 1933 even planned assassination. A week before Ananda's arrival by the SS *Meonia*, FM Pibul was dressing for some occasion and had just put on his boots but not his trousers when his valet pulled a pistol on him, fired and missed. Less than a month later, he and his wife collapsed over their dessert at a luncheon: it had been poisoned by the cook whose lover was in the pay of the Political Prisoners' sympathizers. Again he survived. His repeated escapes were as remarkable as the fact that he alone among modern Siamese leaders has been singled out for the doubtful tribute of attempted assassination.

The tense atmosphere generated by these events emboldened the Assembly to clamour again for the Government's resignation. Exhausted and ill, Colonel Bahol prorogued the Assembly and resigned. FM Pibul succeeded almost as of right. In six years the junior artillery officer had risen to the Premiership of Siam.

But by now Ananda had arrived, and most of the people gave no thought nor felt any emotion while their future was being placed in thrall by these political events. Mind and heart were monopolized by the royal visit, for nothing commands Siamese enthusiasm like a public celebration. In the Festival of Flowers, for example, or the ancient rite of welcoming spring, this enthusiasm is joyful enough: when it is infused with their one enduring unity of loyalty to the throne, then it has pure rapture—the greater now because no king had been among them for five years.

He arrived on 15 November, 1938. His reception was memorable. The pale green Gulf of Siam glistened under the sun as the navy, gathered in full strength at the mouth of the Menam, awaited the SS *Meonia* steaming over the horizon. The Premier and the three-man Regency Council went aboard to greet their thirteen-year-old

monarch, and he who a few weeks before had been tending his vegetable patch at a Swiss school and making his bed in a Swiss villa was
suddenly translated into the transcendence of a demi-god.

They all went on to the pride of *his* navy, the *Ayudhya*, as it thundered out a twenty-one gun salute. A hundred planes of *his* air force
flew overhead; and every kind of river craft, gaily apparelled, escorted
the battleship up-river in a great procession which the official account
says 'was the most magnificent ever seen in this Venice of the Far
East'. At the royal jetty by the Grand Palace members of the royal
family, the cabinet, and ambassadors in full court dress rose to their feet
as music from conch-shell, fife, trumpet and drum accompanied the
appearance on deck of King Ananda. He was 'clad in royal robes and
holding the Golden Sword, symbolic of Power', and the nine-tiered
umbrella to which only a king is entitled was held aloft as he stepped
ashore to the chanting of monks.

After addresses of loyalty, heard on the radio by reverent millions,
he entered the enchanted land of the Grand Palace. In the Temple of
the Emerald Buddha he worshipped at the sacred image. In the
mausoleum he paid homage to his 'August Predecessors of the Royal
House of Chakri'—a collection of statues of doubtful likeness. And in
the Inside his grandmother prostrated herself before him. Leaving the
Grand Palace he did not so much as notice the Barompiman Hall where
his final drama would be played out.

Who could remotely have foreseen that drama as the solemn-faced
boy, dressed in a white uniform with much gold braid and a plumed
helmet, set out in a shiny open carriage down the Rajdamnoen Avenue
for the populace to acclaim him? What hint could there have been in
the illuminations by night, the flags by day, the multitude of people
intent on eating delicacies or watching the entertainments provided on
land and water or with smiling languor relishing—as only the Siamese
know how to relish—every moment of festivity?

During the two months of his visit, while the real power over his
kingdom passed firmly into the hands of FM Pibul, Ananda made up in
composure for what he lacked in years. There was a dignity and
courtesy about him very kingly except when a shyness or slightly
puzzled air briefly betrayed the boy. Everyone could feel satisfaction—
the populace basking in the sun of the Lord of Life's presence, politicians like FM Pibul who could reckon that this gentle fellow would

give them no trouble, and royalists who hoped that the public enthusiasm heralded a return to their own prominence.

When he left on 13 January, 1939, three hundred thousand people lined the banks of the river. Afterwards it could be asked who in that concourse would come to act the killer: but at the time, there was only a tumult of devotion. The unforeseeable stood cloaked and cowled in silence.

IV

THE seven following years were the seven lean years of modern mankind. Yet, though few places on earth—not even the distant temples and palaces of Bangkok—escaped the rasp of World War II, Switzerland remained at peace. At the Villa Watana you would scarcely have guessed that war raged to north, south, east and west, had you not seen two boys and a grown-up intent on an innocent parody of it. In this game the manœuvres of toy soldiers and armaments were ingeniously combined with tiddlywinks; and the two boys, Ananda and his brother Bhoomipol, played intermittently for years with the grown-up, a Monsieur Seraidaris, who was himself its inventor.

In the Introduction I mentioned briefly an extraordinary eighteenth-century Greek named Phaulkon who rose to be the King's right hand —Lord of Cool Knowledge—until vengeful courtiers slew him. M. Seraidaris provides a curious echo of that tale, for he too is a Greek and during the last six years of Ananda's life was his almost constant companion. In Bangkok where he has never been seen, 'the Greek' exists as the legend of a shadow, the nameless subject of conjecture, when not he but the King met a violent end, as if paring a frayed end of history.

Cleon O. Seraidaris—as his visiting card describes him—was born in Germany about 1907. His father, a tobacco merchant, removed him to Switzerland during World War I. He was a supervisor of the smaller children at the Ecole Nouvelle while studying for his doctorate, when he was brought to the Princess Mother's attention shortly before World War II: she wanted someone to help her sons with their homework, and later on she engaged him full-time as their tutor. He did not live-in, having recently married and being in process of acquiring two sons of his own, but he became an integral part of the family. I found him to be a big-boned man with a certain boldness of feature beneath his greying hair. He had a quiet manner and perhaps a too zealous

51

regard for the immaculate infallibility of the royal family; but then many good teachers are only at their best in a boy's world.

He was not simply the brothers' academic coach (his subject was science) but to a great extent he became a substitute father-figure. The three of them—the Greek and the two boys—had what they called their 'club', whose headquarters were a large packing case at the bottom of the garden. There they sat drinking orange juice, and talked or pored over *Jane's Fighting Ships* or played with their white mice and canaries. They also played with their toy electric train system in the garret, or with other toys, and of course their war-game. Toys grown out of—and loyal subjects sent many gifts—were sold by the club for charity, or to buy either new ones or tools, for M. Seraidaris was first-rate at carpentry and gave Ananda a lasting enthusiasm for it.

These activities were restricted in term-time when Ananda did not finish school and homework until six. The mid-week half-day would often be used for a picnic outing by the whole family, and in the holidays they went to the Valais to climb or to Arosa to ski. At other times they had plenty of exercise sailing, rowing and swimming; and at all times M. Seraidaris was by their side.

But behind every detail was the hand, heart and mind of the Princess Mother. It was she who made the decisions, carefully prescribed the family's diet, took them on the picnics and holidays, ensured diligence in their schoolwork. She encouraged them to read everything from detective stories to books on astronomy, and to collect stamps and take an interest in photography as an addition to their 'club' pursuits. M. Seraidaris was her instrument.

She had another confidant, a certain Nai Anek, who has still to be described, and he and the Greek were within the tightly closed circle of the family. There were other tutors—a Swiss music teacher, and an Englishwoman recruited from the young ladies' finishing school next door, and a kindly Siamese *maha* (a sort of doctor of theology) who taught Siamese and held forth on Buddhism. But these were only a degree nearer than the attendants, the officials who came on business, or the visitors who were seen as a rule on Saturdays when the Princess Mother held an at-home. This was almost her only concession to sociability. She took no part in the life of the city. The newspapers, having nothing to report, never mentioned her. Her world was the Villa Watana.

For all its well-regulated activity, life there was very informal. Table talk flowed freely and easily. Servants never had to crawl. And even the background of Swiss equalitarianism did not spare casual visitors their surprise when the front door was sometimes opened to them by the Princess Mother herself, wearing shorts if she had just come in from working in the garden.

She could scarcely have been more different from her predecessors in rank, the eccentric matriarchs of the Inside of the Grand Palace. She got obedience by love and example; the extreme of punishment for the children was usually a fine for any damage caused. Her daughter was perhaps the most 'difficult' of the three, having a shortness of temper in the best Chakri tradition and a most un-Siamese disdain for rice, but for most of the first half of the war she was away from home as a weekly boarder in Geneva. Closest of the children to their mother was the youngest, Bhoomipol, two years Ananda's junior. He played the clown of the family, and no one today would recognize the stern good looks of the present monarch in the irrepressibly comical bespectacled boy. If Ananda felt jealousy or resentment he showed neither. All the evidence attributes the brothers with a strong attachment to each other. They shared their room and their enthusiasm for their 'club'. Ananda's attitude towards his mother seems equally clear: he always asked if she had slept well, urged her not to tire herself, and constantly showed his devotion to her.

He seemed perfectly content in the world of the Villa Watana she had built around him. School-going was but a foray into the outer regions. His school friends were not invited home though very occasionally he visited one or two houses like that of Professor Piccard, the balloonist whose son was also at the Ecole Nouvelle. On such occasions M. Seraidaris accompanied him, a reminder perhaps of Ananda's status of King. Another reminder was the guard placed night and day by a thoughtful Swiss Government at the gates of the Villa Watana. (It was in charge of a powerfully-built inspector, round-faced and black-haired, slow of speech but quick of movement, a former national ju-jitsu champion; he afterwards retired at the age of sixty when he married a girl of twenty-five.)

Within the gates, while the war thundered outside, Ananda shed his adolescence. Picture him—growing taller than most of his compatriots, with pronounced sloping cheekbones set in an oval face, smoothcomplexioned, and with large doe-like eyes for which he required spectacles, though usually only when reading. His habitual expression was serious, his gaze level, yet he had an air of one withdrawn, almost dreamy. If he felt wronged he seldom got angry but after due reflection quietly spoke his mind. He thought before answering. He was not afraid of the dark, and looked carefully before crossing a street, having been taught to do so. He did everything in precisely the way taught him, even to breaking the shell of a boiled egg. For all his seriousness he would have been no Siamese without a strong sense of humour, but he never joked at anybody's expense. His disinclination to discuss sex or to swear make it easier to call him a prig than the facts justify, for at school he enjoyed genuine respect and he made friends easily, being more sensitive to relationships than the rather cleverer Bhoomipol who had some difficulty in understanding other people.

I suspected the perfection of Ananda's portrait that graces royalist memory. Besides, allowance had to be made for the transfiguring effect of tragedy. But from prolonged questioning of his former schoolmasters and others less likely than relations or sentimentalists to distort fact I emerged with my scepticism forgotten. Ananda had no evil and his qualities were great: responsibility, humour, restraint, an honest puzzling over that which he did not understand until he did understand, and especially, a kind of interior gentleness hard to describe except by the approximate word poetic. He was extremely intelligent, not brilliant—'sufficient to good intellectual level' is a former master's classification—but with an open mind quick to learn, and retentive.

In 1943, approaching his eighteenth birthday, he spent the last six months of his schooling at the Ecole Nouvelle as a weekly boarder, for his mother wished him to put out his tentacles a little into the world, as if she recognized the inbred quality of life at the Villa Watana. He matriculated well, enrolled at the Law School of Lausanne University, and embarked on the final round of his youth—of his life, though if there is something within us which intimates our mortality it gave him no hint.

His enrolment at the university brought what appeared to be the merest impingement on the tightness of his family circle. The first day he attended the Law School he found that his class consisted of only a dozen men and one girl, though later there were more. They all became friends, and sometimes they were invited to the Villa Watana.

The Mahidol children had learnt a variety of instruments—Ananda could play the piano, flute, guitar and banjo—and musical friends joined them at jazz-playing sessions. But mostly he went to their houses where they talked with student gusto over glasses of wine and slices of cake. He did not go to restaurants, and except for occasional visits to the cinema or a concert, usually with his mother, he kept himself from the public view.

The nature of his relationships at this crucial period of Ananda's life was frequently stressed to me by members of the royal family and entourage. It was, they insisted, that of student acquaintanceship, nothing else. No one is more insistent about this than M. Seraidaris who was his apparently inseparable companion, becoming a kind of supernumerary student—and the umbilical cord attaching Ananda firmly to his mother.

The family's unity was strikingly expressed when by 1944 all four of them were attending the university. Ananda's sister accepted a friend's idle challenge and enrolled to study chemistry, Prince Bhoomipol entered the faculty of science, and the Princess Mother herself began a course on comparative religion. Attendance at the university thus became simply another family activity. Essentially the Villa Wantana continued, it seemed, to enfold Ananda. It was the warm within; all the rest, the cold without.

True, he no longer shared a room with Bhoomipol. His pocket money soared, if only to ten francs (about 17/6) a week. And though the 'club' had a residual existence he was turning to chess or bridge with the grown-ups. But none of this altered the quality of those years at the Villa Watana, insulated from the world and hence the world's war: an idyll, it would seem, of family contentment and a boy's advance to manhood.

The war scarcely ruffled the domestic surface. The Swiss Government offered to provide extra rations but the Princess Mother only availed herself of extra rice; and petrol, though the black Mercedes had to be sparingly used, so the boys and M. Seraidaris took to bicycles. Another effect was the exodus to Switzerland of Siamese students from all over the Continent, one of whom[3] fell in love with Ananda's sister at a Saturday at-home at the Villa Watana and presently married her (July 1944).

But if these were the direct effects of the war they were merely on

55

the surface. What mattered was the thunder at the gates. It could never be shut out by day or night. It reverberated in every bulletin, every newspaper, every conversation among the students; and especially in the news from Siam.

One day the Japanese Ambassador arrived at the Villa Watana with a gift of rice which the Princess Mother diplomatically accepted and then quietly gave away to a hospital. The visit reflected the convulsive events that had grasped Ananda's oriental kingdom. Some were shameful, some noble, but details for balanced judgement were lacking. This much seemed clear: the unclarity of the future.

Above all, would the monarchy survive in Siam when kings were everywhere in flight from their thrones? The answer given to the Princess Mother came from a source which would scarcely make it worth mentioning had it not proved to be totally accurate. To humour her friends who nagged her into consulting a certain fortune-teller she lightheartedly did so, to be told that although Ananda was King and his coronation only a formality awaiting his majority and peace, not he but his brother Bhoomipol would be crowned!

It made a funny story to pass on to Nai (=Mr) Anek, briefly mentioned before as her confidant. The Siamese Government had appointed a Secretary, nominally Ananda's, to deal with the little State business that got through to its Embassy at Berne, and before 1942 the Princess Mother had gladly dealt with this aristocratic dignitary, but she did not feel in sympathy with his successor, so that more than ever she conferred with this Nai Anek on political as well as family business. And because he holds a possibly even more equivocal place in Bangkok gossip-legend than M. Seraidaris I was bound to investigate further.

Anek Subrabhaya was born into the Bangkok upper-class in 1905 and studied engineering in Manchester and then Paris, where Pridi gave him much help in personal matters. Later he was invalided to Switzerland with tuberculosis. Prince and Princess Mahidol visited him there in 1926, arousing a devotion he has given all the Mahidols ever since. Though he has never fully recovered his health he preserves his smiling good nature, nor has almost permanent expatriation deprived him of the honesty, gentle manners and generosity typical of his countrymen. Petit and dapper, he presents the picture of a loyal Siamese whom Europe has somehow not swallowed up in crusty bachelorhood.

He acted as the Princess Mother's confidential secretary and general friend of the family, cycling daily to the Villa Watana from his apartment. They discussed everything together, but one subject arose more often than any other. It was reflected in the phrase which everywhere in the world was the most over-worked in all those years: *after the war.*

It was both a distant door to unspeakable happiness and a high wall that provided a shelter against the unknown. This ambiguity, existing in the utter uncertainty of when the war *would* end and who would live to see its end, gave the prospect of its ever ending a certain fantasy. The longer the war lasted the more unreal did speculation about what would happen sound. Even the clear indications of the Axis Powers' imminent collapse could not quite sharpen one's focus, for on what was one to focus except a huge question-mark?

And then suddenly the official Secretary brought a cable to the Princess Mother who handed it to Nai Anek, and they were aware of something incredible. *After the war* had become—*now.*

This is what they read. It has never been released but the following text may be accepted as authentic, save that in translation the difference in Siamese between words used for a commoner and those addressed to a King disappears.

6 September
2488 Buddhist Era. [AD 1945]

His Majesty King Ananda Mahidol
Lausanne.

Sire,
With reference to my appointment as Regent by resolution of the Assembly of the People's Representatives as notified by the President of the Assembly on 1 August BE 2487, the day is now approaching when Your Majesty will formally fulfil Your Royal functions in conducting the government of the State, for on 20th September of this year Your Majesty will have completed twenty years of age.

I therefore humbly beseech Your Majesty to return to the capital in order to conduct the government of the State in accordance with the provisions of the Constitution and, as from 20th September of this year, my regency will terminate. I therefore humbly beg to bring the above to Your Majesty's high knowledge.

The name of the Regent who signed this cable will come as a surprise to the reader who harking back to Ananda's official visit to Siam just before the war recalls the political situation which brought FM Pibul triumphantly to the premiership. For a Regent acted as but the rubber-stamp of the Government, and the man who was now Regent surely had not become that—he who had inspired and led the struggle for democracy. Or had he, in the face of FM Pibul's success, given up the fight and descended to being his creature?

If it seemed so, I was to find the reality quite otherwise; and its unravelling will bring us closer to answering the basic question of whether that cable was intended to be what it in fact turned out to be, Ananda's death warrant. For he was to die within nine months of receiving it, and his murderer would be cited as the man who sent it: Pridi.

V

WE must see now what had been happening in Siam while Ananda was growing up in Lausanne—during the years, mostly taken up by the war, between his official visit and his receipt of that momentous cable.

When the royal family left Bangkok in January 1939, the events which had just brought FM Pibul to power were not played out. Men frustrated in their hopes of a democracy plotted rebellion, and getting wind of it FM Pibul seized the chance to purge the army of the last vestige of opposition to himself, on the pretext that the plot was solely by royalists intent on restoring the absolute monarchy—a proposition he confirmed by submitting many noblemen to the un-precedented indignity of the common gaol. There followed eighteen executions; and ten life sentences added to the population of Political Prisoners. These now included a prince of the blood, Ananda's uncle, the artistic, amusing and wholly innocent Prince Rangsit, whose name should be noted.

FM Pibul emerged the undisputed, undisputable overlord of Siam. He achieved not only complete control of the army but, by his final humiliation of the royalists, silenced any rallying-cry for defection. The civilians, especially Pridi's liberals, were powerless. Their represen-tation in the Assembly merely gave the gloss of democracy to an essentially fascist régime. Pridi himself was kept in the Government solely by grace of the man who had once looked to him for leader-ship. It was an ironical outcome of a revolution fermented by Pridi's passion for democracy; and seemingly the final destruction of his hopes.

Yet he accepted the situation with stupendous calm and no bitter-ness. As inscrutably patient as ever, he did his work in the Government, taught at his UMPS, and bided his time.

He was now nearly thirty-eight. By an oversight rare for a Siamese politician he had acquired no wealth in six years of almost continuous office. Sometimes he even forgot to collect his salary for months on end, and his wife's gentle reminders only had an effect when she served a poor table. At the beginning of their married life they had a home in her parents' compound. Later he built a modern house on a piece of land donated by them, selling his law books to help pay the builder. For all his absorption in politics, his was a happy family, largely due to Mrs Pridi, for though he took any major domestic decision he had little time to devote to his children. Of these there were to be altogether two boys and four girls, most of whom in due course went to university and one girl graduated from the Royal College of Music, London.

Omitting his students who worshipped him and the intelligentsia who devotedly followed him he had many friends. Some were uncouth or plain-speaking to the point of un-Siamese bluntness, which was surprising because he himself was infinitely courteous and had an old-fashioned respect for his elders. But there is no easy explanation of Pridi. He liked his friends to drop in for a meal and often cooked the main dish himself, usually from a recipe learnt in France, yet there was something essentially monastic about him. He worked indefatigably, avoided parties, forwent official functions whenever he could, rarely touched liquor. He spoke simply, he lived simply. Because of this and the shy warmth of his manner and his readiness to laugh, anybody felt perfectly relaxed in his company; all the same, no relationship went beyond a slight softening of the austere. He remained a man out of reach.

It was this inaccessibility, more than his remarkably luminous eyes or the brilliance of a mind as lucidly expressive in French and English as Siamese, that accounted for the magnetism of his personality. His opponents speak of stealthy ambition forever stalking the ramparts of power; his supporters, of compassion and idealism: I think the facts will make judgement fairly easy for us but I doubt if this will bring us any closer to him. It is noteworthy that though he sometimes played cards he preferred chess—that is, if necessary he could gamble but he relied less on chance than strategy to defeat his opponent.

That opponent was not FM Pibul. It was the ignorance and cheerful indifference of the masses. He waited on time and event to cure this fundamental defect in the democratic cause and meanwhile he placed himself at the service of the State. FM Pibul was gratified. If Pridi's popularity among the intellectuals irked him—as it did, even though he made himself Dean of the Chulalongkorn University as a riposte to Pridi's founding of UMPS—it did not perturb him when power was solely his: he could afford to indulge his natural tolerance so long as Pridi made no hostile move.

He needed his brains, especially in financial matters: the world was moving into war, and money had to be found for armaments. More armaments, in fact, than simply to meet Siam's defence requirements, for FM Pibul's ambitions were growing. He had a palatial building as his official quarters but he continued to maintain his home near the British Embassy in Bangkapi down one of the alleys beside the equally numerous canals, and here within his large well-groomed compound he had three double storeyed houses—one for his children, one for his marital life, and the smallest one in the middle for his personal use. I recall the expensive but not ostentatious furnishing of its drawing-room where I was recently received by his two engaging sons (their pride in him I gladly record to his and their credit). The chesterfield suite was covered in green leather on wooden frames which were edged with a traditional pattern in gold and reached a Gothic peak at the back. I felt that I was enthroned, rather than merely sitting, amid that somewhat imperial décor. Here it was that FM Pibul dreamt of a new grandeur. Hitler and Mussolini fired his imagination, and nearer home the Japanese gave an example of dynamic nationalism.

He established a Youth Movement modelled on the Hitler Youth, full of aggressive patriotic fervour. He changed the name of Siam to Thailand, and allowed propaganda for a so-called Pan-Thai movement aimed at the recovery of surrounding French and British territories, which once belonged to Siam. He would be the führer of all South-East Asia.

One always suspects of FM Pibul that he backed into ambition, or perhaps that it overtook him when he wasn't looking. Thus, the intention to be führer was not at first overt. When war broke out in Europe he declared Thailand's neutrality. He even signed treaties of non-aggression with France, Great Britain and Japan.

That was in June 1940. But the fall of France offered too great a temptation. Three months later he let loose his army, navy and air force on French-held Cambodia. France's lamentable record in her dealing with Siam nearly justified FM Pibul's vulturine swoop. At all events it seemed a great success, for Japan insisted on 'mediating' and awarded

Thailand a slice of Cambodia. FM Pibul experienced the heady furore surrounding a führer as public enthusiasm was roused, an alleged Western spy-ring smashed, the army sent through Bangkok in a heroes' parade, the hideous Victory Monument erected at a traffic roundabout, and himself made a Field-Marshal (self-appointed).

But Japan's friendliness now knew no bounds: Nippon wanted to embrace Siam in the tightest of economic hugs. Again FM Pibul proclaimed his country's neutrality, and he said he had a million men under arms to defend it. Pridi urged him to go further and pass a law requiring every Thai at home or abroad to defend the country's independence to the death, arguing that this show of determination might deter any would-be aggressor. FM Pibul, who wanted only the privilege of power with the least possible disturbance to anybody, agreed. After all, he could always change the laws if expediency dictated. But to Pridi this law marked an absolute point of no return after he had acquiesced in or kept silent over so much that had happened to the clamant wonder and lavish promise of 1932. The supreme test was nearer than anyone realized. The law had no sooner been passed than Siam was confronted with an ultimatum.

Late at night on 7 December, 1941, the Japanese Ambassador called on the Thai Foreign Minister. His purpose was politely expressed, as polite as the hiss of a snake: he demanded the right of passage for Japanese troops to attack British-controlled Burma and Malaya. An answer had to be given within hours, by 1 a.m.

FM Pibul is either said to have gone into hiding, or departed for a town already under threat of attack. Whatever the truth of that, responsibility for decision devolved upon the next senior minister, who was Pridi. He had no time to call a cabinet meeting, no chance to share the burden of decision. At this remove the anguish of that burden is hard to evoke. A ruthless military power threatened him and his country with annihilation if he, a man of peace, opposed its will. This was the pivotal moment of his life; and it proved him great, for he said, 'We fight.' But it was also the pivotal moment of FM Pibul's life and it proved him small, for next day when the invading Japanese marines encountered stiff opposition, he sent orders countermanding Pridi's. Though isolated fighting continued in the south, costing several hundred Thai lives, the enemy entered Bangkok easily.

A last-minute appeal from Churchill was meaningless. A few miles down the coast Britain's pride, *The Prince of Wales*, sank along with *Repulse*, and her troops had been beaten out of Europe; the US was momentarily paralysed by Pearl Harbour the very day Bangkok was entered: no hope gleamed over any horizon. In preventing the devastation of his country FM Pibul therefore had an arguable case—but not in entering into an actual treaty of alliance with the invader, which is what he proceeded solemnly to do in the Temple of the Emerald Buddha itself. Pridi refused to have anything to do with this treaty. Rather than be party to national dishonour he resigned from the cabinet.

FM Pibul was nervous about Pridi's departure: outside the Government he might rally troublesome support. It chanced that a vacancy had occurred in the rubber-stamping Regency Council so FM Pibul thought Pridi would be sufficiently emasculated if he were appointed to fill it. The Council came in fact to consist solely of him and a prince named Aditya (*pr.* ah-tit)—for easier identification here called Regent Aditya—a weak dandy and literary dilettante with a vivid and vivacious wife.

Having allied himself to Japan FM Pibul had now to declare war on Britain and the US. Always anxious to play the democrat, he put the bill through the National Assembly, though in the absence of a majority of the elected deputies those present were mostly his own nominees. He had it signed by Regent Aditya at a moment when Pridi was out of Bangkok. On completion of these formalities the Japanese were enchanted and presented Thailand with portions of Malaya and Burma, while all British and American belongings were seized and their owners interned.

The Japanese proceeded to use the country at will in their conduct of the war, but they confined their brutality to Western prisoners like those at work on the Burma railway. They usually behaved well towards the Siamese, and as allies they were not, technically at least, in charge of the government, which was under FM Pibul. (He maintained the charade of a National Assembly though martial law prevailed.) Little Allied bombing occurred to upset Bangkok; and all in all, to a country rich in food, the war was comparatively painless.

FM Pibul even managed to introduce some high comedy in his role of local führer. The Bangkok English-language newspaper, now controlled by the Japanese, daily proclaimed: *One country—Thailand. One*

Leader—Pibul. One aim—Victory. 'The sun,' declared one of FM Pibul's sycophantic ministers, 'is powerful, but no more powerful than our Prime Minister.'

As-powerful-as-the-sun announced a new religion called civilization, by which in his blindness to principles he meant Westernization. Women must wear hats, gloves, stockings: penalties were imposed if they did not. No one must chew betel-nut—his own mother had reluctantly to give it up—and he had all the betel-nut trees chopped down. A husband should no longer observe the custom of scarcely noticing his wife when he returned home but must actually kiss her. On the other hand, one should prove one's patriotism at social gatherings, even a private party, by once in the evening performing a traditional dance. The populace gained great if concealed hilarity from these solemn decrees; yet the fact remains that if this were all the story it would all be shame, for Thailand had seemingly pledged herself to a monstrous aggressor and eternal dishonour. But it is not all the story.

When Thailand declared war against Britain and America in January 1940 a member of the Chakri family was Siam's Ambassador in Washington. Seni Pramoj (*pr.* say-nee prer-moat) is one of two distinguished brothers, the sons of a prince and hence entitled one rank lower, *mom rachawan*, usually abbreviated to *mom*. Mom Seni graduated from Oxford University where he won a coveted law award, the Birkenhead Prize, and on his return to Bangkok he joined the Ministry of Justice and lectured on law at UMPS. There he caught the eye of its founder Pridi, at whose suggestion FM Pibul gave him the key appointment of Ambassador in Washington. He had not been long in office when history arrived like a sudden cloudburst descending on a man without an umbrella.

I can picture him: genial and sophisticated, his trim well-rounded figure expensively clothed with calculated carelessness, discreet jewels gleaming on his immaculate cuffs and on the ring-finger of the hand which held the declaration of war he was instructed to hand to the State Department. . . . For the *bon viveur* the *vie* was suddenly not so *bon*. He recollected himself as a lawyer and a Chakri and put away the disagreeable document in a drawer so that as far as the US was concerned Thailand never did declare war on her. He based himself on the law promulgated at Pridi's urging which obliged every Thai to defend his country's independence no matter what. Accordingly he announced over the radio in a famous broadcast from San Francisco, that he did not recognize Japan's puppet government led by FM Pibul and was forming a Free Thai Movement to help rescue his country.

Upwards of a hundred Thai students in the US joined this Free Thai Movement (FTM) and began training with the US Army. In Britain a similar number gathered round a man of particular interest to this story. He was King Mongkut's grandson and brother to the widow of King Prajadhipok whose bodyguard he had commanded: Woolwich-trained Prince Subha Svasti (pr. soober ser-wot, though he is best known by the sobriquet *Tahn Chin*). At the outbreak of the war in Europe he had offered his services to Winston Churchill who got him a post in the British Army. Now he helped train his young countrymen and would share their hardships and perils.

Meanwhile Mom Seni Pramoj's broadcast from San Francisco had achieved an even more momentous result. The BBC relayed it to the Far East. Pridi heard it. As he listened, his thoughts throbbed with a daring response. His new position of Regent could be used both to inform himself on the inner counsels of the Government and as a cover for private activity: why not, then, a FTM *within* Thailand—an underground resistance against the Japanese?

With cool deliberation that is what he set about organizing.

All over the country from the hot alleys of Bangkok to remote jungles, groups were recruited for guerrilla action and sabotage. In the towns shopkeepers, civil servants and professional men secretly met at group-leaders' houses for instruction in the use of weapons, and they developed a sudden enthusiasm for 'picnics' in the countryside where they drilled and practised. In the country districts administrative officials and peasants joined in. All through 1942 the FTM gathered strength. By early 1943 senior officers in the navy, which had kept itself aloof from the politics-ridden army, were also participating. Eventually it numbered sixty thousand men, though so far lacking arms. Each man took his life in his hands by joining; but none more than Pridi, the heart and soul of the movement.

If FM Pibul knew nothing of the secret organization at work all around him he was aware of his declining popularity. At one stage, to assure his position, he actually thought of crowning himself king— had not the first Chakri been a general?—but the Japanese, reverential in their monarchism, dissuaded him. So he resorted to various shifts of pressure and deceit. In February 1943, trying to make the Assembly a wholly nominated body with no elected members who might oppose his will, he sought to coerce Regent Aditya; but this time Aditya ran away to the official residence of his co-Regent, Pridi, on the bank of the Menam close to UMPS and the Grand Palace. Pridi's FTM friends in the navy promptly patrolled the river and put marines ashore to guard the landward approach, effectively deterring FM Pibul from pushing matters to a bloody conclusion. The episode lasted scarcely more than a weekend but it had important results. Among the naval officers who now met Pridi for the first time was a certain Lieutenant Vacharachai (*pr.* watcher-er-chy). A few months later he became Pridi's ADC and here was doom because between him and the killing of Ananda was to arise a connection little guessed at in the breathless urgency of affairs in the FTM. A result also of FM Pibul's latest move was that Pridi felt the moment ripe for the FTM to act, if only he could provide it with arms.

He therefore sent out two emissaries. Each had a thousand pounds in cash sewn into his belt for the purpose of smoothing his way into China where Chiang Kai-shek was fighting the Japanese. After a journey of extreme danger one emissary got through to Chiang's Headquarters at Chungking in about May 1943.

The West has most of it conveniently forgotten Chiang Kai-shek's covetousness, and little was known of his ambition to extend China's power over South-East Asia including Siam: because of this ambition he discouraged Pridi's emissary from contacting the West's representatives. Pridi's man nevertheless did so, though it resulted in his sudden death from, said the Chinese, 'cancer of the stomach'.

But the Allies now had vital inside data on Siam and knew who their friends were. By this time numbers of the FTM were arriving in Chungking as part of the America OSS, while those from Britain were in India as part of Force 136. Both were under Lord Louis Mountbatten's South East Asia Command (SEAC), intent on the long-awaited offensive to throw out the Japanese.

In Europe the tide had already turned, and with the fall of Mussolini FM Pibul began to think twice about his own future. That is, he prepared to change sides. He decided to build a new capital in the northwest which could be defended against the Japanese but was open to the

Allies campaigning in Burma. The Japanese were not fooled. A cable from their Ambassador in Bangkok—intercepted by SEAC—told their high command his suspicion of FM Pibul's intentions and they became less reliable in their support of his régime.

In May 1944 the FTM members in the OSS began a march from China into northern Thailand. They suffered much privation. At about the same time members of the FTM in Force 136 also went into action. A man equipped with a radio transmitter made a parachute descent into Thailand, but FM Pibul's soldiers captured him. He was put into Bangkok gaol. This turned out to be wonderfully fortunate: his warders were FTM men and on Pridi's instructions they kept him in comfort and helped turn his cell into a secret broadcasting station. By this means Pridi got into direct communication with Mountbatten, and at SEAC headquarters a name grew into a legend—Ruth, the code-name for Pridi. Soon arrangements were made for an important meeting touching the future of Siam and of Ananda. The leader of the FTM contingent in the British forces, Prince Subha Svasti (Tahn Chin), one night arrived off the southern coast of Siam by an RAF seaplane. A launch awaited him. As history would have it, the officer in charge of the vessel was the same Lt Vacharachai we shall meet as Ananda's alleged assassin; but that by the way. He guided Tahn Chin safely up the Menam, dodging FM Pibul's and the Japanese patrols to reach Pridi's riverside house in Bangkok.

Their military talks need not detain us, but relevant to the events and allegations surrounding Ananda's death was their discussion on the country's post-war aims. Before Tahn Chin made safely away from that night of dark peril Pridi pledged himself that if he survived in a position of authority he would try to achieve national unity under King Ananda and based on democratic principles: and to this end he would try to get the Political Prisoners—i.e. predominantly royalists—released and the ban lifted from princes' taking part in politics.

The very next month FM Pibul's régime collapsed.

The new capital he was building had already cost twenty thousand forced labourers' lives lost through disease, and the Assembly, by now sewn thick with FTM sympathizers, refused to sanction the project. *It is hard to get a tiger out of a cave*, holds a Thai maxim, but the deed was done: FM Pibul, outvoted by the previously docile Assembly and deprived of Japanese support, finally resigned. Regent Aditya also resigned, leaving Pridi sole Regent. Through the FTM he was the secret master of Thailand.

But the Japanese were present in ruthless strength and, until the time came for the intended uprising, had to be bluffed. Therefore the cabinet Pridi formed of liberal civilians and naval officers loudly asserted their loyalty to the Japanese alliance while quietly fostering the FTM, which was steadily being officered and armed by air-drops. And further to bluff the Japanese Pridi appointed as temporary Premier a man who will increasingly require our attention.

Kuang Abhaiwongsi is a tall, scrawny, bespectacled man. The visitor to his house is likely to find him dressed in coffee-pink Chinese silk pyjamas, and either blissfully sniffing his roses which grow with a rare bloom for Thailand, or seated in his drawing-room surrounded by Thai antiques, which include a fine collection of the miniature tea-sets so many upper-class homes display in glass-fronted cabinets. He is a man of contrasts; but above all he is a man of mirth.

The son of a Siamese-Cambodian aristocrat, Kuang (*pr.* coo-ung) had gone to Paris in the 'twenties to study engineering and so joined the germinal group of students led by Pridi. Subsequently he became one of the Promoters, playing an important part in the 1932 Revolution by using his position in the Department of Posts and Telegraphs to help secure communications. Since then he had acquired some political experience as a Pridi protégé in FM Pibul's cabinet. His function now was to jolly the Japanese along by using his histrionic abilities as a buffoon, for it is scarcely possible for Kuang to express himself except in terms of drollery with immense gestures and grim-aces. His nickname in Thai means Great Comedian and laughable stories about him abound. When FM Pibul decreed that everyone had to wear hats, Kuang attended cabinet meetings in a hat which he declined to remove because, he said, having to remember when to put it on or take it off disturbed his concentration. Again, when FM Pibul sought to flatter him by creating him a major in the army, Kuang himself started the rumour that he wore his spurs back to front. But a shrewd mind lay behind his antics, and upon Pridi's appointment of him as Premier he proceeded to deceive the Japanese with as steady a flow of original lies as ever flowed from the mouth of a prime minister. For example, when the Japanese angrily announced their discovery of a secret airfield which the FTM was building, he laughed at them:

'What nonsense. It's a field being cleared for growing chillies.' The FTM had then quickly to sow the place with chillies to confirm Kuang's story. As the Japanese became increasingly suspicious they bluntly asked whether his Government planned to double-cross them. Kuang immediately retorted, 'Extraordinary you should ask that. We've just been debating whether *you* intend to double-cross *us*.' The Japanese implored him not to listen to Allied propaganda aimed at creating mistrust, and withdrew satisfied.

By such means Kuang the Great Comedian helped gain precious time for the FTM to gird itself. The testing moment was at hand. By mid-1945 the Japanese grip on South-East Asia had been loosened by the battles in Burma, and the Allies prepared to liberate Malaya. Thailand's internal security was essential to the Japanese use of it as a base and bastion. At the last moment their knowledge of the FTM went beyond suspicion and they had to smash the movement to forestall an uprising which Pridi was in fact to trigger off the moment SEAC informed him that the Allied advance had begun. But before either the Allies or the Japanese could move, while Pridi and the FTM and Thailand were screwed up to the last pitch of nervous tension, the history of the world was changed. On 6 and 9 August atomic bombs fell on Hiroshima and Nagasaki.

Japan capitulated. In Thailand the FTM was thereby cheated of its final consummation; but countless women were saved from widow-hood.

All was joy—relief—excitement. The promise and challenge of *after the war* became here and now. But as the 7th Indian Division flew into Bangkok to take possession on behalf of the Allies many people viewed the prospect of continued occupation with dismay, for Thailand was technically an enemy country. They need not have worried. For one thing, the US ignored the declaration of war. For another, the British acted with an understanding of the FTM's bid to salvage national honour, and although their interests had been gravely affected —far worse than the US's—they regarded their military occupation as nominal while they repatriated the Japanese troops and negotiated a peace treaty with Thailand, the while maintaining cordial liaison with Pridi through Prince Subha Svasti (Tahn Chin).

Pridi wasted no time in starting to build a new democracy. The name 'Thailand' was dropped, a distasteful memory of FM Pibul, and

'Siam' was unwrapped like so many other treasures kept in safe storage for the period of the war, and seemed to emit a greater radiance for its release from the vaults. But what was Siam without a King? And she had a King. On September Pridi sent the cable we have already seen (page 57), inviting Ananda to return.

So were the lives of Pridi and Ananda and with them many other lives disposed to come together and be destroyed at the very time they could rejoice in the safety which the ending of the war seemed to assure. Not fear, then, greeted the arrival of Pridi's cable at the Villa Watana, merely the opening up of the future so glaringly before them that they held up their hands to shield their eyes. A full week passed before Ananda's reply:

The Regent,
Bangkok.

I have received your telegram asking me to take up my duty. Although I am anxious to serve my country, I feel that I shall be more fitted to do so if I may be allowed to finish my studies. I passed my first examination at the law school last July and I still have another, more difficult, in order to pass in over a year and a half, and I will need at least another year to prepare a thesis for the doctorate. I know that you understand my desire to complete my studies. If you and the Government agree, I should like to go home at once for a visit before completion of my studies. I beg you to accept my heart-felt thanks and gratitude for the difficult work you have done and are still doing with success in my name.

Ananda Mahidol

Pridi pondered this. He wanted Ananda in Bangkok. The lad's presence would complete the national unity created by the war, and give in popular sentiment an impetus to the new democracy Pridi envisaged, especially as he planned to liberalize the 1932 constitution. Also, he was thinking of some form of South-East Asian federation in the same way that Western thought was turning to a united states of Europe. It was to be a fresh start, the beginning of a great new era, and the King should be there for it.

Your Majesty's gracious telegram of the 14 September has been received with loyal sentiments and heart-felt gratitude by myself and Your Majesty's Government. We are particularly happy to learn of Your Majesty's desire to return to the capital once for a visit before completion of Your Majesty's studies. I now humbly beg to place before Your Majesty the following circumstances [concerning the proposed constitutional changes]. I consider that it will be most highly desirable in the national interest for Your Majesty to return to Your country, even on a short visit, so that the fundamental issues above referred to may be decided with Your Majesty's personal participation and consent.

He added that he was trying to arrange with the British for a plane to fly the King out—a tactful hint that Ananda's visit should be soon—and he concluded: 'I ardently trust that Your Majesty will be pleased to accede to my invitation and return on a short visit to Your Kingdom.'

The reply prepared for Ananda was brief. He was sure that Pridi and the Government would deal with the constitutional problems 'justly and efficiently', and that his own presence would not be of great use 'as I am still inexperienced'; however, 'if you think it appropriate for me to return for a short visit I will be glad to accept your invitation.' But there was a qualification added by the Secretary:

Princess Mother suggests that if it will be convenient in every respect arrangements should be made that His Majesty may leave in the beginning of December next and return to Switzerland in the first week of January in order that the period of absence may not greatly affect his studies.

The Princess Mother did not know it but she was asking in that postscript a favour which Providence would not grant. Yet seemingly the arrangements were as she wished and the visit would be quickly over. In the first week of December 1945, Ananda left the Villa Watana with her and his brother. As his sister had recently given birth to a daughter she did not accompany them. At the airport there was a crowd to see them off and Ananda had difficulty in disappearing for a moment to telephone a student friend.

With journalists swarming about he had time but to say *au revoir*. He told no one of the call.

VI

BENEATH Ananda the world, spinning out the days which took him to his inheritance of a dynasty grown from the ruins of Ayudhya, had been devastated on a scale appalling even to the shade of the Chakri who founded the dynasty.

For Britain it was a world of Austerity; for the US, of Discontent. And both countries, mourning their dead and struggling through their internal convalescence, grappled with international near-chaos. Their partner, Stalin's Russia, shocked the first United Nations Assembly meeting in George VI's London with hints of dropping what Churchill christened the Iron Curtain. It was a world shuddering and uncomprehending before photographs of Buchenwald and Belsen. A world of the Nuremberg war trials, the executions of Nazis, collaborators, Quislings, traitors: an all-ticket audience of four thousand watched Hermann Frank hanged in poor doomed Masaryk's Prague. A world of shadow people, from black marketeers to refugees. Of trembling hope for what blessings nuclear energy, the jet engine and penicillin might bring. Of civil war in China and Greece; the struggle between Jew and Arab in the British mandate of Palestine; anti-colonial riots in Gandhi's India, Farouk's Egypt, the Sudan, Burma, Indonesia. It was a world rubbing the red of Britain's Empire off the map, and the red of communism on. But above all it was a world of hunger and homelessness. Two of Russia's soviets alone—White Russia and the Ukraine—had twenty-five million people without shelter as winter closed in; in China, fifteen million faced death from starvation: and these were but part of a hideous tale.

By comparison, the kingdom in which Ananda alighted on 5 December 1945 was a paradise. Though the Japanese had upset the economy and caused wild inflation, scarcely a stick or stone had been violently displaced. His people had abundant food, warmth, shelter. And they

72

had him. Even more than in 1938—for now he was of age, and so King indeed—his coming aroused among peasant and sophisticate alike an exaltation, a mystical reverence, out of all proportion to his political importance. He brought rain, he brought good luck, he brought the blessings of heaven.

Tall and slender; intelligent, liberally educated, well travelled; serious, while possessing a sense of humour without sarcasm or malice; gentle and yet direct in his manner which removed any notion of the sly oriental potentate, and at the same time self-possessed, with a reserve that became his rank: this was the highly attractive twenty-year-old student from Lausanne who, metamorphosed into the Lord of Life, descended the aeroplane gangway to be greeted by all the leading representatives of his people.

The Prime Minister prostrating himself before him was not Kuang the Great Comedian, whose office ended with the Japanese collapse, but Mom Seni Pramoj. Returning from his ambassadorship in Washington a national hero for starting the FTM, he had accepted Pridi's invitation to head the administration. As a lawyer and standing well in with the West he readily qualified for the immediate job of negotiating a peace treaty with the British.

Pridi himself, his regency over with the King's arrival, received at the ripe age of forty-five the title of Senior Statesman. He held undisputed sway over the nation though he preferred to hold it unseen, through the cabinet headed by Mom Seni Pramoj. Whether the reason was deviousness of character, as his opponents say, or simple shyness as his friends insist, scarcely matters: the solid fact is that he alone of Siam's leaders from first to last espoused the cause of the common man and the ideal of parliamentary democracy.

The ideal was now all but a reality. A fine free wind of unity and democratic aspiration blew through almost all the population: the bad old days of FM Pibul's fascism were over. To prove it, Mom Seni Pramoj's Government passed legislation against war crimes and FM Pibul himself was arrested. For this, some say, he never forgave Pridi, though in fact the arrest forestalled the Allies who would have given him shorter shrift besides depriving the Siamese of much face. So three times a week FM Pibul travelled from gaol in a black maria for his leisurely trial before the War Crimes Tribunal, and in the long hours between he composed bad verse bemoaning his fate:

73

Even the mighty ocean, deep and mysterious,
Looking green with fearful mixture of water and sky,
Cannot be compared with the misery and the heartache
Of seeing only the sky and the prison bars.

A few minutes away from that melancholy prospect was the altogether different prospect known to Ananda. The day he arrived back in Bangkok he was driven to the Barompiman Hall in the Grand Palace.

Suppose, that day, you and I had followed him as he approached what would prove to be his last home. Outside the Palace is a famous plain, tree-fringed but dusty, called the Pramane Ground where royal cremations and public fairs and other spectacles are held. On three sides stand ministries, UMPS, the National Library and Museum; on the fourth, the Grand Palace. The latter occupies a square mile of the riverside. A great white wall surrounds it, crenellated with leaf-shaped merlons and sometimes twelve feet thick with tiny forts built into it at intervals, each with a tiered and tapering spire like the head-dress of a Siamese dancer. Entering by the main gate, called Glorious Precious Victory, we would have passed down a hundred-yard avenue of small trees: on our right the Treasury, royal elephant stables, and the palace school; on our left a lawn in front of the compound of the Temple of the Emerald Buddha, and then the Crown Property Offices. The avenue gives way to an alley between the royal equerries' quarters and the Royal Household Secretariat. So we would have come to the courtyard at the heart of the Outside: before us, a range of edifices of impossible splendour, mainly used for the coronation and funeral ceremonies of kings. Beyond them lies the Inside where the royal women, children and attendants totalled as many as three thousand, but it was practically deserted by the time of Ananda's arrival and in any event he did not enter it but turned left out of the courtyard. Through an iron gateway he reached the Barompiman Hall.

How urbane—unsinister—it looked under the sun-drenched sky! It was a product of King Chulalongkorn's travels in Europe. You would think it an Edwardian millionaire's mansion in Monte Carlo or Geneva, which must have made it seem not unfamiliar to the Swiss law student. Double-storeyed, it lies east and west, with a projecting

74

front entrance and a curved bay at the back; a central dome similarly breaks up the straightness of the roof-line. The building is over two hundred feet long by about eighty, but for its size has relatively few rooms, these being high and big.

Now the internal arrangement was to receive, over and over, the most fervent attention for what it might mutely reveal. In most investigations the scene of the crime is important enough but here its importance cannot be exaggerated.

The ground floor was taken up by a dining-room, audience room and ante-chambers, but mostly it was used by pages, servants and guards; the catering staff occupied kitchens in a separate building in accordance with Siamese custom. On the ground floor also was the bedroom of the Royal Nanny, now resuming service with the royal family after she had not returned to Switzerland with them in 1939 because of illness.

The upper floor—our chief concern—was reached from the central entrance hall by a massive staircase emerging onto a wide landing called the Main Balustrade, or by two minor staircases in the west wing. This wide landing, the Main Balustrade, was the hub of the upper floor which may roughly be represented by the diagram on page 76, for the sake of clarity only Ananda's quarters being indicated in any detail since each part of them would assume significance.

The whole of the upper floor was therefore in two distinct sections—the east wing on the left and the west wing on the right. They were directly connected, via the Main Balustrade between them, by the front and back corridors which were each forty yards long. And they provided the living quarters of only four people: Ananda had the east wing, and his brother, mother and the latter's lady-in-waiting were in the west.

From this many-windowed upper floor of the Barompiman Hall they had wonderful, unforgettable views. Who would think of murder, here where every day shone bright from limpid dawn at seven o'clock until six when the setting sun drew colossal streamers of gold, flamingo and turquoise across a sky that had held cloudlessly blue all the hours between? At first the saffron-, rose-, and green-glazed tiles of roofs, and the ceramic and glass embellishments on gables, spires and columns, and the gilded bell-shaped towers, all dazzled the eye too greatly for detail to be picked out. By night the

75

Ananda's Quarters
in East Wing

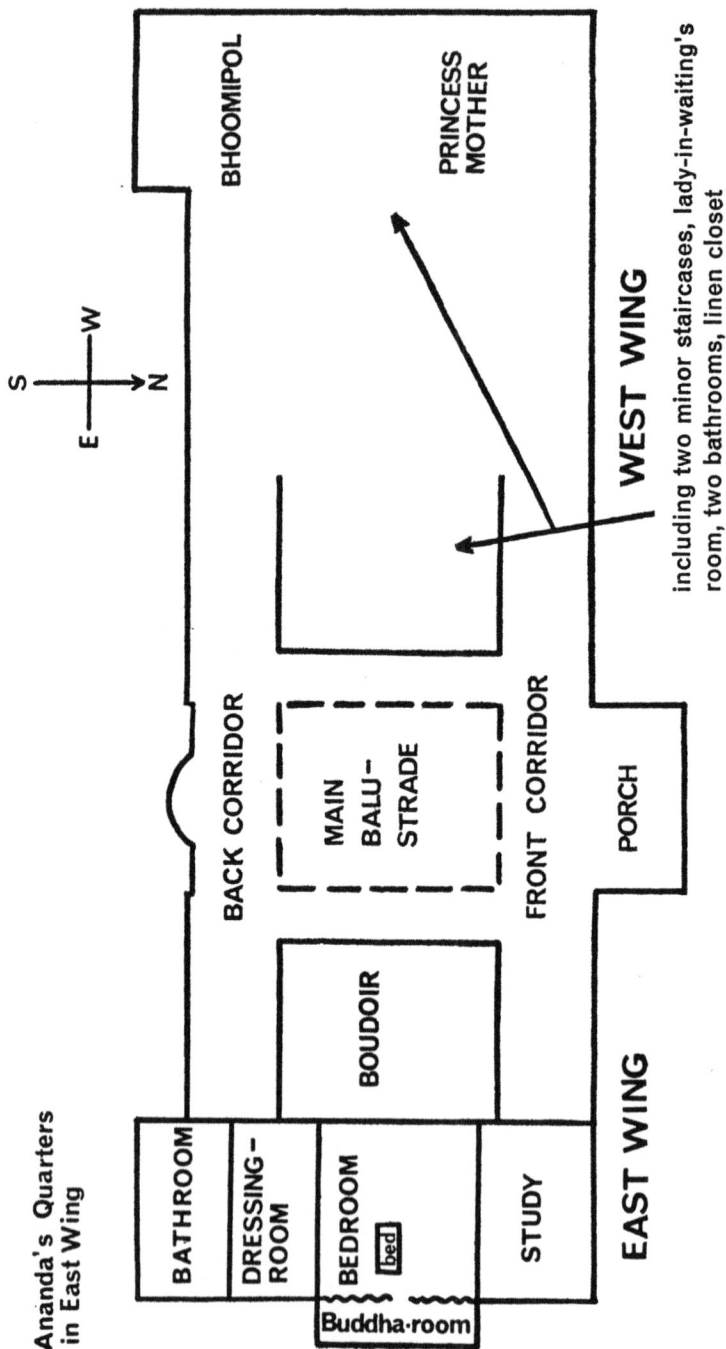

N↑ E←→W ↓S

BHOOMIPOL

PRINCESS
MOTHER

WEST WING

including two minor staircases, lady-in-waiting's
room, two bathrooms, linen closet

BACK CORRIDOR

MAIN
BALU-
STRADE

FRONT CORRIDOR

PORCH

BATHROOM

DRESSING-
ROOM

BEDROOM

bed

Buddha·room

BOUDOIR

STUDY

EAST WING

See also the photograph of the Barompiman Hall facing page 43

moon brought the strangeness of shapes into their own—upswept eaves and telescoped roofs, towers like gigantic cacti, spires tapered as sharp as needles thrust at the sky. In front of the Barompiman Hall, beyond the Secretariat, was the compound of the Temple of the Emerald Buddha with its many other fantastical structures like the Mausoleum, the sacred library, and the seven columns representing the planets. Behind the Barompiman Hall lay a pleasance called the Tortoise Garden; beyond this, the royal theatre and other buildings extending to the boundaries of Wat Po with its immense Reclining Buddha. Or if the observer turned from this southern view to the south-west, there lay the buildings of the Inside and the Garden of Heaven, and beyond the limits of the Grand Palace the broad teeming Menam yielded on the further bank to the soaring Temple of the Dawn.

Such was the magnificence of Ananda's domestic surroundings. And the people around him, his personal attendants, were aides-de-camp, pages and secretaries. These formed part of a whole hierarchy of functionaries in the Royal Household Bureau. Some will make a fitful appearance in this story, but four were to become the cynosure of the nation.

One was the Lt Vacharachai who first met Pridi while helping to patrol his house to protect the Regents from FM Pibul and who later became Pridi's ADC. Pridi now included him as the navy's representative among the King's equerries drawn from the three services.

He directly made another appointment, equally significant in the aftermath. This was of a political follower named Chaleo (*pr.* cherlieu), whom I shall call Secretary Chaleo because the post Pridi gave him was that of Ananda's Private Secretary.

The other two names destined to be on everybody's lips were those of the pages of the royal bedchamber and hence the persons most intimately concerned with Ananda. The families of both men had been in royal service for generations; and both, aged about forty, had served Ananda in his childhood in Bangkok. One was called Butr and the other Chit—though Butr was actually more of a chit of a man than Chit, who was bigger, more educated and brighter, and so is here referred to as Nai Chit to distinguish him from Butr. The section of royal attendants to which they belonged was headed by a functionary called the Silk Bearer, and its members came to the job largely through

77

inheritance. They alone were allowed to touch the King, and then only in carrying out such duties as barbering and manicuring. An exception was the King's physician who had of necessity to break the taboo of royal untouchability; but no one else.

Ananda's arrival in the Barompiman Hall at the Grand Palace marks a stage in the story at which I might usefully list the people who have so far appeared. His violent end was now less than six months away, turning the joyous overture of his arrival into a derisory knell that sounds down the years. In Bangkok were:

King Ananda, living at the Barompiman Hall in the Grand Palace with his brother *Prince Bhoomipol* and the *Princess Mother*.

A *Lady-in-Waiting* to the Princess Mother, living close to her on the upper floor of the Barompiman Hall.

The *Royal Nanny*, former fellow nursing student of the Princess Mother, now re-united with the royal family; also living in the Barompiman Hall.

Pridi, Senior Statesman, still occupying the official residence allotted to him during his Regency—i.e. by the riverside near the University of Moral and Political Sciences (UMPS) and the Grand Palace.

Secretary Chaleo, Private Secretary to the King, appointed by Pridi.

Nai Chit and *Butr*, pages of the royal bedchamber.

Lt Vacharachai, one of the King's ADCs, appointed by Pridi.

FM Pibul, former dictator, now held in gaol on war crime indictments.

Mom Seni Pramoj, Prime Minister, lawyer, former Ambassador in Washington and founder of the Free Thai Movement.

Kuang, Great Comedian, a leading politician, Prime Minister after FM Pibul's fall.

Princes—ex-Regent *Aditya*; *Subha Svasti* (Tahn Chin), soldier grandson of Mongkut, head of the British end of the FTM;

78

Rangsit, Ananda's uncle who had been falsely sentenced to life imprisonment in 1939 but now freed by Pridi along with the other royalist Political Prisoners.

And in Lausanne, Switzerland:

Nai Anek, friend and personal secretary to the Princess Mother.

M. Seraidaris, tutor.

Princess Galyani, the King's sister, with her husband and new-born child.

Student friends.

Newly arrived at the Barompiman Hall with its spacious rooms and magnificent views, Ananda quickly settled down to a daily routine. He got up between eight-thirty and nine in the mornings—not early by normal Bangkok standards but early enough for a Chakri. He breakfasted with his mother and brother on the first floor porch. At ten he discussed official matters with Secretary Chaleo, then he studied Siamese and Buddhism with a lay priest (no longer the *maha* who had been with him in Lausanne and who had now returned to private life). After that, ministers and civil servants had audience of him to report on their departments of State. Before lunch he read or wrote, or sometimes drove a car in the palace grounds. Lunch, with his mother and brother and occasionally a relation or cabinet minister, was at twelve-thirty. A rest, another session of Siamese or Buddhism or the reception of diplomats and officials, and then it was tea-time, often spent in the Tortoise Garden behind the Barompiman Hall. In the late afternoon he either visited his paternal grandmother or enjoyed some form of recreation with Bhoomipol. After dinner at seven the evening was occupied by guests, or Ananda played music with his brother and others, watched a play or film in the royal theatre, or walked in the palace grounds with his brother and pages. At ten-thirty, before going to bed, he visited his mother in her quarters.

This was the quiet outwardness of Ananda's days within the Grand Palace but we shall see that politics gave them an increasingly unquiet inwardness.

Daily routine was often varied by excursions into the surrounding city. Driven in a Nash or blue Rolls-Royce he called at all the principal monasteries to pay his respects to the Buddha's many images. He visited government buildings, factories, and places of interest. Sometimes at night he was driven incognito around his capital with Lt Vacharachai or even Pridi as his guide.

He also travelled outside Bangkok, to make a number of formal visits to the provinces. One of these trips, actually the first, must be recalled in some detail because of its fateful consequence.

It was on 23 December, to Cholburi on the eastern side of the Gulf of Siam, and he went there to review a farewell rally by members of the FTM. Pridi went with him. The royal entourage included Ananda's page Nai Chit, his Secretary Chaleo, and, among his ADCs, Lt Vacharachai. Pridi had the idea of taking a jeep along as a gift for the King who might wish to drive it himself but on the way it overturned and killed the chief ADC and injured Lt Vacharachai and Secretary Chaleo. Despite this unhappy start the parade was a success. An especially applauded event was the FTM's presentation to the King of a souvenir selection of their weapons. Among them may have been an American ·45 service pistol numbered 2 C 81459. Accounts vary. Some say that an American OSS officer gave it to Pridi who gave it to Ananda, while Bhoomipol was to recall that a certain page gave it to him. At all events the ·45 came into Ananda's possession at about this time and the FTM's gifts stimulated both him and Bhoomipol into starting a pastime which became almost a passion with them.

Using automatics, revolvers and rifles in Ananda's collection they sometimes fired from the windows of the back corridor on the upper floor of the Barompiman Hall. More often they chose the Tortoise Garden behind it, which provided a perfect shooting gallery. The naval ADC, Lt Vacharachai, set up targets for them, got in ammunition and acted as instructor. He was kept busy, since there were days when they shot off as many as five and six hundred rounds.

VII

WE have reached the last months of Ananda's life.

Events and people call for sharper delineation.

The negotiations for a peace treaty ran into trouble when Mom Seni Pramoj, as Prime Minister and chief Siamese delegate, viewed the British proposals with legalistic horror. Though the Siamese Government and armed forces were to function freely, the British wanted continued military occupation and reserve powers over the country's resources—lest trouble arose in disposing of the Japanese. These proposals were in fact milder than the Allies imposed on any other occupied or defeated country.

Now Mom Seni Pramoj's aristocratic origins and Oxford education combined to produce a strong sense of humour, easy good manners, and an equal pleasure in music, good books, and frivolous gossip. Even the impregnable self-satisfaction which I found in all except one or two members of the Siamese aristocracy has in him a disarming charm. He is a successful man—as a lawyer, as a university professor, and in private life. He once gave a lecture on the Art of Living. I have a copy before me: its sentiments are admirable though it betrays no knowledge of the Art of Leading, and perhaps the two arts are mutually exclusive. Though he is secure in his country's history for starting the FTM, former members of the movement are qualified in their regard for him.

The British peace treaty proposals shocked an understanding limited not only by a lawyer's suspicion of every whereas and wherefore, but by suspicion of fundamental motive. He had spent the war in the US where belief in Britain's predatory imperialism ran deep even after the forthright Atlantic Charter, and he had got hold of something said at the Quebec Conference which convinced him that Britain wanted to make Siam a mandate or colony. The British proposals, therefore, seemed to him a cloak for this malign scheme which he deemed it his patriotic duty to frustrate. The US *chargé d'affaires* encouraged him with the assurance that Congress, then debating the question of aid for Britain, would support him.

He vexed Pridi who was anxious for the treaty to be signed quickly so that the country could go forward and was himself prepared to rely on British reasonableness. He had been the Foreign Minister who negotiated the ending of all foreign extra-territorial rights before the war, and he more than any man had risked his life to end foreign occupation during it, so you might think him rather better fitted to judge than Mom Seni Pramoj. But not in Mom Seni Pramoj's opinion; and Pridi showed less than his usual patience in prodding his Prime Minister, especially when the British came back with a second set of proposals more severe than the first. In the result there was some tinkering with words and the Treaty was signed on 1 January 1946*, but more irreparable damage had been done to political relationships than was immediately apparent during a period of celebration.

Although British troops were to be about for most of the year to deal with the Japanese, Ananda was now king of a wholly unfettered nation. As such he was host a few weeks later when Lord Louis Mountbatten arrived on a proconsular visit. It was Ananda's first big official public function—'a somewhat trying experience,' observed the *Times* correspondent of an untried young king who nevertheless 'displayed great poise, and he impressed those he met with his intelligence, sincerity and wide reading.' There were three days of ceremonies and entertainment including a state ball attended by the nobility whose women, said the *Times*, were 'dressed with almost Parisienne chic.'

The presence of the King and Pridi's release of the Political Prisoners in accordance with his wartime promise had indeed brought the royalists back into the swim. What the *Times* man noticed most at the time of Mountbatten's visit, however, was the atmosphere of pro-American and anti-British sentiment caused by the popular belief that the US had forced Britain to moderate her peace treaty demands. Mom Seni Pramoj's suspicions had been widely aired.

The rift which this had begun between Pridi and Mom Seni had also other origins. Mom Seni never forgot something FM Pibul

---

* Its essential provision was the supply, free, of a quantity of Siamese rice for starving Asia. The supply was eventually got—but mostly by the British paying a substantial price. (See Sir Geoffrey Thompson's memoirs[4].) At no time, before or after the Treaty, did Mom Seni's fears prove to have the slightest justification in fact or even possibility.

whispered in his ear when appointing him Ambassador to the US—
that Pridi had recommended the appointment because he was jealous
of Mom Seni's growing popularity among the law students. In this
manner, though FM Pibul lay in gaol, his mischief continued to do its
work. And there was something else: Mom Seni wished to make his
brother-in-law the Chief of Police, but Pridi refused. Long afterwards
this refusal was to have as ironic a sequel as any novelist could dream
up.

A general election followed within a week of the Peace Treaty, and
Mom Seni Pramoj formally resigned his premiership. The deputies
elected to the new Assembly were mainly independents since party
organization scarcely existed yet, and their first task was to vote in a
premier. The widening rift between Pridi and Mom Seni caused
Pridi to support the candidature of another of his associates as Mom
Seni's successor. Kuang the Great Comedian confidently expected
that he was to be the anointed and would resume the premiership he
had ably held after FM Pibul's fall. But Pridi disillusioned him,
believing that another would be a better head of the new democracy.
Nevertheless, when the name of Pridi's nominee came before the
Assembly not he but Kuang, to his own great surprise, found himself
with a narrow majority vote. Pridi had not tried to influence the
deputies and, equally accepting the situation, got on with the next
important task, which was liberalizing the constitution.

Prominent among his collaborators in this work, but siding with
Mom Seni Pramoj, was the latter's brother, Kukrit Pramoj. Besides
his brilliant satirical journalism—he still runs the country's leading
newspaper—Mom Kukrit's rôle of *enfant terrible* in Siamese politics
has long been a feature of Bangkok life, tiresome though some find
this role sustained into middle age. His conversation is highly diverting
with its gloomy wit of the unconfessed sentimentalist. Unlike his
brother who enjoys the happiness of a united family he is a divorcé,
the father of two children. Educated at Oxford, of noble birth, he has
an agile intellect which thinks of the generous, compassionate or
idealistic act more often perhaps than a character weakened by a
certain vanity and immaturity permits him to carry out. This may be
why Mom Kukrit Pramoj arouses admiration in some and fear in
others, when he has it in him to arouse love in all.

While work on the constitution went forward, the new Assembly proceeded to tear down the fabric of national unity. Since the debris was to surround the tragedy of Ananda we must examine what happened.

In the Assembly's vote on the premiership Pridi's nominee had gained sixty-five votes to Mom Seni's four, yet the latter was taken over the former's head into the cabinet formed by Kuang without consulting Pridi. He also gave a portfolio to one of the principals in the rightist government which had exiled Pridi in 1933. Kuang the Great Comedian had claws, bared now in bitter hostility towards Pridi for having rejected him, his protégé. And on Pridi's side there was not only the deep hurt of Kuang's cabinet appointments but the revival of old fears of royalist revenge against the 1932 Promoters: Kuang's actions, coinciding with the royalist comeback, suggested that maybe the Great Comedian was trying to 'get off the tiger's back', as a Siamese saying has it, by turning on him, the arch-Promoter.

And then, if Kuang and Mom Seni Pramoj's break with Pridi was not already complete it was quickly made so by the quite immoderate attacks by Pridi's indignant followers at the very first Assembly debate after the election. This led to outrageous personal abuse on both sides, drowning the infant voice of democracy. On 18 March Pridi's supporters asserted their strength and defeated Kuang on the minor issue of his refusal to make shopkeepers display price-tags. Kuang resigned a premiership that had lasted only two months.

What was happening was a division less through intellectual conviction than emotion. Kuang, Mom Seni Pramoj, his brother Kukrit, and their friends, forming what came to be called the Democrat Party, were rightists. They shared the monarchist sentiment of the aristocratic class to which they belonged and which the ex-Political Prisoners augmented. It was ironical that Pridi should come to be so bitterly opposed by a class he had rescued from repression by freeing the Political Prisoners, re-admitting princes to public life, and restoring the posthumous honours of the late King Prajadhipok refused by previous régimes. But he was too much of the people, preferring the company of plain-spoken men and, while never himself lacking the courtesies, paying little regard to courtly servility. So he was suspected and mistrusted as a communist or fellow traveller though the only faint connection with truth in this belief was that if the Democrat Party, with which we may roughly group all royalists, was on the right, Pridi's followers were on the left. But with them we must also group most liberals, and in fact all these labels are misleading in the context of Siamese politics unless you remember that the essential struggle was between personalities and their supporters. Pridi's included not only Bangkok intellectuals but humbler people throughout the country who once belonged to the FTM. This infuriated his opponents who believed that he was wickedly exploiting something started by them all in the national interest. Another result of the war was that many people, including most of the army and others who had not noticeably opposed the Japanese, found a psychological comfort in joining the opposition to him. And opposition was not lessened by the Democrat Party's propaganda that he aimed at establishing a communist republic. Curiously, though, he acquired more respect even from his most rabid critics than any modern Siamese politician has ever received. But this very ascendancy fed his opponents' antagonism. And the fact that all through the deteriorating political situation he kept out of sight was interpreted by them not as expressive of his desire to teach and guide, but to conceal his grasping ambition. Suddenly this belief appeared to be completely justified, for when Kuang resigned Pridi promptly became Prime Minister himself.

Why? Especially why when the aftermath would show it to have been a fatal step? And most especially why when he could have been Premier at any time after FM Pibul's fall?

The reason, I believe, is that he staked his hope on the proposed new constitution creating a responsible democratic parliament devoted to principle rather than personality, and in order to make sure of getting it through the Assembly and then carrying out its reforms he entered the arena himself. Such was the importance he attached to this new order which was about to be ushered in, that to place the royal seal on it he persuaded Ananda to prolong his stay. The visit first mooted for one month thus lengthened into many months, during which the political dissonance seemed even more jarring because of the harmony that had accompanied his arrival.

No one close to the throne regretted the dissonance more than that brave and devout patriot Prince Subha Svasti (Tahn Chin), himself politically uncommitted. Since Pridi had honoured in the letter and spirit the pledges he gave him on the hazardous night of his wartime descent on Bangkok, Tahn Chin believed in Pridi's sincerity. Feeling

85

deeply the tragedy for Siam of the split between its leaders, he and others of like mind tried to effect a reconciliation between them. We shall see how this well-meant move was to be used in evidence, but here I need only note that all they got for their pains was the taunt of having been bought by Pridi.

This was hardly, however, something that could be said of the King, who had at least until now—that is, March 1946 when Kuang the Great Comedian resigned and Pridi took office—shown the utmost cordiality towards Pridi. During the previous month, going for a few days with his mother and brother to the royal seaside palace at Hua Hin, he invited Pridi to holiday with him. Events were closer to tragedy than anyone could remotely have guessed from the relaxed and intimate atmosphere. Despite their difference in age they had much in common. There was their interest in law, of which one was a student and the other a professor. There was the problem which confronted them both of how best to exercise Authority. There was the strong sense of duty both felt towards all their people. And both were serious men. Besides, Ananda had a good deal to learn which the Mentor was glad to impart, and wartime excitements to hear about which the FTM leader was glad to relate. Dining daily together, and swimming or walking together, they reached out towards each other from the deep reserve of their inner selves. Or was Pridi hiding his true and evil thoughts?

It is relevant here to consider how he was regarded by the Princess Mother. In a family so close-knit she could not be indifferent to Pridi's influence which to some extent overshadowed herself as the one to whom Ananda always turned for advice and direction; and she was naturally concerned for the prerogatives and dignities of his position. On the other hand her background, and the obvious desirability of friendship between Ananda and his most powerful subject, made a counterbalance. And anyway the family would soon be back in her own kingdom of the Villa Watana in Lausanne. Yet—yet, did the question obtrude itself, Can Pridi be trusted?

Afterwards there were said to have been straws in the wind, but it does not follow that she was aware of them at the time, or even that they ever did mean anything to her. However, let us here conveniently glance at some. The official secretary at the Villa Watana, appointed during the war (page 56) and whom she did not like, turned out to have been sent by Pridi in the course of his duties as a Regent, and this fact led to mischievous whispers that the man had been sent to spy for him. Then there was his behaviour at the recent state banquet for Lord Louis Mountbatten: Pridi was not seated at the main table, being at the time neither Regent nor Prime Minister, but such disregard of the national resistance hero seemed an unduly niggling observance of protocol, and pique rather than his declared excuse of illness was said by some to have been the reason for his apparent breach of etiquette in leaving before the King rose. And then, during this Hua Hin holiday itself, later to be so intensively recalled, there were incidents we have yet to examine which seemed straws as big as faggots to set conjecture ablaze. Though all this raised mere suppositions of disrespect, apparently too trivial to have any part in a sober tale, men's lives were to depend upon them. For the same reason attention was to be concentrated on certain incidents which though not directly involving Pridi involved people closely connected with him.

For example, his appointment of Chaleo as the King's Private Secretary turned sour. Secretary Chaleo had general charge of the royal garage, and when one of the royal cars was stolen the theft was considered a dereliction of duty, even though thefts were an everyday occurrence in the post-war crime wave. Having already incurred the royal family's displeasure for alleged disrespectful behaviour, he either resigned or was sacked—the distinction was to be fatally controversial. At about the same time Lt Vacharachai was dismissed from his post as one of Ananda's ADCs. He had absented himself on the excuse of illness, but when the Princess Mother sent a doctor to see how he fared he was found all too healthily playing cards with friends. Thus the two officials appointed by Pridi both left the King's service under a cloud.

However, these departures from the Palace occurred in May, and if the Princess Mother had in fact any suspicion of Pridi my guess is that it arose only long afterwards, in recollection if at all, and certainly not at the time of Pridi's accession to the premiership when Kuang resigned in March.

A day or two before Pridi took office the courts gave judgement on FM Pibul. Or rather, they decreed the legislation against war crimes invalid because it was retrospective—an objection which, incidentally, the Nuremberg War Crimes Tribunal crisply rejected. So FM Pibul walked out of gaol a free man. Still, he had fallen on hard times, being discredited and powerless. Pridi, believing that a sufficient gesture had been made, left him alone. Pibul himself always protested that in his own fashion he had secretly worked for the Allies. Be that as it may, he was now free again, but in the shadows. He retired to the country, watching from afar the growth of personal animosities for any opportunity they might present to his still unslaked ambitions.

Pridi duly achieved the immediate object of his becoming Prime Minister: he put through the new constitution. Among other things it created a senate, the election of which was highly important since both Houses had to approve future governments. The challenge to intriguers on all sides was great and duly accepted but the result was fair, for Pridi's followers who formed a majority in the lower house duly gained a majority in the senate. The relevance of this to our inquiry is that Pridi had then formally to resign, submit his government to a vote of both Houses, and then be invited by the King to renew his premiership: and thus it happened that the royal proclamation of this appointment was Ananda's last official act on earth.

The document was dated 8 June but probably signed by Ananda the previous evening. Up to that evening, 7 June, there is no evidence of any lessening of the cordiality between him and Pridi. He had stood aloof from the heat and dust of the political struggle. The Democrat Party claimed that it enjoyed his favour, and they used this claim to recruit support against Pridi, but though prominent members of the party often visited the Barompiman Hall, their claim is wholly unsubstantiated. Besides, once the new constitution was promulgated Ananda was absorbed in preparations for his long-delayed departure.

There was particular excitement about this departure because the American and British Governments had sent invitations for a state visit before he settled down again to his studies in Switzerland. He proposed to leave Bangkok on 13 June. A superstitious Westerner might have viewed such a date with misgiving but the Siamese do not consider it inauspicious. In fact it was fixed by the Royal Astrologer.

Few Siamese in their everyday lives do anything important without first consulting an astrologer. Similarly no State event, such as elections, coronations, arrivals and departures of the King, and so forth, is fixed without the recommendation of the Brahmin who holds the office of Royal Astrologer. (The Siamese, uncertain whether to be

THE LIFE AND DEATH OF ANANDA

embarrassed by this official sanction of superstition or delighted by
the survival of ancient tradition, delicately steered me off when I
tried to see him.) However, he receives very clear official guidance in
his mysterious calculations, and significantly the date of Ananda's
intended departure was publicly announced to have been fixed by the
Royal Astrologer 'with royal approval'.

As it happens, royal approval was in fact given with surprising
abruptness. Those concerned with arrangements for the state visits to
the West wanted a later date because they needed time to find out the
right things for the King to do and the right hands to shake. But
Ananda, displaying uncharacteristic imperiousness, insisted on the
earliest possible date. So 13 June.

In the weeks before this he made half a dozen journeys to places in
the country. Huge crowds thronged every route. They crouched in
the dust for hours to proffer their poor gifts of a bunch of flowers or a
trussed chicken. Of the realities of the struggle for political power in
Bangkok they knew nothing and cared nothing. Here was their
young King, compassion manifest in his every shy half-smile, ensuring
their greater prosperity by his mere presence and enabling them to
acquire much merit by their grateful acceptance of this opportunity to
show their loyalty. To be loved so greatly, even if Ananda told himself
that the reason was hysteria born of ignorance, warmed the heart; but
it was humbling also—even if his presence *did* sometimes bring rain
as if in proof of his special relationship with the gods.

On 3 June he made his last, most memorable, public visit. It was in
Bangkok itself within a few minutes of the Grand Palace. He went
to the Chinese quarter—that part of the central city distinguished by
its blaze of neon lights; and its vast advertisement cut-outs in front of
cinemas; and its thronged shops, from those of opulent jewellers to
the purveyors of grisly medical cures. Afterwards there was to be some
controversy as to whether Pridi approved of the visit. What is certain
is that Ananda carried through with it although he was not feeling
well. The Chinese, always sensitive about their position which had
been threatened by the nationalistic decrees of former régimes,
interpreted his visit as a gesture of royal protection. They gave themselves over to scenes of astonishing enthusiasm. Some Chinese even
brushed handfuls of dust off the streets he walked, to keep for purposes
of veneration.

Three days later, 6 June, he attended the Oxford and Cambridge Dinner, a private function at the palace of one of the princes and attended by prominent Western-educated Siamese and a number of Westerners. He appeared quite recovered from his indisposition.

Next evening, 7 June, Pridi had a private discussion with him after dinner. It was probably then that Ananda signed or arranged to sign next day's royal proclamation of Pridi's re-appointment to the premiership. They talked also about the Regency Council which would have to be instituted after Ananda's departure in a week's time. This discussion was afterwards to assume gargantuan significance. Pridi had suggested Prajadhipok's widowed Queen; Ananda preferred or proposed the most prominent of the ex-Political Prisoners, his uncle Prince Rangsit. The precise degree of difference, if any, between them on this issue was to be fatefully controversial.

The following day Ananda felt ill and had a stomach ache. He breakfasted and lunched with his mother and brother as usual but felt steadily worse. In his engagement book two functions outside the Palace were noted for that day, the cremation of ex-Regent Aditya and the Household Guards' Dinner, so arrangements were made for Prince Bhoomipol to deputize for him at both. As the afternoon passed, the Princess Mother became anxious about Ananda and sent for the Royal Physician, Dr Nit.

Dr Nitayavejvisidh (to give him only part of his full name) had been a friend of the Mahidols in the US where he was a student on one of Ananda's father's scholarships, and when the family first settled in Bangkok, Dr Nit became their doctor. His appointment during Ananda's present visit had, therefore, been a natural choice.

Summoned to the Barompiman Hall he found Ananda lying on a sofa in the royal boudoir (see plan on page 76). He said he felt rotten and kept wanting to vomit. His tongue was thickly furred, his stomach was swollen and he was a little feverish with a temperature of 99°. Dr Nit found nothing in this to worry about. He knew that Ananda had suffered such upsets before—'intestinal upsets', he called them, caused by indigestion. He prescribed a tablet ('Novanyin') to be taken at once to lower the youth's temperature, directed that an enema should be given later in the evening, and left sleeping pills ('Optalidon'); in the morning, he said, Ananda should be given castor oil.

The Princess Mother took charge of supervising this course of treatment. She had her dinner with Ananda in the boudoir, ordering a dish of oatmeal for him. The Royal Nanny was there, and the page on duty was in the offing.

The two pages of the bedchamber previously mentioned, Nai Chit and Butr, alternated in being on duty. Each was on call for twenty-four hours. The 'shift' began about 11 a.m., though when the King retired for the night the page on duty could leave him and go to sleep in special quarters outside the Barompiman Hall but within the Grand Palace. The page who had come on duty that morning was Butr.

Butr had been in the service of King Prajadhipok, and his father and grandfather served in the royal family before him. He was a simple fellow, rather thin and small, with a little, expressive face and bright eyes, and Ananda was fond of him with a child's remembered fondness, for Butr had acted as 'horse' for him when he first came to Bangkok, and so attached to him still was he that he often got him to comb his hair or dry his body after bathing, and indeed he had chosen him to accompany him on his state visits abroad and back to Switzerland. For this purpose the Princess Mother had given him money for his clothes and arranged to pay half his salary to his family during his absence, which he also prepared for like any pious Siamese by going to the temple to take a holy bath for good fortune, though afterwards the sinister question arose as to what particular enterprise it was that he sought good fortune in.

Being on duty, then, that night when Ananda was ill, he was directed by the Princess Mother to administer the enema, and between nine and ten o'clock he helped Ananda prepare for bed. Together the two of them went into the Buddha Room, which as the plan shows was really a large recess divided by a curtain from the bedchamber. Butr lit the candles and handed them to Ananda for the latter's obeisances.

Butr next held open the mosquito net, by which Ananda's bed was surrounded at a distance of one pace, for him to enter. He was attired for the night in blue Chinese silk trousers and a light T-shirt or vest. The Princess Mother was on hand to give him one of the sleeping pills. 'Nand,' she said, 'if there's anything just ring the bell.' He replied, 'Yes, Mam.' So she left him. Shortly afterwards Butr did likewise.

It was the night of 8–9 June, a Saturday night in the Year of the Dog, Buddhist Era 2489, AD 1946, and Ananda would not know another.

VIII

ABOUT six o'clock next morning the Princess Mother left her quarters in the north-west wing of the Barompiman Hall to attend to Ananda. The front corridor which led from her room ended at the door of his study, but this was normally kept locked at night so she crossed over to the back corridor which ended at his dressing-room. The palace was already astir even on this upper floor. The night guard, which had changed at two-hour intervals throughout the night, was going off duty: it consisted of two men stationed by the Main Balustrade where they had a view both ways down the front and back corridors, two other men stationed at the foot of the staircase below them, and the Inspector of the Watch. The cleaning staff was coming on duty. In addition, an Assistant Chief of Royal Pages was at hand to bring up the hot water, milk, brandy and two small glasses ordered by the Princess Mother to take with her via the dressing-room to Ananda's bedroom.

According to her account, Ananda was still asleep. She shook him and asked, 'Had a good night?' He replied, 'Good.' She then gave him a dose of castor oil mixed with brandy, followed by a little hot milk. He proceeded to brush his teeth; and the Princess Mother, thinking he still wanted to sleep, returned to her own bed.

Shortly before seven o'clock, two pages of the royal table began preparing the porch—it led, remember, off the front corridor in front of the Main Balustrade—for breakfast. One of them was not feeling well and left with the permission of the Chief of the Night Attendants, who himself took his place, going downstairs once but returning before seven-thirty.

Between seven and seven-thirty Butr returned to resume his duties. He would claim that as usual when on his twenty-four hour stint he had slept in the Service Section of the Royal Household Bureau just beyond the iron gates leading from the grounds of the Barompiman Hall to the central courtyard of the Outside.

By now the sun was getting up. The temperature, which had scarcely fallen below 80° through the night, was rising. Sunday was little different from other days and the whole city round about was beginning to swarm with activity. The 'floating markets' of loaded sampans on the canals were offering their foodstuffs. Shopkeeping families were rolling up their sleeping gear off floor and counter before taking down their shutters. Monks were returning to their monasteries with filled bowls from their dawn round of alms-gathering. The streets were growing louder with the noise of motor-cars, trams, over-loaded single-decker buses, and bumping trishaws, frightening away the packs of pariah dogs who still scavenge the streets at night.

Butr set about the routine which he, like Nai Chit, always followed when on duty. He saw that the cleaners were about their work (they did not go into the east wing while the King was there), and he opened a section of the screen door which gave access from the back corridor to Ananda's dressing-room. This was to enable him to see when the King woke, because usually on waking up between eight and eight-thirty Ananda crossed the dressing-room to reach the bathroom. Butr would then go into the bedroom with a glass of orange juice to put on a small bedside cabinet, hook up the mosquito net around the bed, put the morning newspapers—in which, to save Ananda time, he would have marked with red or blue pencil all duplicated items—on the table in the study, and unlock the study door to the front corridor. In preparation for this ritual the page got the orange juice, already waiting for him on a service table near the Main Balustrade, and placed it on the window sill outside the partly open door of the dressing-room where he sat down to wait. Shortly before eight the newspapers were delivered to him, and a little later someone brought a book on the Royal Page Service which Ananda had expressed a wish to read.

According to Butr, what happened next was that at about eight-thirty while he waited in the corridor outside the dressing-room he looked into the room and saw Ananda standing there. The King was facing his bedroom, which is to say with his back to the bathroom, and though he glanced across at Butr he said nothing. Butr assumed he must just have returned from the bathroom, so picking up the orange juice he followed Ananda who had gone wordlessly into his bedroom. At the door between it and the dressing-room Butr paused. Ananda

93

lay in his bed, which was in the centre of the room with its headboard towards the Buddha-room: he had his knees drawn up and he was gazing towards the foot of the bed, and with his hand nearest Butr— that is, his left hand—he waved a gesture of dismissal.

Butr therefore returned to his station in the back corridor outside the door of the dressing-room. After about a quarter of an hour someone unexpected arrived. It was Nai Chit—unexpected because he was not due to take over from Butr for a couple of hours yet. He explained that he had earlier that morning been to a jeweller about having a box made for the royal family's Chakri orders and decorations, and that as the exact dimensions were needed he proposed using a piece of paper he had just obtained from the royal kitchen to measure the decorations, which were kept in a safe in Ananda's dressing-room. Butr told him that the King had been to the bathroom but refused his orange juice and gone back to bed. Nai Chit, not wanting to risk disturbing the King, decided to wait with Butr at the door of the dressing-room. That, at least, was to be the two pages' story.

Ten minutes later, round about nine o'clock, Prince Bhoomipol came along the back corridor. He had finished breakfast on the porch and encountering the two pages he asked after his brother. Butr replied: 'There appears to be nothing serious, sire. After toilet His Majesty retired again to bed and hasn't yet taken his orange juice.' Bhoomipol turned and disappeared along the back corridor to his own room.

Ten more minutes passed. Time: say, 9.20 a.m.

A single, startling sound rent the air. Unmistakably a pistol shot. And it came from Ananda's bedroom.

In the opposite wing of the building the Princess Mother was about to leave her room with her lady-in-waiting to go to breakfast. Suddenly Nai Chit burst in. 'The King's shot himself!' he wrenched out.

The words that rose from the Princess Mother's lips were quite mechanical: 'My poor Nand.' Horror, terror, pity and desperate incredulity held her for an instant transfixed before she began to run, asking no questions, and running through her crashing world grasped at the hope that the page was foolishly mistaken, or that 'shot' meant merely a graze, and that her son would greet her with a rueful smile at having been careless with one of his pistols. But the spectacle in the bedroom obliterated hope.

Ananda lay in bed as if asleep. His flowered coverlet was drawn up. He lay on his back, his legs stretched out straight together. His arms, extended fairly close to his sides, were outside the coverlet. On his left wrist was his watch, on a finger of his left hand his ring, and an inch or two from his left hand a pistol, the American Army ·45. Not that the Princess Mother took in all these details. Her entire being was concentrated on the blood oozing from Ananda's forehead. Nai Chit opened the mosquito net for her and with a scream she flung herself on her son's body.

Not far behind came the Royal Nanny. Her account of her movements would be that she was putting away some cine-film in Bhoomipol's room when she heard what she thought might be a shot followed by running footsteps. Seeing the Princess Mother making for the King's quarters she hurried after her. She saw her distraught on the bed, endlessly repeating through her sobs, 'My dear Nand, my dear Nand.' The Nanny half lifted her away but she again bent keening and weeping over her son, across whose face, shoulder and pillow the blood freely flowed, until the Nanny moved her towards the foot of the bed where she lay half on the floor.

The Nanny took hold of Ananda's wrist. Though the Palace Law of 1450 had but recently given way to the Penal Code which no longer made anyone who touched the royal person guilty of a capital offence, there was still a powerful taboo and this she defied by feeling the King's pulse. *It was beating.* At this same moment of discovery—everything was confused, confusing and indescribably terrible—the Nanny was aware of the pistol close to the wrist she held. The barrel pointed towards the Princess Mother at the foot of the bed, and fearing an accident the Nanny quickly picked it up with three fingers and put it on the bedside cabinet where Ananda had placed his spectacles and where a small clock ticked off his final seconds, for when the Nanny again took his wrist the pulse had stopped.

Told this, the Princess Mother, whose weeping had momentarily been arrested by the Nanny's first discovery, cried more unrestrainedly than before, and with a corner of the coverlet tried to staunch the flow of blood. She called for another piece of cloth and continued her efforts.

Meanwhile Bhoomipol—he himself was to testify—had been in his playroom, as distinct from his bedroom near by, when he had

95

heard someone cry out. He went towards the porch and encountered the lady-in-waiting who told him his brother had shot himself. He at once went into the royal bedroom, entering very soon after the Royal Nanny. He then hurried out and met Butr whom he asked to fetch a doctor. Returning to the bedroom he saw his mother trying to staunch the flow of blood. He comforted her and took her to a chair at the foot of the bed. For a boy of eighteen he kept remarkably self-composed.

The Royal Nanny applied herself to stopping the blood. She too kept calm despite watching a young man die whom she had nursed in infancy; but she was a woman of uncomplicated piety, taught by Buddhism that death is inevitable and transitory.

When Butr got downstairs to carry out Bhoomipol's instructions, he was told that the doctor had already been sent for. Thus it was that the Royal Physician, Dr Nit, who had something of his late patron Prince Mahidol's simple habits and was busy cleaning his car in the grounds of his house, received an urgent message from a royal page summoning him at the Princess Mother's behest to the Grand Palace. He washed and set out for the Barompiman Hall, arriving there shortly before ten.

When he entered the royal bedchamber the Princess Mother was sitting down—either in that room or just beyond the open doorway to the study—and Bhoomipol sat on the floor by her feet, looking sad but calm. The doctor quickly and reverently crawled across the floor to the bed. A moment's examination and he helplessly pronounced himself unable to do anything. The Princess Mother's voice, broken with grief, exclaimed—demanding an answer not of him but Fate—'Did you ever think such a thing could happen?'

She asked him if he would stay to clean the body. With the help of the Royal Nanny, the two pages being in attendance, he did so. He found that the wound on Ananda's forehead, above the left eye-brow, was shaped like a small cross of the kind put at the end of a letter to signify a kiss.

Fresh bed linen and apparel were brought; and blocks of ice ranged down either side of the bed, together with an electric fan to blow cold air continuously across the corpse. Except for the whirring of the fan and the weeping of the mother, everything, everyone in the royal suite was extraordinarily still about him who had been Lord of Life.

But downstairs, and beyond in the city, fact and rumour were spreading amazement, incredulity, shock, and the seeds of suspicion unbounded. This process, which in the end would dominate the situation, was initially but a faint *obbligato* to the sequence of events in the Grand Palace.

At the time that Dr Nit was being sent for, the Chief of the Palace Guards telephoned news of the tragedy to the aristocrat who held the office of Chief Major Domo and Protocol. He was at his private house and before setting out for the Palace he instructed another dignitary, the Chief of the Royal Fanfare and Paraphernalia Section, to report to Pridi at the latter's official residence by the riverside. Pridi immediately called in the King's Secretary-General, the Minister of the Interior, and the Police Chief (entitled Director-General of the Police Department). The first of these was to give the only account of Pridi at this moment: 'He was very agitated and pacing the floor. He said to me in English, "The King is a suicide".'

They all went straight to the Barompiman Hall where five senior princes together with leading cabinet ministers and courtiers were fast assembling. During the ensuing hours, after they had made obeisance before Ananda's body, they gathered downstairs and anxiously debated the situation.

The Police Chief and his top-ranking officers had meanwhile been busy. An attempt to examine Ananda's body was sharply stopped by Prince Rangsit, Ananda's uncle, whose term of imprisonment had not removed the encrustations of tradition from his mind: royalty must not be touched by anybody. The premises, however, were carefully inspected and the servants, guard and officials questioned. The Police Chief had started by suspecting assassination, but after this investigation he was satisfied that Ananda had committed suicide.

His conclusion was shared by all the princes and statesmen and officials assembled downstairs. As this prolonged and agitated meeting will crop up constantly it may conveniently be referred to as the Palace Meeting. Some of those present were afterwards to say they had reservations about the conclusion of suicide; but any doubts were no more, in those stupefying hours, than a vague unease at the back of the mind. No sign could be found of an assassin's entry or exit, and Pridi said the King had quarrelled with nobody, including himself. In the course of the discussion the two pages of the bed-

97

chamber were sent for, Nai Chit being told to bring down the pistol. It had always been kept, the meeting was informed, in Ananda's small bedside cabinet. When the Royal Nanny picked it up from the bed she had put it on top of this cabinet, but fearing that the Princess Mother might turn it on herself Butr had subsequently put it away in a drawer in the dressing-room. Summoned to the meeting, Nai Chit brought this drawer with him, and in it was also a spent cartridge-case supposedly belonging to the bullet which had killed Ananda, though no one actually asked about it or how it got into the drawer (Nai Chit was later to explain that he had put it there after finding it on the floor near Ananda's bed). Instead, Nai Chit was asked to show how he thought Ananda must have committed suicide, and this he demonstrated lying on the floor. Butr appeared to be too distressed to speak. The pistol was examined and handled by many of those present. It was cocked ready for firing, and fully loaded except for one missing round.

The problem agitating the princes and statesmen was not, however, the cause of death, which seemed plainly an open-and-shut case of suicide, but what to tell the public. An announcement of suicide was too shocking to the repute and dignity of the throne to be contemplated. Prince Rangsit expressed himself strongly to this effect and the others agreed. What explanation, then, were they to give the nation?

Under the duress of uncertainty and grief the various suggestions put forward were scarcely satisfactory: they ranged from cholera to stomach ache. Dr Nit especially was against any suggestion of an internal malady: he knew how monstrous rumour mushrooms quicker in Bangkok than almost any city in the world, and he was not going to provoke whispers of poisoning. Time passed; they had to make up their minds; the afternoon was far advanced before at last a communiqué was drafted, agreed by them all, and issued by the Royal Household Bureau.

Since the 2nd June of this year the King has had an intestinal upset and suffered loss of vitality. Nevertheless the King has continued to carry out His functions in making visits to the people. Later, as the upset had not subsided the King was obliged to remain in bed and was unable to attend the royal ceremonies scheduled. On the 9th June this year after rising at six in the morning the King, after taking castor oil, attended to His toilet as usual and then returned to bed. At about nine a shot was heard in the Palace by the royal pages attached to the Royal Bedchamber who immediately rushed in to investigate. They saw the King lying dead on His bed with blood over His body. They therefore reported to the Princess Mother and then proceeded to attend the royal remains. An examination thereof was made by the Director-Generals of the Police Department and the Department of Medical Sciences, as the result of which it is concluded that the King must have played with his pistol as he was fond of doing, resulting in an accident.

The minor inaccuracies in this communiqué reflect not only a typical Siamese disregard for the strict niceties of fact but the agitation of at least a majority of the subscribers to this extraordinarily inept document. They wanted above everything to preserve the sanctity of the throne. Therefore they strove to present an acceptable story: the King had been ill, he was weak, making more likely that while he played with a gun, which he often did, he met with an accident.

The communiqué was broadcast over the radio early in the evening. For many it confirmed dreadful rumour. For others this had already been done by signs and portents which even Western-educated Siamese sometimes believe in—like Mom Seni and his brother Kukrit Pramoj who were together when at sunset they wept to see across the sky a great band of yellow resembling the sash of the Chakri Order. But for most people the radio provided the first news, flooding them with anguish. From stilted teak houses poised over canals, from sampan homes lilting on the river, from the shady modern villas of the well-to-do, from the slits of shops and cluttered workshops, Bangkok delivered up thousands upon thousands of people who made their way in sorrow and fear and curiosity to stand outside the white walls of the Grand Palace. And through the countryside, across rice-field, jungle, and mountain, the news travelled via the monasteries and the few other possessors of radio sets, causing even greater consternation because of the greater veneration of the countrypeople.

When Prince Rangsit arrived at the Barompiman Hall that morning he had burst out to his sister-in-law the Princess Mother, with scant regard for tact, 'So it's turned out true what the fortune-teller told you, that Bhoomipol and not Ananda would be crowned King!' As the day wore on, persons coming to help or condole prostrated themselves before Bhoomipol. The implication was not lost on the Princess Mother. At first she set her mind against her now only son becoming King, but then recalling herself to the demands of their family position she acquiesced when he himself said he would deem it his duty to accept if he were invited. There was no automatic right of succession: the National Assembly had to propose and approve.

Dr Nit's day, that had begun so casually with his cleaning his car, was not over with the end of the interminable Palace Meeting and the issuing of the communiqué. At nine o'clock that evening he returned to the Barompiman Hall with sedatives for the Princess Mother. He intended to hand them over to the Royal Nanny but Bhoomipol said he would deliver them. The young celestial prince was in a sad, ruminative mood. There was already upon him the unsmiling gravity which would henceforward make him a stranger to the exuberant Bhoomipol everyone had previously known. The kindly, cautious, bespectacled Dr Nit had been a friend of both his parents in America before his birth, physician to the family whenever they had been in Bangkok, and he could almost be regarded as a relation. Bhoomipol said to him: 'I think there's no other explanation than accident for my brother's death. I can't help clinging to superstition because four or five days ago he was very tender towards me, especially when he led me by the hand into the dining-room. He'd never done that before.'

He paused. Then he said: 'You must help me, Luang [a minor title like a baronetcy, bestowed before the 1932 revolutionaries abolished titles] Nit. Don't leave me in a situation like this.'

Long afterwards the doctor was closely questioned about Bhoomipol's precise meaning, but he could attach no meaning to it beyond a young man's need for help as he tried to square up to a new and totally unexpected life. Even as he talked with the doctor, Pridi arrived. A special session of the Assembly that evening had unanimously asked him to invite Bhoomipol to be King.

'I accept the invitation,' Bhoomipol answered, 'and I will do my best to lead Siam to a glorious future.' So he became the ninth monarch in the dynasty of Chakri. Nor for the best part of fifteen years would he publicly be seen to smile.

Next day, doctors and nurses from the Chulalongkorn Hospital came to inject Ananda's thigh with a preservative and to prepare the body. Tradition demanded prolonged rites spread over many weeks. Those observed at the death of any Siamese are elaborate; the higher you go in rank, the more elaborate; and for a king they are passing strange. But the basic assumption for all is that though the physical being is dead the astral body continues alive and present for forty-nine days.

The first ceremony was ritual bathing. The new King, his mother, senior princes and officers of the State in turn poured scented water, which had been blessed by monks and kept in crystal vessels, over Ananda's feet. Next, the special section of pages permitted to touch the royal person dressed him in the glittering robes he would have worn for his coronation.

After this majestic state the rest is bathos, for he was placed in a sitting posture with his legs crossed and drawn close to his body, his hands clasped together holding incense sticks and a candle as if he prayed to the Buddha, and strips of white cloth were tightly wrapped round him like the bandaging of a mummy. Thus trussed and swathed he was put, still upright, in a silver urn—wedged, rather, for the fit was very tight. All this had to be watched by Bhoomipol, who then placed a crown on the corpse's head, before finally the lid of the urn, following the contoured spire of the Siamese crown, was locked shut.

In solemn procession attendants carried the silver urn on a royal palanquin across the long courtyard of the Outside and deposited it five tiers high in the beautiful building called the Dusit Hall*. Here the silver urn was enclosed by an intricately chased golden urn, known as the Big Golden One, put together in eight sections because of its immense weight. (It was made on the orders of the first Chakri in 1808 and he was so pleased with it that for some days he had it in his bedroom. When one of his wives wept at what she took to be a sign of ill-omen, he sharply retorted that if he did not see it while he was still alive how could he ever expect to see it?) The white Umbrella of State, consisting of nine silk bands of diminishing circumference in ascending order, was raised above.

There in the Dusit Hall the monks started the official ceremony of One Hundred Days. The new King attended before the golden urn each evening for an hour. Every morning princes came to feed the four monks who had chanted all through the night, as others would through the day. In the afternoons the public filed past, awed and sorrowful. On the seventh, the fiftieth and the hundredth day big full-dress ceremonies took place in the presence of the royal family, the

* Not to be confused with the Dusit Palace, the centre of the 1932 Revolution and since used for the Assembly.

royal relatives, high ministers and officials, the diplomatic corps, and always the saffron cloister of head-shaven monks. But the conclusion of these ceremonies did not mean that the cremation would take place yet. Ananda was to stay in his golden urn for almost four years; and by then his own tragedy was to have become merged in the even more bizarre tragedy of its sequel.

For the doctors and nurses who came from the Chulalongkorn Hospital to prepare the body the day after Ananda's death returned with disquieting information. They had found in the back of his head a wound smaller than that in his forehead, and from the belief that the exit mark of a bullet is greater than its entry mark deduced that Ananda died neither from accident nor suicide. He had been shot from behind.

IX

THE Chulalongkorn Hospital doctors' conclusion appeared in the popular press. It conferred 'scientific' confirmation on sinister rumours which had been started by anonymous telephone calls. These had been made, perhaps on the Sunday of Ananda's death but certainly by Monday, to the American and British diplomatic representatives, the heads of the armed services, and others. Some named the assassin. That name was shouted out by an unknown man in the darkness of a cinema: *'Pridi killed the King!'*

The words flung Bangkok into a state of seething anger, speculation, disbelief. The violent death of a king was appalling enough to the Siamese mind but here it occurred in an atmosphere of intense political animosity; and the suspicion caused by certain surrounding circumstances, instead of silencing suspicion merely increased it. First of these was the communiqué: it said a great deal about everything except what really mattered—how the 'accident' befell a cautious young man well used to firearms. Secondly, fanatical royalists demanded to know why not even a single arrest had been made when historical precedent required the immediate execution of everyone concerned with the care of the King if he died by violence however arising. Finally, by issuing a further communiqué the day after the first the authorities exposed their own uncertainty.

This communiqué came from the police as the result of a conference largely duplicating Sunday's Palace Meeting. In an attempt to deal frontally with the rumours already shaking the city, it referred to the three possibilities—assassination, suicide, and accident. And it insisted that investigation had revealed nothing suggestive of anything but accident: lying in bed playing with the pistol Ananda probably checked whether it was cocked and in doing so he accidentally touched the trigger.

Next day, yet another communiqué came out, again from the

103

police. It listed the King's engagements for the day of his death: in the morning a prince was to have taken his leave before entering the priesthood, at noon Prince Subha Svasti (Tahn Chin) was due for lunch, and lastly a Professor of Philosophy in the Royal Secretariat was to have called to arrange for the leavetaking of the Prince Patriarch (head of the Buddhist Church) on the King's departure. The fact that Ananda had made these arrangements, said the communiqué, suggested accidental death, or at all events 'clearly precluded any presumption of suicide'.

The fatuousness of this reasoning satisfied only the gullible, but its conclusion accorded with the universal rejection of suicide. This was not only because the idea was abhorrent in connection with a king but because there appeared not the slightest reason why Ananda should have wanted to kill himself, or the slightest indication of mental unbalance which could have driven him to it on the very eve of his departure.

So rumours of murder and murderers swirled night and day round the city and overflowed abroad, baffling some, infuriating others, appalling all, and submerging the whole of political life in a morass of suspicion and counter-suspicion. Pridi's supporters have ever since blamed these rumours on the deliberate activity of the royalists in general and the Democrat Party in particular. The mysterious telephone calls and the shout in the cinema are attributed to them; and even the employment of a group of men to go about in public places spreading the allegation of Pridi's complicity. Kuang the Great Comedian and the Pramoj brothers hotly assert, however, that the outcry was the spontaneous and inevitable reaction of the public at large once any suspicion of foul play arose. As the Prime Minister responsible for the King's safety, as well as the man who had both invited Ananda to Siam and extended his stay, Pridi was obviously answerable to the nation, especially as allegations of his direct complicity multiplied, and their plain duty was to call him to account. This attitude, while perfectly proper even if it angered Pridi's supporters with its coincidence of duty and political advantage, was hardly calculated to still public perturbation. Besides, many royalists mistrusted Pridi so readily that they accepted his alleged guilt as proven fact.

Other suspects were likewise tried by rumour—his own followers had their ideas, and foreigners like the British had theirs, and generally the range of suspects included almost everyone we have met—but within Siam the weight of information, true and false, piled up primarily against Pridi. It amounted to this: a named assassin had with inside help killed Ananda as the result of a conspiracy either headed by Pridi or to satisfy his wishes.

Ambition was his motive; inordinate ambition. It was so great that he did not even respect the throne—a number of incidents had betrayed his contempt for it—and he wanted a leftist republic headed by himself, especially since the monarchy impeded his scheme for a South-East Asia federation.

This theory about Pridi's alleged motive was elaborated by the conjecture that the conspiracy had probably aimed at wiping out the whole royal family, but that the conspirators had been moved to premature action when a bitter quarrel between Pridi and Ananda over who was to be Regent after Ananda's departure touched off one of Pridi's pathological rages which, it was said, the public never saw but which jealousy over Ananda's popularity and superior rank had already aroused. An alternative or additional motive was also whispered about, and in time became increasingly insisted on: Ananda, if not actually afraid of Pridi's ambitiousness, had become exasperated by it and had decided to abdicate in favour of his brother in order to enter the political arena where his popularity would overwhelm Pridi; and getting wind of this scheme, Pridi had struck.

Such were the reasons given to damn Pridi. But they are more important for a Westerner than an Oriental, who cares little about logical motive and is readier to accept without question an eruption, however irrational, from the depths of the human psyche.

Now Pridi's own reaction to the conclusion reached by the Chulalongkorn Hospital doctors, which was the essential origin of the storm about his head, could be interpreted according to one's belief in his guilt or innocence. That is, it was as consistent with guilt as with a Prime Minister's proper concern about the rumours disturbing the peace of the whole nation. He sent for the doctors, and expressed himself forcibly on their conduct in talking so freely to the popular press. He considered arresting them but, dissuaded by the Police Chief, confined himself to a warning. So at the start he and the medical profession got on the wrong side of each other.

One distinguished member of the profession, however, kept a cool head. While noisy speculation filled the corridors of the Assembly—a pro-Pridi deputy was actually assaulted by a colleague—and almost everywhere in the whole city when any two people came together, the Royal Physician applied himself to practicalities. Dr Nit went shooting pigs.

He wanted to test the belief that a bullet always makes a bigger wound at its exit than its entry. By arrangement with the Police Chief three or four pigs were taken to the compound of Police Headquarters. It is unlikely that history had a precedent for porkers being called upon to stand-in for a king, and indeed there was criticism of such an heretical procedure, but Dr Nit's experiment proved an important point. When the pigs were shot by the same kind of pistol as that found next to Ananda, the Chulalongkorn Hospital doctors were shown to have been poor forensic experts. Their conclusion had been quite unsound, and in fact confirmation that Ananda had after all been shot from the front came with discovery of the lethal bullet embedded in the mattress beneath where his head had lain.

It was discovered on Wednesday by the investigating police under Nai Chit's guidance, for public agitation had far from allowed them to close their file. They next sought out the bed linen. The flowered coverlet, the sheet on which Ananda had been lying when shot, and the pillow case, had already, like his nightclothes and even the mosquito net, been laundered and were spotless. But the royal launderer, considering the pillow itself blood-soaked beyond redemption, had by no one's leave but his own buried it in the golf course. It was dug out, and found to confirm the evidence of the pillow case that the bullet had missed it when travelling from Ananda's head into the mattress.

None of these discoveries or experiments made any difference once the suspicion of murder had taken root in the public mind. Even if Ananda had not been shot from the back the assassin could have fired from the front, and this seemed in fact a more likely happening while Ananda dozed. As the storm around Pridi blew up more fiercely, fanned by a bellowing popular press, he took action. He set up a Commission of Inquiry. By a notice issued on 18 June 1946 with the approval of the Regency Council (appointed during Bhoomipol's minority and headed by his uncle Prince Rangsit) the Commission was entrusted with investigating Ananda's death of nine days before. The Police Chief had to present the evidence, supplementing it with any further evidence the Commission might want, and he could enforce the attendance of witnesses. The chairman was the President of the Dikka Court, the highest court of appeal in the country. His colleagues were three senior princes; the respective heads of the Appeal Court, the Criminal Court, the Department of Prosecution, and the three armed services; and the president of the two houses of parliament.

This formidable array began work the day after the notice. They first inspected the Barompiman Hall and appointed an advisory medical panel of a dozen or more doctors, including four Westerners. The panel was allowed to do something unprecedented and unthinkable in Siamese history: it carried out a post-mortem on Ananda's body.

The great golden urn was unjointed in its eight sections, the lid of the silver urn unlocked, the poor fetid bundle eased out, the juice-sodden bandages unwrapped; and the mouldering remains were subjected to X-ray photography in ten positions, and to the scalpel, the probe, and all the gleaming instruments of dissection. The x-shaped wound starting an inch above the left eye was measured at an inch and a half each way. A surgical pin then traced the course of the bullet: after gouging a hole of half an inch diameter in the bone it followed a perfectly straight but slightly downward-inclining course until its emergence from the left occiput (one of the two bulges at the back of one's head, between the ears) near the nape of the neck. Both holes were surrounded by broken bone; there was no metal in them. Death had been instantaneous because the bullet destroyed a vital area of the brain. Under a small square of skin taken from the forehead wound the doctors found not only a burn but pistol powder, proving conclusively that the bullet entered from the front. The intestines and parts of the liver and kidneys were removed for analysis but produced no trace of poison, so disposing of one of the rumours concerning Ananda's illness during his last days.

The medical panel also experimented to determine the distance at which the pistol had been fired. At the Siriraj Hospital where the Princess Mother once trained, bullets were fired into the heads of half a dozen human corpses. These were of people aged between twenty and forty, some newly dead and some not. The conclusion reached was that the muzzle of the pistol had been held no more than an inch and a half from Ananda's face.

THE DEVIL'S DISCUS

On 26 June the Commission began public hearings in a building at the other end of the Pramane Ground from the Grand Palace. The crowds which flocked to it spilt over onto the Pramane Ground where they made a gigantic picnic of the occasion. To that dusty plain at the sweltering height of the hot season they came with their families, children and all, to squat, stroll, chatter, and part with their ticals to itinerant restaurateurs who conjured up little food-stalls complete with stove and crockery and stools, or to hawkers of fruit and sweet-meats; and old people who, too poor to eat fully, or from simple addiction, sucked pellets of opium rolled in their pale, seamed palms.

In contrast with the festivity outside, the proceedings of the Commission went gravely forward. Yet now and then, as at the entry of the two pages Nai Chit and Butr and ex-Secretary Chaleo, angry outbursts from the public showed that rumour and the popular press had already singled out some at least of those concerned in the alleged plot to kill Ananda. And when the Royal Nanny went into the witness-box, applause greeted her declaration that the King had been murdered.

Such incidents were magnified by the popular press, worsening the condition into which public life had sunk. Note that the Siamese press has little in common with the complex organizations of the West, being for the most part incredibly disorganized in a few cluttered rickety rooms with some printing machines and a handful of staff more ebullient than professional, even readier to invent scandal than to report it, and so conscious of their fleeting existence that the keeping of picture-blocks and copies of back numbers and such basic sources of reference as a clippings library is almost unknown.

Pridi clamped down a temporary censorship. The spate of irresponsible allegations even while the Commission sat was bad enough, but worse when an election was about to be held, since the new constitution required the nominated half of the Assembly to be replaced by popularly elected deputies the same as the other half. Despite the curb on the press, the election—in August—was dominated by what had become known as the King's Death Case.

The Democrat Party's campaign was loud with accusations against Pridi's government for not clarifying the matter, and heavy with implications of his and his associates' guilt. There were two pro-Pridi parties and they were equally vociferous in denouncing this apparent exploitation of a national tragedy. Expressive of the prevailing frenzy, a bomb was thrown into a crowd listening to the Democrat Party, costing one of its leading personalities a leg. In the result, such of the electorate who bothered to go to the polls expressed massive approval of Pridi: his supporters won 57 seats, the Democrat Party 11, and Independents 7.

Pridi felt himself vindicated: the great majority of at least the politically conscious electorate rejected the calumny of his opponents. With the new constitution now fully operative, his object in taking on the Premiership was accomplished. Tired out, he resigned and reverted to his position of Senior Statesman while a new government was formed under his friend the liberal Admiral Dhamrong.

Before this, one of his last functions as Prime Minister was to attend the departure of King Bhoomipol and the Princess Mother. To the grief of the past few months had been added fears of more killing. Security had tightened; Bhoomipol gave instructions for anything or anyone suspicious to be reported immediately; and when at night the lights sometimes failed, the Royal Nanny rushed to wake him and the Princess Mother. On the arrival of an RAF York aircraft sent by the British to fly the King to Switzerland, British troops guarded it continuously, it was floodlit at night, and the crew were forbidden the city. The time of day fixed by the Royal Astrologer for the royal departure bothered the pilot, who wanted an earlier time in order to cross the mountainous border before the south-west monsoon turned the weather against him. But the Royal Astrologer could not be moved, and indeed Bhoomipol and his mother were safely carried from the scene of such dreadful memory.

Back at the Villa Watana there were memories of a different kind to live with as mother and son, rejoined by the former's personal secretary Nai Anek and the latter's tutor M. Seraidaris, tried to pick up the threads of their Swiss life. But for over a year she could seldom stop crying, he had prematurely shed his youth, and for neither could life ever be the same again. Returning to the university, Bhoomipol switched from Science to Law in preparation for his new responsibilities.

In Bangkok on 31 October the Commission of Inquiry presented its report on Ananda's death. *It completely rejected any idea of accident.* Beyond this sensational verdict it could go little further, being unconvinced of suicide and finding insufficient evidence of assassination.

It complained that it had been hampered by not knowing whether there was more evidence than the police had chosen or been asked by it to produce. It had merely conducted a preliminary investigation, which had yielded the doubts which it reported 'for the benefit of further investigation to find out the truth'.

Rejection of the accident theory could scarcely have been more embarrassing to Pridi and the authorities who had set so much store by it in trying to hush up the whole affair. The theory was in fact scarcely to be heard of again, and if the American Army ·45 pistol found by Ananda's hand is briefly considered, the reasons become clear.

The American Army ·45 is usually called a Colt Forty-five, though two companies besides Colt make it. First produced before World War I, huge quantities were poured out for the GI in World War II. It is a veritable piece of miniature artillery: black, with a brown hatchwork grip on either side the butt, the overall length nearly nine inches, weight nearly three pounds when fully loaded, barrel nearly an inch in diameter. The inch-long bullets are loaded into a magazine which slips into the butt from underneath. On being fired, a flash and a puff of smoke precede powder fumes; the spent cartridge is ejected anywhere and the next round slides automatically into the breach, ready for firing.

The fearsome power of the weapon, which has been known to blow off much of a man's head, is hinted at when the trigger is pressed. The instant explosion almost deafens one in a firing chamber, and the kick when I tried it for the first time jerked my arm high in the air. The kick can actually shift a weight of seven pounds a distance of two feet as the bullet emerges at close on supersonic velocity—840 feet per second, to be exact. This fact would prove to be important, but the feature of the ·45 to note here is the small panel on the back edge of the butt. This is the safety spring and it *has* to be pressed at the same time as the trigger in order to fire the pistol. The pressure of an uncomfortably strong handshake is needed, *simultaneously on two different places*, the trigger and the safety spring. If Ananda, lying in bed, was holding the pistol up in front of him to look at or play with and it slipped and he clutched it, then only by highly improbable misfortune could he both have pulled the trigger and pressed the safety catch. But even so he would not have been killed unless by a well-nigh incredible concatenation of chances the barrel was in that very instant pointed at a mortal spot. Even if the accident theory were not related to a cautious and experienced person like Ananda, it only becomes tenable in the total absence of any other explanation.

Rejection of the theory by the Commission of Inquiry was not less embarrassing to Pridi, since the police had tended to steer the evidence in support of it. The result was that instead of public agitation being stilled the opposite happened. The Government had no choice now but to act on the Commission's clear hint and instruct the police (though only on 7 December) to investigate further. The police, following their practice, set up an internal committee under a senior officer—but they did not do this for over seven months, and they were still deliberating and investigating without anything to show for it sixteen months later when the events of November 1947 rudely stopped them.

Pridi had hoped that by his resignation of the premiership and withdrawal from public view the storm of suspicion would abate, but the Commission's report hardly encouraged this. And the police investigating committee's slowness did not help either, any more than did the accumulation of unanswered questions concerning certain individuals.

Foremost of these was Lt Vacharachai. Having been sacked from his post of ADC to Ananda he soon became secretary first to Pridi and then to the new Premier, Admiral Dhamrong. Such preferment seemed the odder when the popular press, which had been released from censorship after the election, came out with the plain hint that his was the actual hand that killed the King. Ex-Secretary Chaleo, likewise the subject of public disquiet, had also received preferment after leaving the royal service, for Pridi had got him into the Senate. Why had Pridi positively rewarded these two men whom persistent rumour linked with the murder of Ananda? Why did a government of Pridi's followers also leave the two pages of the bedchamber at large when rumour linked them too with the crime? Why—above all—had no one whatever been so much as arrested?

The continuing agitation, especially in the Assembly, harassed Admiral Dhamrong's administration in its struggle with post-war economic difficulties. Huge profits in rice-smuggling to a hungry Asia involved government officials in corruption stimulated by every kind of consumer shortage. It spread to some deputies, supporting Siamese popular belief that men go into politics to make money. Punitive legislation failed to sweeten the smell that increased through 1947. Still, a parliamentary democracy was at work and, given time, could grow strong. The question was whether it would have time.

All British troops left by the end of 1946. The army would have been free again to start playing politics but for the new constitution which forbade it. However, the ban did not apply to *ex*-army men, and one such suddenly stepped out of the shadows: in March 1947 FM Pibul re-entered public life with a new party called the Might is Right Party. Some militarist nostalgia and right-wing extremism gave him a measure of support, but with the Democrat Party swearing devotion to democratic principles as staunchly as Pridi's followers, any return to fascism—any real comeback by FM Pibul—could scarcely be thought practical politics.

So in spite of the mistrust created by the King's Death Case, Pridi appeared securely in power even though he remained out of sight—counselling, urging, encouraging. As Senior Statesman he continued to live in his official residence. Being on the river bank close to UMPS and the Grand Palace it was more convenient than impressive: the sparse grounds were surrounded by a high wall with a strong pair of wooden gates, and wore little adornment other than a few trees and a fringe of garden along the low river wall. There were two houses. He used the older, wooden one for official receptions, the newer one alongside as his home. The latter, a product of the 1920s when architecture was imprisoned in a concrete box, included on its upper floor his study lined with bookshelves which, I found, concealed a secret door. This was a relic of his FTM days when towards the end he actually had a transmitter in the house.

That hazardous time seemed long past now. His protégé democracy was going forward, however falteringly, and if only the tragedy of Ananda's death could be forgotten he was happy enough. Certainly, had you seen him at home you would scarcely have taken him for a murderer: a man profoundly serious yet quickly given to laughter, patiently explaining things to a disciple, or vigorously chatting with his family, or making *crêpes suzettes* for his friends, or playing chess with an intimate. If he was ambitious it could not have been for material gain. He was even making careful inquiries among the English colony about the exact cost of schooling in England, since he hoped to save enough from his salary to send his children over; he would not hear of the State paying.

One night, the night of 7 November 1947, to his house by the river bank came the Prime Minister, Admiral Dhamrong, together with the chiefs of the armed services and police. He had asked them to call because rumours were about that army elements planned a *coup d'état* and he wanted to be sure that all precautions had been taken. Rumours are as plentiful as rice in Siam and precautions were merely prudent. His visitors assured him that he had no cause for anxiety and soon departed. The Prime Minister indeed left rather hurriedly, being late for a charity ball where the gaiety of the music and the shimmering gowns of jewelled beauties quickly put the fanciful rumours quite out of mind. But at Pridi's house the telephone was ringing; and this twentieth-century bell, tolling, tolled for Pridi.

X

NIGHT over Bangkok has its particular alchemy. The air that by day wrings you out with its cloying heat becomes a balm, the sky is rich with stars, voices turn softly murmurous, the canals yield up languid gold reflections, and in scented gardens a man is at his best—mosquitoes permitting—with his lover or his god. Pridi's favourite place for musing was on the low river wall. Close by were moored covered-over sampans with families come to the city with their up-country produce. On the opposite bank about six hundred yards away few lights showed, and these faintly, like the tip of the Gauloise she sat smoking, for there were mainly orchards in that area. Now and then some river craft glided by, propelled by oarsmen standing up.

Inside the house the telephone was ringing. Someone wanted urgently to speak to Pridi. Reluctantly he left the peacefulness of the night; but then mind and senses were brought rigidly to the alert. His informant had catastrophic news. The *coup d'état* had been sprung after all. The army was everywhere seizing control. It was out to kill or capture him and he must flee, at once, for his life.

The warning seemed too late. Tanks were rumbling up the street. Shots rang out. The crash of splintering wood announced that the gates were being battered down. Soldiers swarmed in, all over the grounds, into both houses, into every room.

But they could not find him. Hailing a sampan he had leapt onto it from the river wall and disappeared into the darkness of the other side of the river.

Through the night the search for him went on, while the military occupied all public buildings, set up roadblocks, and arrested leading officials and cabinet ministers. Next morning soldiers carried FM Pibul shoulder high into the Ministry of Defence, where he was proclaimed Commander of Siam's Armed Forces. He was to deny planning the *coup*. Its chief executants were the head of the air force,

Pridi, photographed in 1946, a few months before Ananda's death

Mom Seni Pramoj

Kuang, 'Great Comedian', on his way to accept office as Prime Minister after the 1947 *coup d'état*

Police-General Pao, during the brief period of free speech permitted at 'Speakers' Corner' on the Pramane Ground, protesting his devotion to non-violence, democracy, and honest administration

the commander of the Bangkok garrison, another army general and his son-in-law who was a senior police officer. We need bother about the name only of the latter, which spatters like blood over the years: Police General Pao (*pr.* pow). But privy to the plot or not, FM Pibul was back in power.

Declaring that the purpose of the *coup d'état* was to clear up the mystery of the King's Death Case, he placed before the Regent, Prince Rangsit, a new constitution abrogating the liberalizing provisions of Pridi's. Prince Rangsit signed. Since, however, the Western Powers refused to recognize the Pibul junta, FM Pibul had to resort to an expedient. He sent for the leaders of the Democrat Party, Kuang the Great Comedian and Mom Seni Pramoj, and proposed that they form a government. It was clear that it would exist by his grace and under his protection.

Now these political leaders had a distinguished record in opposing this same FM Pibul's sell-out to the Japanese. For them to receive such a proposal after the violent overthrow of the legally elected government and the arbitrary scrapping of the liberalizing constitution they themselves had helped give birth to, must have severely strained even Kuang's highly developed sense of comedy. After prolonged internal debate they accepted the offer in the interests, they believed, of the nation; and doubtless their decision reflected a wistful hope that democracy might yet be salvaged. So Kuang became Premier again.

But had Pridi been toppled? He was still missing. So was his Prime Minister, Admiral Dhamrong, whom a message had reached at the charity ball and prompted his departure by the back door even faster than the arrival of soldiers by the front. The hunted Premier had then driven all night along the maze of alleys off the Bangkok highways, and having eluded all the road blocks he entered the compound of the British Embassy at 6.30 a.m.

The Ambassador at that time was burly, hawk-nosed Sir Geoffrey Thompson. A doughty northern Irishman schooled in the mud of Flanders, he had illumined the Diplomatic Service in many parts of the world with his humour and sagacity. He belongs to a generation before diplomats were neutered by rapid direct consultation between governments; and confronted by the exhausted Admiral Dhamrong he reacted with characteristic humanity: on his own initiative he offered him asylum. Dhamrong appeared to accept but while Sir

Geoffrey was attending to business the Prime Minister, shaved and breakfasted, spared him any embarrassment by quietly disappearing—crouched down behind the front seat of a car that drove him out of the compound.

He and those of Pridi's leading supporters who had also so far evaded arrest held meetings at a secret rendezvous in Bangkok, their loaded revolvers on the table before them, and planned a counter-*coup*. Or rather, they relied on the navy. The one truth in Bangkok's hectic rumours about Pridi's whereabouts was that the navy now sheltered him, for it had consistently despised the political machinations of the army. So few people had been educated in the demands of a democracy that there could be no massive civil uprising; and Pridi himself, faithful to his wartime promises, had disarmed the FTM whose members adored him. Hence only the navy held out any prospect of effective counter-action. But at the prospect of civil war it hesitated, and so did Pridi. And aware that his presence might cause it difficulties, and even result in his being given up as the price of peace, he left the naval base down-river at Suttaheep and disappeared to await developments.

These turned wholly against him. The Democrat Party's acceptance of FM Pibul's offer destroyed any chance of a united political stand. The fugitive Prime Minister, Admiral Dhamrong, quitting Bangkok for the south-east, failed to rally support for lack of the fangs of armed strength. The British and Americans urged the navy not to precipitate a civil war. And the *coup* leaders, by lavishly spending money, cleverly mixing arrests with promotions, and finally asserting their military might, achieved complete control.

They made redoubled attempts to catch Pridi. In justification of the *coup* they now freely named him the chief conspirator in Ananda's murder. He would be brought to justice, they said, along with his actual instrument of assassination, Lt Vacharachai—who was also missing. As an earnest of their intention, three men were arrested* and held in the city gaol, heavily chained to thwart any attempt at rescue or escape. These men, Pridi's alleged co-conspirators, were the two pages of the royal bedchamber, Nai Chit and Butr, and ex-Secretary Chaleo.

* Two other people—a high-ranking Palace official and Lt Vacharachai's wife—were also arrested but released after prolonged interrogation.

For years they were to stand at the centre of an extraordinary national spectacle, but for the moment all attention was on the search for Pridi and Lt Vacharachai. Rumour was so prolific that Pridi was often reported, with absolute certainty, in several places simultaneously. Yet even rumour fell short of what actually happened.

The story should now be told.

The British naval attaché at this period was Captain Stratford Hercules Dennis, aged nearly fifty. Son of an Irish horse-breeder; five times a rider in the Grand National; educated at St John's, Cambridge. A short, wiry, sun-browned man with a keen lean face and a quiet manner little indicative of a perfectly undaunted courage. Served at Jutland in World War I, and in some of the most violent episodes of World War II—Narvik, Dunkirk, Dieppe, Sicily, Salerno, Normandy. Ferried agents into occupied France, and from being one of the first commandos became SEAC's deputy head of Combined Operations at Delhi by the time Japan surrendered. By then he had three DSCs, the Polish Cross of Valour, and five mentions in dispatches. Arrived in Bangkok with six Gurkhas to help disarm the Japanese and reorganize the Siamese navy, and thus met Pridi.

So much for the past.

On 19 November 1947 at about 6 a.m., Captain Dennis was roused at his house near the British Embassy. At his door stood a Siamese naval officer. The man said: 'Ruth is here.' Dennis immediately asked him in. The car outside disgorged five other occupants in naval uniform. They had two Thompson sub-machine guns, half a dozen bombs, and other armaments besides the pistol which each carried in a shoulder holster. Dennis recognized Lt Vacharachai in the party, but the man with a big cap, thick spectacles, moustache and sunken cheeks was new to him until Pridi convinced him of his identity—the final touch to his disguise having been achieved by his keeping his teeth in his pocket.

He had driven two hundred miles along indifferent roads from his last hiding place to make Dennis's house before daybreak. Strained and exhausted, he unwontedly accepted a whisky and soda. His mortal need was to get out of the country. The instinct which warned him that otherwise his life would be forfeit was to be proved no delusion by subsequent events. Bluntly he asked Dennis for help. Dennis ushered

117

him and his companions into an upstairs room, and telling them to keep clear of the window he went across to the British Embassy, exchanging like any good Irishman a wink with the statue of Queen Victoria.

Sir Geoffrey Thompson was about to address himself to his breakfast when his Chinese butler announced, 'Cap'n Dennis want come topside dam' quick.' Sir Geoffrey received the attaché at once, listened to his story, and proceeded to confer with the US Ambassador, Edwin Stanton. The niceties of diplomatic usage were considered second to the need for helping a wartime comrade whom the British and Americans both admired and refused to believe guilty of regicide. The American naval attaché, 'Skeats' Gardas, was called in, and so was William Adam, the Shell Company's local chief who had worked on the Burma railway as a prisoner of war and felt no love for FM Pibul. Adam ascertained that by chance a Singapore-bound Shell tanker was at the mouth of the Menam waiting for the tide to carry it across the bar to the open Gulf. Plans were quickly laid which Dennis relayed to Pridi.

Scarcely had he done so than he was summoned to the front door by a certain prince friendly with the Pibul junta. This man said there were rumours that Pridi was in Bangkok and about to attempt an escape by river: what did Dennis know? Dennis promptly confirmed the rumours, adding that Pridi was leaving from a jetty at the other side of the city to reach his home town of Ayudhya in the north. With the prince's departure on this false trail, a nerve-racking pause followed until one o'clock.

At that hour Dennis and the fugitives set off for the main docks at the southern outskirts of the city. Dennis drove a jeep, and behind him as if by way of an escort the others travelled in the saloon. They had left most of their arms behind lest suspicion were aroused if they were searched at a roadblock. They were in fact stopped at barricades but agony was ended when the soldiers, having glanced at the European officer and his Siamese naval escort, and being under instructions to avoid clashes with the navy, stepped back to salute. Exactly on schedule at one-thirty, the party drew up beside a launch moored at the main docks, Klong Toi.

The launch belonged to 'Skeats' Gardas. It was an ex-submarine chaser with twin propellers, ideal for the intended purpose. To avoid the risk of betrayal, Gardas had given his Siamese crew a holiday. His wife and his pretty blonde nineteen-year-old sister would be the crew. With Pridi and his companions aboard, and the Stars and Stripes flying, the launch set off on the first stage of its perilous journey, the twenty-odd miles down the well-guarded and patrolled river to the sea.

Meanwhile Dennis returned to his house, just in time to receive a telephone call from the US military attaché who was concerned by considerable Siamese military activity around the US Embassy. He had no arms for defence should the situation turn ugly, and he asked if Dennis could help. Dennis put the arsenal Pridi and his companions had left behind into diplomatic mail bags which he sent round to the US Embassy (where happily no need in fact arose).

The two ambassadors and Captain Dennis and Adam could do nothing but wait. And pray. The tanker was due to reach the open sea at about 4 p.m. and her captain had agreed that if he were hailed outside territorial waters by the occupants of a certain launch he would take them aboard with no questions asked. To the men waiting in Bangkok the afternoon seemed interminably long. William Adam was to receive a radio report from the tanker but the hours passed in silence.

But at last, about 6 p.m., he telephoned Sir Geoffrey. 'A radio signal from the master of the tanker M.V. ——— reports that after a short stop due to engine trouble she is now running smoothly.' This was the pre-arranged code to convey that the operation had succeeded. Pridi was safely away. (How wrong things might have gone was not known to the relieved British and American officials at the time. No sooner had the Gardases discharged their cargo than they had real engine trouble, and then they hit a sandbank, so that they only returned to Bangkok at ten o'clock next morning, to complete a neat paragraph in the annals of Anglo-American adventure.)

Any anxiety the British Ambassador might have had about Whitehall's reaction to his diplomatic unorthodoxy was dispelled by a message of approval from Ernest Bevin, then Britain's Foreign Secretary. And the morning after the escape-bid the Ambassador composed a letter which, with the US Ambassador's concurrence, he handed to Kuang as head of Siam's unrecognized but *ad hoc* Government. It stated that the two ambassadors felt themselves unable to

THE DEVIL'S DISCUS

reject Pridi's appeal for help in view of their obligations to a wartime comrade, and they had, therefore, facilitated his exit from the country, which would, besides, help restore internal peace. Recollection of this forthright admission still infuriates some royalists, indignant at alleged Anglo-American perfidy.

All the same, Pridi's departure did lead to a lowering of the political temperature, and the Western Powers recognized the Kuang Government after elections in January at which supporters of Pridi scarcely dared show their faces. They nevertheless gained 18 seats (Democrat Party, 54; FM Pibul's 7). By scrapping Pridi's constitution and reverting to the system whereby half the Assembly was not elected but nominated by himself, FM Pibul ensured the parliamentary form as well as the military substance of control. But plainly so long as Pridi remained at large he posed a permanent threat to the régime.

The way to insure against that threat was simple. If Pridi's complicity in the King's death were proved, the whole nation would be so roused against him that any return to public life would forever be impossible. This idea was not dictated by political expediency alone. Most royalists were becoming genuinely convinced by the accumulating evidence of Pridi's guilt, and many other people were honestly perplexed and anxious for all the evidence to be gathered. Ironically, the man gathering it was Mom Seni Pramoj's brother-in-law—the same man Pridi had refused to have as Police Chief during Mom Seni's premiership.

Answering an inner call to duty, he was recalled from retirement at his own request to lead the investigations by a reconstituted police committee. This man, named Phra Phinich (*pr.* prah pin-it)—let us call him Detective Phinich—began preparations for the prosecution case against the three men in captivity. But if the names of ex-Secretary Chaleo and the two pages Nai Chit and Butr were those appearing on the indictment, the case was directed squarely at Pridi and his henchman Lt Vacharachai. Though they had vanished they would stand, as much as though they were present, not only in the dock but at the bar of history. The proceedings, strange and challenging through all the years they lasted, were to filter almost every circumstance relating to the King's death. If Pridi were guilty, so he would be proved.

The Shell tanker had delivered him safely at Singapore. At first given 'hospitality' on the quarantine island off-shore, he is said to have been presented with the electric light bill on his departure. The British authorities, as also the Americans presently, felt themselves embarrassed by his presence anywhere under their jurisdiction pending clarification of the mystery of Ananda's death. With a few companions, including Lt Vacharachai, he therefore disappeared for the present, though not before writing a letter to his host, Lord Killearn, Britain's Special Commissioner in South-East Asia:

I hereby deny absolutely that I was in any way implicated in the death of His late Majesty King Ananda, which I most sincerely deplore. I further declare that to the best of my knowledge and belief no member of my present entourage was implicated in that unhappy event.

Was he speaking the truth? The regicide case against the three arrested men would tell. It was finally to start in September 1948.

By then Kuang the Great Comedian had once again provided a little comic relief. Only a few months after his acceptance of the premiership, having served FM Pibul's purpose of maintaining a government acceptable to the Western Powers during the immediate period following Pridi's violent and illegal overthrow, he was visited by four army officers who suggested that he should seriously consider retiring. Kuang had little choice but to take the hint. FM Pibul, put in gaol less than three years before amid universal odium, installed himself once again as 'Prime Minister'. And confidently he awaited the regicide trial to complete the destruction of Pridi.

The Trial

I

A COMPLETE record of the trial does not exist. There is no transcript of the evidence. The judges relied on their own notes in arriving at a verdict.

The prosecution, however, had a pile of papers three feet high, besides hundreds of photographs, models and exhibits. If anything of all this remains, inquiries are not welcome. I was politely put off with the let's-be-reasonable query of why I should wish to revive the unpleasant past. But with indelicate persistence, and with dependable help in defiance of both official obstruction and the pall of fear and reticence that Ananda's death still casts over the Siamese, I can piece together the substance of a trial which was not only unique in its own right but an essential guide to the final solution.

It began on the afternoon of Wednesday, 28 September, 1948.

So close to the scene of the crime was retribution sought that the bedroom where Ananda died almost overlooked the courthouse. The Court of Criminal Causes in Bangkok is in the large grey buildings of the Ministry of Justice, across the road from the same side of the Grand Palace wall which bounds the Barompiman Hall. By chance, there is at one end of the Ministry a small separate building set aside for the guardian spirit of Bangkok—just as every house is believed to have its own guardian spirit, so is every hamlet and city. This animistic concept blends with Buddhism, whose founder's image is the chief furnishing of the tawdry interior, being daubed with gold-leaf by the devout and surrounded by glowing joss-sticks, though people throng the place less to make merit than to get their fortunes told. But oracular vision would have been severely overstrained if called upon to foresee the course of the trial which began at the other end of the Ministry, near the Barompiman Hall, in another separate single-storeyed building dominated by an image of the Buddha and filled with an unseen presence.

The long, many-windowed, hall-like court was called Room 24. Against the wall opposite the entrance was the large Buddha image with a group of red-lacquered and gilt wooden footstools with jars of flowers in front of it: here witnesses vowed to tell the truth. For the rest—the judges' dais beneath a portrait of King Bhoomipol, the dock, witness-stand, places for counsel, and so forth—the setting was unexceptional. Westernization came early to Siam's legal institutions and in fact some of the judges had been to Oxford or Cambridge.

The usual quota in a criminal case was three judges but here there were four presided over by a fifth, the Chief Judge of the Criminal Court. As if explaining the disparity he said at the outset that this was the most important case in the history of Thailand. It also looked likely to be the longest. At preliminary hearings during the month or two before 28 September, the prosecution announced that they would call over three hundred witnesses. Even though the court decided to sit thrice weekly instead of keeping to the practice of once weekly for any one case, it could only hope to finish in a year.

The formal charges by now laid against ex-Secretary Chaleo and the pages Nai Chit and Butr were in three groups. The first asserted, in brief, that between 9 April and 9 June 1946 all the accused had treasonably *plotted* with others to kill King Ananda. The second group, from which Chaleo was excluded, charged the pages and unnamed but easily identifiable 'accomplices who are still abroad', with actually committing the crime by shooting the King through the head on 9 June 1946 'in accordance with their premeditated intention and plan'; alternatively, the pages not only failed in their duty to prevent the crime but gave 'aid and abetment material to the success of the crime'.

The third group of charges was against Nai Chit alone, and they were very surprising indeed. It may be recalled that when he was summoned to the Palace Meeting after Ananda's death he brought down a drawer, containing the ·45 pistol found by the body and also a spent cartridge which he later said he had found near the bed. But, said the indictment, while this was indeed the spent cartridge of a bullet fired from the ·45, Nai Chit knew perfectly well that the ·45 *was not the pistol which fired the fatal shot*. In other words the ·45 was a 'plant', and the deception had been bolstered by Nai Chit's production of a spent cartridge which had once been fired from it, his object being to 'protect his accomplices from lawful punishment and to conceal the crime of compassing the King's death' by pretending that Ananda had committed suicide.

This disclosure of a subtlety in the assassination plot greater than anyone had guessed brought excitement over the impending trial to the boil. On the Wednesday afternoon a thousand spectators jammed Room 24 and the approaches, where the proceedings were relayed through a loudspeaker. The building was tightly guarded by special police. Everyone going in was searched. The Pibul Government did not intend risking the escape of the accused when it was so confident of the overwhelming nature of the evidence that the trial was being publicly conducted in proper form. The three men themselves were escorted by guards carrying sub-machine guns.

They took their places in the dock. Accused No. 1. Accused No. 2. Accused No. 3. What dull digits to hide so many beating hearts, for all the men had families. Each was dressed in khaki drill trousers and a white shirt; and they were of an age—in their forties—but there resemblance ended. Little Butr with his worried bright-eyed face has already been described. His bespectacled colleague Nai Chit had a much more alert mind, was better built and taller, and good-looking. He came in fact from a superior family to Butr but like him had succeeded to several generations in the royal service; he had six daughters, a reputation for practical jokes, and a fondness for knitting. Ex-Secretary Chaleo, man of business and politics, was the least attractive of the three. He was portly and puffy, and somewhat coarse-grained. But we must not hang people for their appearance or few of us would be alive.

In turn each of the accused pleaded not guilty. And while they stood before their judges and declared their innocence, no one failed to see the invisible figures of Pridi and Lt Vacharachai looming huge behind them. They were the chief accused: Pridi especially: *he* was standing trial, before his people and his people's history. This fact, reaching out with the terror of political or police reprisal to everyone connected with him or who might speak in his favour, made the task of the defence no easier.

It had been made hard enough at the start by the fact that defending counsel had only been allowed to interview the accused for the first time less than two months before, and when on the eve of the trial they were presented with the voluminous documents the prosecution intended to put into evidence they asked for an extension of time. The court rejected their application, and perhaps it was with relief that the counsel seized on the rejection and asked leave to withdraw because, they protested, the time given them for preparation was unfair to their clients and injurious to their own reputation.

The court adjourned while fresh counsel were sought. An unusual silence and self-effacement settled on the legal profession in Bangkok. The search seemed in vain.

It chanced, however, that a young criminal lawyer named Fak Nasongkhla was in the disrobing room of the law courts when he heard that no one would take on the accused's defence. He was himself fully occupied by an increasingly lucrative practice, yet he at once volunteered. A certain pugnacity attached to his appearance, for he had a short sturdy figure with a somewhat square face and small nose, but he spoke very quietly as if absorbed in trying to convey what he wished to say, and he was gentle-mannered, hesitant, almost shy. Because he was brave and passionate for justice he set an example that was followed by several other barristers, able followers of Pridi. With the accused thus defended more strongly than they had dared hope, the trial at last began.

The Chief Prosecutor briefly outlined his case. There had been, he said, a skilfully conceived murder-plot by a band of conspirators. They had subsequently carried out their dreadful enterprise—except for the reckoning which now awaited them. He would prove his case, he said, by evidence not only of what they let slip to other people, but by what they said among themselves: they had actually been overheard. Other kinds of evidence would be produced also, which he could promise would be equally conclusive; but first—the conspiracy.

The damning testimony of what had been overheard first became known to the authorities only a few months before the trial. It happened this way. A market is held every Sunday on the Pramane Ground outside the Grand Palace, and while wandering about the stalls a police colonel met a childhood friend who unburdened himself of a tale weighing heavily on his mind.

Said the friend, he had an acquaintance named Tee, a northern timber-dealer. This Tee had been staying with him for a few days a couple of months before. One evening, when another guest was also present, they fell to talking about the King's death, and an argument flared up about Pridi's complicity. Suddenly Tee burst out: 'You two don't know the truth about who killed the King. I do!' Pressed to explain, he reluctantly said that he had overheard Pridi and a group of men conspiring against the King's life while meeting at the house of a high official where he, Tee, had been staying at the time. Being, he said, under a debt of gratitude to this official he would not reveal his identity and he made the two men promise to keep the information to themselves. However, after the other guest had gone, his host asked Tee if his suspicion were correct that the official was a certain Rear-Admiral, Speaker of the Assembly during Pridi's premiership and a former royal ADC. Tee answered affirmatively, adding that of the conspirators meeting with Pridi the names he caught were Chaleo, Nai Chit, and Too—Lt Vacharachai's nickname.

This was the secret story of which Tee's host unburdened himself to the police colonel on the Pramane Ground. Detective Phinich, chief investigator, had immediately sent for Tee from Paknam Po in the north. The police investigating committee interrogated him and the other witnesses, and they were among the first to appear in the witness-stand in Room 24.

They included the Rear-Admiral. He freely admitted that Pridi had indeed visited his house—first in about 1945, when he presided over a wedding*, and then once or twice in about April 1946, two months before Ananda's death (9 June). The Rear-Admiral also agreed that Tee the timberman was staying with him at the time—in connection with some business relating to railway sleepers—and he further confirmed Tee's story by recalling Pridi's arrival one evening with Chaleo, Lt Vacharachai and others he had forgotten. He invited them all into his drawing-room but only Pridi and perhaps Chaleo and Vacharachai went in. After this point the Rear-Admiral could not corroborate Tee's story. He said that his guests, who stayed a mere quarter of an hour, talked about his timber venture and were normally sociable; if there was any treasonable conversation he heard none. But then he had to admit that he had left the room for a few minutes to see about refreshments—and the incriminating words Tee claimed to have overheard needed only those few minutes.

* It is a custom to invite to a wedding—combination of marriage ceremony and reception—a distinguished person who acts as a nominal host, thereby conferring auspiciousness on the occasion and honour on the family, besides ensuring a good turn-out of other guests.

However, the defence had seemingly decisive evidence, for it produced certain letters written in *July* 1946 to the Rear-Admiral by another participant in the timber venture, stating that the writer would bring Tee down to Bangkok on the 15th of *that* month. Tee could scarcely have overheard a regicidal plot if his visit was after Ananda's death. The Rear-Admiral readily accepted that his memory must have been at fault, and he roundly declared that in any event the idea of Pridi's complicity in a murder plot was absurd and the result of agitation by the Democrat Party.

But the defence's exaltation at this blow struck for it by a prosecution witness was short-lived. The letter-writer, called to the witness-stand, said that on the last day of the third month of the Year of the Dog (2 March 1946) he got a letter from the Rear-Admiral, as a result of which he took Tee down to see him and returned home alone on the 14th day of the Waning Moon in the fourth month (31 March). Tee was therefore with the Rear-Admiral before Ananda's death. The letters produced by the defence related, he said, to a later and quite different transaction. Besides, the prosecution called one of the Rear-Admiral's housemaids who testified that in the last week of May at about 6 p.m. her master's young son asked her to go out and buy roasted corn (yellow corn-on-the-cob is cooked over an open fire until almost black, when the grain is chewed like nuts or sweets), and on her way she noticed guests in the drawing-room, including Chaleo who sat at the table in the centre; and outside the drawing-room, under a mango tree, sat Tee.

But, of course, even if the evidence proved that Pridi and company had visited the house prior to Ananda's death and that Tee the timberman was staying there at the time, this did not prove Tee's account of what he alleged he overheard. Proof of *that* largely depended on the credibility of Tee himself. And what exactly was it that he had overheard? As if the evidence so far had served as a fanfare for the star player, he at last entered the witness-stand.

Three times, he said, had he been at the house when Pridi visited. In the sixth month of the Waxing Moon (first half of May) Pridi had arrived at about 6 p.m. with two men, and about ten days later he called again at the same time and with the same two men, whom Tee later knew as Lt Vacharachai and Chaleo, plus two others of whom one was identified by Tee as Nai Chit. Tee said he was introduced to

The five judges in the regicide trial, beneath a portrait of King Bhoomipol

Ex-Secretary Chaleo, Butr and Nai Chit in Room 24

Chaleo leaving the court after a day's hearing

Lt Vacharachai in 1946

Pridi but left the house before there was much talk, though he did hear someone say, 'The departure [presumably Ananda's] is getting near. Whatever's got to be done should be done.' Finally, at the end of May, Pridi arrived about 7 p.m. with the same four men. They all went into the drawing-room, which was divided by a partition from another room where Tee, according to his evidence, sat unseen and overheard snatches of the conversation at a time when the Rear-Admiral was apparently not present.

Someone said: 'I've never imagined a mere child could be so astute.'

Someone else said: 'I heard it because I was near. The elder brother said he'd abdicate in favour of his younger brother, then he'd stand for the Assembly so's to become President of the Council of Ministers [Prime Minister].'

Following this echo of George Bernard Shaw's *The Apple Cart* in which a king brings his prime minister to heel by precisely this threat attributed to, presumably, Ananda, Tee could not make out the conversation until a voice remarked: 'That's just it. If their plan succeeded we'd be in a lot of trouble. Therefore we should get rid of him before he leaves.' (Ananda's departure was scheduled for 13 June.)

'Leave that to me,' someone promptly replied.

Another said: 'If this thing goes through we hope we'll be well looked after.'

'If I don't keep my promise you'd better shoot *me* dead.'

'If the job's done successfully, the reward will come up to everyone's expectations.'

After this, Tee said, he heard nothing more. Ten minutes later Pridi left and the others sat under the mango tree chatting and drinking, when Tee sat with them.

'Look at the accused,' prosecuting counsel said. 'Can you recognize any of them?'

Tee pointed out Chaleo and Nai Chit. He had never seen Butr.

The prosecutor asked him: 'Did you speak to the Rear-Admiral about what you'd overheard?'

'Yes. I asked him, "Are you also taking part in what Pridi and them were talking about?" He answered me, "No, I've nothing to say to them except 'Quite right' and 'Yes', because they're in power and they've done me a good turn." I was very worried. I advised him, "It'd seem better if you have nothing to do with them".'

With this, Tee's evidence-in-chief ended. The defence now had the formidable task of trying to shake it. They extracted from him the fact that he had no fixed address, and that since sending for him the police had supported him and his wife. They put to him something the Rear-Admiral had said, that the window through which Tee claimed to have seen the conspirators in the drawing-room was blocked up by the belongings of the Rear-Admiral's mother-in-law, but Tee stuck to this detail as he did to every other in his story: and such detail, and the unlikelihood of a petty provincial concocting it out of thin air, left a powerful impression.

The prosecution was quick to add to it with other if less dramatic evidence which suggested that at least two of the accused had sinister inside information prior to Ananda's death.

This evidence was given in the first place by the Princess Mother's lady-in-waiting, who recounted a conversation she had with Nai Chit, shortly before the tragic Sunday, about the King's intended departure. Nai Chit, she testified, said: 'I tell you he won't be leaving on the thirteenth.'

'What do you mean? Why do you say that?' she asked. He made no reply, so she retorted, 'I don't believe you.'

Nai Chit laughed. 'As you will. But just wait and see!'

The lady-in-waiting was herself going abroad with the royal family, which inclined her to think that Nai Chit merely teased her—until the tragedy of 9 June put his words in a very different light. Moreover, on the very eve of the tragedy he had a similar conversation with one of the pages of the royal table. This man, named Mee, repeated in court the following dialogue:

Nai Chit: I'm surprised the King's going on the thirteenth. Westerners regard it as an unlucky day.

Mee: But the King's a Thai. Why should he believe in Western superstition and delay going?

Nai Chit: He won't be going.

Mee: But the day's been fixed by the astrologers. He must be going.

Nai Chit: Mark my word—he'll *not* be going!

The prosecution had similar evidence against Chaleo. They called a certain army officer, an old friend of Chaleo's—in fact while serving his term as a monk he had been asked by Chaleo, according to custom, to bless Chaleo's house by having a meal there. This witness said that meeting Chaleo at ex-Regent Aditya's cremation (at which Bhoomipol had deputized for the ill Ananda on 8 June) he asked him, 'Why is the royal departure fixed for the thirteenth?' Chaleo replied: 'No, he won't leave.' But he would give no explanation, merely saying, 'Just wait and see.'

Chaleo's words quoted by his army officer friend fell startlingly upon the silence of that packed intent courtroom, and like Nai Chit's all too accurate prognostication added credibility to Tee the timberman's story of their participation in a conspiracy.

Thus, slowly but with compulsive effect on public attention, the prosecution continued to pile up the evidence. Then, on the morning of 1 December, the proceedings were suddenly interrupted by an announcement that despite a twenty-four-hour guard the prosecutor's office had been broken into. The custodian had vanished, but the huge pile of papers appeared to be intact. There has never been an explanation of the incident. Was it due to friends of Pridi or the accused giving way to despair? By the police to suggest this? Whatever the explanation, the episode generated an insecure feeling which was particularly unfortunate for Chaleo, since he had just applied for bail. He offered security of 400,000 baht (about £7,000) in order to attend the cremation of his son, to have his false teeth repaired, and to recover from the year's immurement in prison since his arrest. His request was rejected. A week or two later he fell ill with pneumonia.

Nor was this the end of his immediate misfortunes. Bangkok was agog over a manifesto entitled *The Red Jar* by no less a person than the Deputy Commander-in-Chief of the army, purporting to take the lid off the conspiracy headed by Pridi and including Chaleo among its members. When extracts actually appeared in the press the accused petitioned the court to protect itself from contempt and themselves from prejudice. The author of the manifesto claimed that a friend had helped himself to it from his desk and published it without permission. Public suspicion of Chaleo was little allayed by the nominal fines inflicted—200 baht on the author, 400 on the friend: scarcely more than shillings.

The trial reverted to its leisurely course, acquiring in time an identity almost of its own, almost divorced from reality, except now and then when reminders of what it might mean broke in. Such was news of the death-sentence passed on Gandhi's assassin early in February 1949. Then its dreamlike quality vanished, and anguish dully asked when would the end be. By that February, twenty-five witnesses had in fact been heard, but mostly of a formal nature or to establish the veracity of others who had something material to say. The latter, after the dramatic revelations of the alleged conspiracy, were relatively few. Among them was the Royal Nanny, who was questioned in the witness-box for seven days.

This simple and pious friend of the Princess Mother had been the constant companion of the royal family throughout their stay at the Barompiman Hall. Pridi, she said, had been on good terms with them —she instanced his holiday with them at Hua Hin, to which the King invited him. Nor had there been any dissatisfaction with Nai Chit and Butr. All the same, she had heard ominous things said. The man who said them is new to us—a senior page who had himself died, from fever, two months before the King. The Royal Nanny told the court that he had often voiced fears of his master's safety because he doubted the loyalty of Ananda's immediate entourage. She had previously dismissed his anxiety as due to his failing health, but the sequel proved him right. His name was Senior Page Chan, and his shade will be found to spread darkly over this narrative.

The Royal Nanny waxed indignant at what she regarded as an attempt by the police, in their inquiries after Ananda's death, to prove the King mentally unbalanced. She insisted that he was 'silent, thoughtful, and clever'. His behaviour the day before his death was perfectly normal: he was cheerful and spent much of the time packing his personal belongings.

Only the most simple-minded member of the public could have missed the implication in the questions which elicited these answers. Proof of the alleged regicidal conspiracy did not of course depend on, but it clearly would be strengthened by, the elimination of any other explanation of Ananda's death. The lingering theory of suicide was one such explanation, which the Nanny's replies helped refute; and now the prosecution turned to another, never for a moment publicly acknowledged but whispered about the world to this day.

What, the Royal Nanny was asked, were Ananda's relations with Bhoomipol?

She answered without hesitation: the royal brothers were deeply attached to each other. In their childhood she herself gave them religious instruction so that they might grow up, as they did, 'meek, mild and dutiful'. When Bhoomipol was told on the day of Ananda's death that he would succeed to the throne he showed great sadness: she felt certain that he had no other wish than to lead the life of an ordinary citizen.

She was taken next over the events of the fateful Sunday morning. She described how she was in Bhoomipol's quarters when she heard the shot, and how she ran in the wake of the Princess Mother, and held Ananda's still beating pulse. She described the prolonged distress of the Princess Mother; and the atmosphere of fear which prompted her, the Royal Nanny, to wake the Princess Mother and the new King whenever there was a failure of electric power, lest harm came to them too. For of one thing she was positive: Ananda had been murdered. She did not believe that either Nai Chit or Butr was the killer—but they must know who he was since they were sitting outside the door when the shot was fired.

Was this a valid conclusion? If so the two pages were done for. The answer depended on another question. How and where did the assassin contrive his entrance and his exit?

The judges, counsel and the accused made a lengthy inspection of the site. They found that there were several entrances to the grounds of the Barompiman Hall, which itself could be entered from back or front: and inside it, there was a choice of stairways to the upper floor and hence of routes to Ananda's quarters (see plan, page 76). The five guards on duty behind and in front of the Hall, the night watch within, and all the domestic staff, gardeners and officials were closely interrogated. Their replies made clear that no strict security system operated: the Hall was big, guards and officials were not everywhere, and people known to them were not bothered to produce any authorization before being admitted. The judges were to find as facts that 'anybody with knowledge of the entrances and exits could enter the Hall by the exercise of little effort. Success in committing the crime would be more assured if assistance were given by people inside the Palace. . . . Should treason be suddenly committed against the person of the King there would be little chance of its being witnessed or prevented by anyone else.'

This group of witnesses—staff etc. in and around the palace—was closely questioned on the vital point of whether they saw anybody in the precincts of the Hall, the night before or the morning after Ananda's death, who had no business there. No one was seen inside the Hall; but one of the gardeners saw somebody a little distance *behind* it shortly before the shot was fired; and after the shot a page looking out of a ground floor window at the back saw the same person, a man, hurriedly descending the steps from the back veranda of the Hall to the garden. Moreover, immediately before being seen by the gardener in the Palace grounds this man had been seen arriving by car at a near-by point outside the Grand Palace; and his own chauffeur confirmed driving him to that point. Furthermore his laundress said she washed blood from his sleeve after the King's death.

The man was Lt Vacharachai.

Later other evidence was brought against him, but by now the framework of the prosecution case was erected. At the centre was Pridi: his creature, the actual killer, was Lt Vacharachai, helped at the critical time by the pages Nai Chit and Butr, the latter being under the influence of the former who in turn was shown to have been friendly with ex-Secretary Chaleo, another of Pridi's creatures. The strength of this framework was that each strut supported and gained support from the next. For example, the clearer Lt Vacharachai emerged as the assassin, the more was Tee the timberman's story corroborated with its incrimination of the others. Evidence against any one increased the evidence against all.

In mid-February Dr Nit, Ananda's doctor, occupied the witness-stand for many days. Besides recalling his attendances on the King the day before and on the morning of his death, he supplied details of Ananda's health up to that time: he had given both him and the Princess Mother a course of calcium injections, but apart from a proneness to colds and stomach aches Ananda had been perfectly healthy. Asked about events after the tragedy Dr Nit said he was in frequent touch with Pridi and served on the medical panel for the Commission of Inquiry. He agreed that the majority of doctors on the panel believed that the cause of death was murder, but he himself believed in the accident theory. In his opinion the number of pages and guards in the Palace made the entry of an outsider impossible, and he could not accept the notion of treason from within; and suicide was totally out of keeping with Ananda's upbringing or personality: he was, Dr Nit said, 'a thoughtful and happy King'. One of the five prosecuting counsel asked him about politics. He replied that neither Ananda nor Bhoomipol ever discussed politics with him but two months after their arrival the Princess Mother asked him for his opinion of Pridi.

'What answer did you give Her Royal Highness?'

Dr Nit could have told a tale convenient to his safety and to his post of Royal Physician (from which in fact he was quietly dropped) and certainly to his popularity, since to speak favourably of Pridi was as if to speak favourably of evil. He chose instead to speak from the core of an honest kindly nature: 'I answered that people liked him for his great knowledge, his cleverness, and his compassion, though he is regarded as leftist because of his 1933 Economic Plan.'

Fak Nasongkhla, who in the five months since volunteering to lead the defence had given up all his practice to concentrate on the case, put a number of questions to him concerning Pridi's actions after Ananda's death. The doctor said that he had never gained the impression that Pridi tried to stop or influence investigation into the tragedy. Fak asked him: 'The allegation has been made that Pridi tried to force you to sign a statement that the King died of cholora. Is that true?' Dr Nit replied that it was not.

He finished his evidence on 26 February with a cryptic reference to someone's suggestion that the Princess Mother should have been advised to read history books which told of younger brothers killing elder brothers. But speculation on this startling information was given little time to bloom, for that night's events in Bangkok abruptly superseded the drama of the trial.

II

PRIDI had been watching from afar.

Almost a year had passed since the November 1947 *coup d'état* and his escape down the Menam in the US naval attaché's launch. From Singapore he had sailed the Yellow Sea and with Lt Vacharachai and others wandered to the British colony of Hong Kong, the Portuguese territory of Macao, and finally sought haven in the cities of Canton and Shanghai during the last days of their possession by Chiang Kai-shek. Patiently he had waited on events to end his exile.

By early 1949 secret messages of support from his friends in the Navy, firmly hostile to the political influence of the army supporting FM Pibul, assured him that the moment was come. His homeland called with a great and growing cry of discontent.

A few months before, Bangkok's English-language newspaper had catalogued the Government's neglect of public needs. Roads were everywhere rutted, bridges unrepaired; electric power was insufficient; there was a tremendous syphilis rate among the newborn, and only one hospital in the whole country took in TB cases; banditry prospered. All this, said the newspaper's editor, was because the leaders of the nation were engrossed in playing politics. He was quickly silenced by a reminder of the danger to anyone speaking his mind in FM Pibul's Thailand: a week or so later the editor of another newspaper went into hospital after a beating up by army thugs for publishing an anti-army cartoon, and increasing censorship either shut down hostile newspapers or ensured a proper servility.

To the charges of administrative backwardness FM Pibul had some defence in the protracted post-war shortages on top of wartime neglect. But he had none to the unspoken charge of corruption and secret police activity which was making his régime one of the most dreadful in Siam's history—or rather, Thailand's, since he celebrated his remarkable comeback by restoring that chauvinistic title. By

October 1948 when the regicide trial was getting under way, discontent began to surface. A group of military officers was arrested for plotting a *coup d'état*. Later in the same month a group of deputies was arrested for plotting a breakaway state in the north-east. In February 1949 a State of Emergency was declared as two army officers and eight Chinese alleged communists were arrested for plotting treason. Similar arrests were to follow with monotonous regularity, but meanwhile Pridi, seizing time by the forelock, had left China.

In great secrecy he had boarded an American yacht named *The Bluebird* and sailed for Thailand.

Accompanied by Lt Vacharachai he reached the mouth of the Menam safely and made contact with his friends at the naval base at Suttaheep. They laid their plans and then Pridi's party, still unbeknown to FM Pibul, filtered into Bangkok.

On the night of 26 February 1949 Pridi quietly entered the University of Moral and Political Sciences. He had no time to reflect on the irony of using this institution, which he had founded to promote the the ideals of democracy, as the headquarters for an enterprise of desperate force. The lecture halls he had known packed and ardent to hear him were balefully deserted. Nor would any of his students have recognized their Mentor in his disguise as a naval warrant officer with a neatly trimmed moustache. Around him assembled about two dozen armed men. At zero hour Lt Vacharachai led them towards the Grand Palace a minute or two away.

They surprised the few guards and took possession with little effort; Pridi himself arrived on the scene shortly after midnight. Another group of men at the same time seized the radio station in the Public Relations Building at the opposite end of the Pramane Ground. The first the public knew of anything untoward was the repeated broadcast announcing that a provisional government had taken control under a new prime minister pledged to restore a democratic constitution.

So far, for Pridi, so good; and he had the knowledge that the navy was swinging into action with ships and marines to support him.

At the other side of the city, in the fashionable quarter of Bangkapi, the British Ambassador's wife came home from a concert 'much disturbed and on the verge of tears', relates Sir Geoffrey Thompson[4]:

'There's a *coup* going on,' she said. 'We were held up for half an hour at a barricade and a marine stuck a tommy-gun through the window and kept us covered all the time.' I poured her a substantial whisky-and-soda. . . . Because of the heat we always slept on the veranda. Shortly before 3 a.m. that night we awoke to a series of vivid flashes and loud reports as something like a small field-gun opened fire in unpleasantly close proximity to the Embassy. . . . I said: 'I think we had at least better get a wall between ourselves and this bloody noise.' . . . Tea was ordered as dawn began to break. Then as it was being served by the imperturbable Keepokh, loud firing began again from mortars and automatic weapons. Tracers flighted over the compound lawns. Our police guard crouched behind the statue of Queen Victoria . . . the firing continued till about 10 a.m., when it ceased.

When it ceased. . . . It ceased because Pridi had fled.

During the early hours of the morning FM Pibul's army, hurriedly alerted, had counter-attacked Pridi and his party in the Grand Palace. This was the crucial period when the navy was to have intervened in strength, but it did not do enough or in time. Confronted by tanks, artillery and superior numbers, Pridi withdrew to avoid the letting of Siamese blood and damage to the priceless Grand Palace.

Elsewhere a number of clashes between marines and soldiers occurred, in which there were some casualties (including six civilians killed), but the basic technique of a *coup d'état*, which is the seizure of leaders and communications, had been neglected. Though for some days the navy and the Pibul Government remained at armed arm's length, the attempted *coup* had clearly failed. Pressure by the British and others, and conciliatory gestures by FM Pibul, brought about a *rapprochement*: by mid-March he was inviting all high-ranking officers of the three services to come, dressed in mufti, to a garden party to forget their little misunderstanding; and the mass of people, as unconcerned as ever by the struggle for power at the top, quickly found life returning to its usual serenity.

Pridi, with Lt Vacharachai, again disappeared into the void after his forlorn venture into violence. Again reports poured in of his presence simultaneously in several places, and a newspaper statement that he was in a certain foreign embassy brought a prompt disclaimer from the British. He was in fact returning to China. Forced back into exile he again had to wait, watching the spindle upon which, now more than ever, his fortune revolved—the regicide trial in Room 24, Bangkok.

III

AFTER the prolonged adjournment enforced by the abortive *coup d'état*, the prosecution consolidated its basic allegation of a conspiracy. For further proof it looked to common motives and mutual association between the alleged conspirators.

Lt Vacharachai, for example—evidence of his association with Pridi could scarcely have been stronger: first he had been his ADC, then his nominee to the corps of Ananda's ADCs, finally his own secretary. Chaleo similarly was bound to Pridi, having been his political supporter, appointed by him to the post of Ananda's Private Secretary, and finally elevated by him to the Senate. Now, argued the prosecution, if it were furthermore shown that Lt Vacharachai and Chaleo had been sacked from the royal service, and that Pridi too had reasons for hostility to the throne, could anyone deny that here was fertile ground for the seeds of a treasonable conspiracy?

The ex-ADC's dismissal was indisputable; but when a palace official was giving evidence that Chaleo had been dismissed, defending counsel challenged him. Chaleo, he submitted firmly, had resigned for genuine reasons of ill-health. The official insisted that he had been dismissed because of unbecoming behaviour, the evidence on which must briefly be summarized. Refusing to do obeisance before the King, it was alleged, he always entered the royal presence without ceremony and stood upright before him like an equal, not hesitating even to smoke—or to flirt openly with one of the female attendants. He was also said to have driven into the inner court of the Barompiman Hall, a privilege reserved for only the most exalted. Almost worse, he had sat in the car *with his legs crossed*, the impropriety of which I discussed in the introduction. But, asked defending counsel, if all this was so and the palace official right in his insistence that Chaleo had been sacked, how was a certain silver cigarette case to be explained? Produced in court, it was seen to bear the King's initials and the legend,

THE DEVIL'S DISCUS

Conferred by Royal grace upon Mr Chaleo Patoomros for having rendered satisfactory service as the King's private secretary. B.E.2489 (1946). To this the official replied that because an outgoing secretary customarily received such a gift he had submitted the matter, at Chaleo's request, to Ananda, who only agreed when the official urged that His Majesty's favour might be granted to avoid unpleasant comment.

It is fascinating to follow the intricacies of reasoning by which evidence may be wrung dry of every implication it might yield. Accept that Chaleo and Lt Vacharachai had been dismissed, then Pridi also had some spur to treason in that fact alone—because the dismissal of his protégés argued an affront to him. And if that argument is tenuous, his appointment of unsatisfactory servants of the King suggested a want of care in the royal interest, just as his subsequent appointment of those same men to superior posts suggested at least an ambiguous state of mind towards the throne.

But more direct and damaging evidence on the subject of his loyalty was soon forthcoming. During Ananda's sojourn in the Barompiman Hall he had a Buddhist tutor, a former priest, and this man came into the witness-stand with a damning disclosure. He said that following Pridi's visit after dinner on 7 June when Pridi and the King apparently differed over who should be Regent upon Ananda's departure, Pridi emerged in a frightful rage. He told the witness he was far from satisfied. More: he declared that he *would not support the throne again.* This threat greatly distressed him, the witness said, and he repeated it to the Princess Mother, urging her to tell the King. She refused, as her own testimony was to confirm, because of her son's illness. The ex-tutor could not be shaken from this story under cross-examination, and before he left the witness-stand he also described the atmosphere of nervousness following Ananda's death; King Bhoomipol, he said, even asked him whether the new appointments of secretaries and other officials were safe.

The question of Pridi's loyalty, so fundamental to the prosecution case, was returned to again and again. Years gone by were raked over to show that his dislike of any superior was of long standing. To begin with there was his alleged communism—notorious enemy of kings. An aristocrat in the royal service recalled the famous story of Pridi's quarrel with the Ambassador in Paris during his student days, and the reports from the Embassy that Pridi had attended communist meetings.* But the witness's value to the prosecution was a little tarnished during cross-examination when he conceded his own admiration for Pridi's talents, and the respect in which many members of the royal family held him for his personal help, especially during the war.

While Pridi's attitude towards other members of the royal family was not strictly relevant to the issue, in an atmosphere where fact could scarcely be distinguished from emotional opinion it was hungrily seized on by the defence, who repeatedly returned to it as several prominent princes followed each other into the witness-stand. But if they ackowledged Pridi's help to themselves as students or later to their families this did not inhibit their evidence on behalf of the prosecution.

One such prince declared that Pridi, having set up the Commission of Inquiry only because of public agitation, 'fixed' the police to deal evasively with any evidence contrary to the official accident theory (he was supported by other witnesses who said they had been made afraid to speak out against it), and that he had information—albeit anonymous—that the one doctor on the commission's medical panel who strongly supported the accident theory was under orders by Pridi's Government. (The doctor referred to—Dr Nit—had already emphatically denied any attempt by Pridi to interfere.)

Now Pridi had appeared to subscribe to the accident theory not out of belief in it but to suppress the notion of suicide. Therefore if he had tried to influence the commission to support the theory, the attempt condemned him only if he had guilty knowledge of the one remaining explanation, murder. The trial was in fact approaching a prolonged and fine-meshed investigation into the fundamental question, Murder or Suicide?

The next prince called, one in the inner counsels of the royal family, was questioned about Ananda's attitude towards the intended state visits abroad, and replied that the King had talked eagerly of meeting President Truman and the British monarchy. This scarcely argued suicide four days before his date of departure. Indeed anyone knowing

* Since that time the political proclivities of Eastern students in Paris during the 'twenties had acquired added significance because of the communist revolution in China which was largely generated by such students under the influence of French communists— who were similarly inspiring other former students to throw off French control of Cambodia and Vietnam.

him well scorned the idea, said his uncle, Prince Rangsit the Regent. This personage told how when he got to the Barompiman Hall after Ananda's death he asked the Princess Mother and Bhoomipol whether anyone had a grudge against Ananda, and they gave him no answer, but at the Palace Meeting downstairs Pridi declared emphatically that neither he nor anyone else had quarrelled with the King. Because of this, and the presence of the pistol by Ananda's hand, and the (Pridi-appointed) Police Chief's rejection of murder, everyone had to con-clude that Ananda was a suicide. Yet when he, Prince Rangsit, saw the large pistol Nai Chit brought down he felt sure that anyone com-mitting suicide would surely point it at the side of the head instead of awkwardly doing it from the front, and only because he was not an expert did he agree to the cover-up story of accident.

However, experts were at hand to dispel doubts once and for all. Some forty-odd witnesses had so far been heard, too many in the grip of prejudice or emotion. But now dispassionate Science was to speak. Ballistics, forensic medicine, and the austere probity of the test tube could claim to reveal the unadorned truth.

There is first the story of how this evidence itself came to be revealed. It starts during the agitated Palace Meeting, after Nai Chit had brought down the ·45 pistol. Among the police there was a certain captain who examined the ·45 and privately decided that it seemed dirty and rusty, and that the barrel smelt stale. Could it really have been fired only an hour or two before? Two days later his chief sent the pistol to the Director-General of the Science Department, asking him his opinion of when last it had been fired.

The Director-General was to become a key-witness. A pleasant square-faced man with thick eyebrows and long ears, he had graduated in natural sciences (physics, chemistry, metallurgy) in Germany, where he stayed on for two years to teach chemistry and practise metallurgy, and then back home he spent eighteen years in the Army Science Department on his way to the top post. Upon getting the ·45 from the police he handed it over to the head of the Legal Chemistry Section (who held a medical degree and a diploma in pharmacy from the local university): a certain test was made and a swab pulled through the barrel. The findings disconcerted them. Later in the day a naval friend of the Director-General dropped by, an engineering and science graduate of Cambridge who happened to have served in the Danish navy to study pistol powder and explosives. Given the ·45 he squinted through the barrel and confirmed the morning's findings: *the pistol had last been fired many days, perhaps weeks, before the time of the King's death.*

The Director-General hesitated before sending his report to the police. He held a meeting of his colleagues. The communiqués kept saying there had been an accident. But the pistol involved in the accident had not been fired! Something, somewhere was wrong. As officials, however, theirs was not to make trouble. The Director-General would feel his way with the police. So in his report three days after receiving the pistol he communicated the unremarkable conclusion that the pistol had *at some time* been fired; but as to *when*, 'the Science Department is not at present properly equipped with apparatus and chemicals to enable it to produce a definite conclusion.' But he concluded with a pregnant orientalism: 'It therefore mentions this for your information.'

The hint was not taken. There was no further contact between the Director-General and the police for a long time.

But the Director-General, intrigued by the test performed by the head of the Legal Chemistry Section, quietly obtained two similar ·45s. After firing them and then applying the same tests at varying intervals during the next few months, he came to the 'definite conclusion' which the police had shied at demanding.

These tests were based on the fact that when a pistol is fired particles of matter are deposited in the barrel. Among them are nitrite which, however, gradually disappears. Its presence is detected if boiling water, poured down the barrel and then into a beaker with certain chemicals, turns pink. A solution which turns pink quickly and very pinky indicates that a lot of nitrite is present and hence that the pistol has been fired recently; a slow pallid reaction would mean the opposite. The Director-General found that to get the same result as the test on Ananda's pistol had produced, it was necessary to fire a pistol at least eight days before. This fixed the last date on which Ananda's pistol had been fired as 4 June; he died on 9 June.

The Director-General's report with this perplexing information was complete by November 1946. He said nothing to the police because his superior advised him not to put his neck out, or as he expressed himself in Thai, not to cast his foot for splinters. But a year later came

FM Pibul's *coup d'état* which had as its professed aim the clearing-up
of the King's Death Case. The Director-General decided at last to send
in his report. Later he repeated the tests three or four times over a
period of months for the benefit of the new police investigating
committee under Detective Phinich.

For Detective Phinich this had been the start of as subtle a reconstruction of a crime as any in the annals of real or fictional detection.
Whether it was sound or illusory was the court's function to determine;
and the defence, trying by every means to discredit the prosecution
case in order to secure the accused's acquittal, questioned it from the
start. In their rigorous cross-examination of the Director-General they
attacked his statistical method: vital, valid deductions could not be
made from only two pistols, and each for different periods. In any
event the amount of nitrite revealed depends on the amount of oil
which happens to be in a particular barrel. And whether for this or
any other reason, in one of the tests the pink reaction had actually
occurred quicker after fourteen days than eight days. In view of these
facts, the defence cried, of what use were the Director-General's
tests? He answered that as to the number of pistols tested, after the
coup d'état he used more than ten, and that the delayed pink reaction
seized on by the defence was a freak result which occurred only once in
innumerable tests. He was then challenged on the worth of tests so
inexactly measured that he could not tell by how much the nitrite in
one test exceeded that in another, the only assessment having been a
description of the degrees of pinkness such as 'pale', 'light', 'barely
perceptible'—all arrived at merely by eye until towards the end of the
series of tests a photometer was used. However, he held firmly to his
conclusion, and it was not only shared by his fellow experts but
supported by tests of another kind.

These concerned the rust which, whenever a pistol is fired, forms in
the barrel at a rate dependent on the quality of the metal. Immediately
before the initial nitrite test on Ananda's pistol two days after the
tragedy, a swab drawn through the barrel contained what the Director-
General took to be particles of pistol powder but which the head of the
Legal Chemistry Section said were rust. So in carrying out the nitrite
tests the Director-General also tested for rust. He found none for at
least two days after firing, while a quality equal to that in Ananda's
pistol needed four to eight days to accumulate, thus confirming the

The catafalque bearing the urn with Ananda's body, drawn by marines outside the Grand Palace. The Temple of the Emerald Buddha is on the right, and in the background left may be seen the roof of the Barompiman Hall

Under the white nine-tiered umbrella, the gold urn holding the remains of King Ananda is moved up the staircase (*right*) of the pavilion on the Pramane Ground

Above the heads of the crowd rises the temporary pavilion on the Pramane Ground, where the cremation of Ananda's remains lasted all night

nitrite tests. The prosecution also called an ordnance colonel who had been an expert on small arms for over twenty years: he declared that to judge from the quality of metal from which Ananda's pistol was made the inside of the barrel would have had a colour like white smoke and only after four or five days assumed the red-earth appearance of rust seen by the police captain at the Palace Meeting and the officials in the Science Department. The defence could not move him from this statement, but he conceded that rust forms quicker if a gun has not been properly cleaned after any previous use.

The evidence on this point was that prior to the fatal Sunday the last occasion on which Ananda was known to have fired the gun was months before, but whether or how well it had been cleaned the prosecution could not say. They could only bring evidence of Ananda's habit of leaving any weapon he had been using to an official for cleaning—which, the court was to conclude, 'presumably must have been done well and not in the slipshod way usual with privately owned pistols'. The question might have been decisively answered in the light of something else the ordnance colonel said, namely that a pistol barrel already rusted at the time of firing betrays the fact by leaving marks on the bullet. But the bullet itself was as intriguing a subject of uncertainty as any at the trial.

Among the innumerable exhibits before the court, ranging from a model of Ananda's bedroom to the blue Chinese silk trousers he had worn and the mangled remains of his pillow dug up from the golf course, were his ·45 pistol, the spent cartridge which Nai Chit said he had picked up near the royal bed, and the bullet found embedded in the mattress three days later. A police expert, unchallenged by the defence, vouched that the spent cartridge and the bullet had both been fired by the ·45. Curiously, no evidence was led to show whether the bullet in the mattress had belonged to the spent cartridge, but the prosecution brought witnesses who testified on the one hand that Nai Chit gave contradictory explanations of where exactly he picked up the spent cartridge; and on the other that the bullet in the mattress had not been the one which killed Ananda but had been 'planted' there in substitution for the fatal bullet fired by the assassin's own weapon.

This conclusion had originated with one of the members of the medical panel advising the Commission of Inquiry. He noted that the bullet thought to have killed Ananda was unmarked, undented, undeformed in any way, yet when bullets were fired through the skulls of unclaimed corpses at the Siriraj Hospital all were badly dented. Nothing seems to have been made of this at the Commission of Inquiry, but Detective Phinich immediately recognized its importance. Two enlarged photographs—Exhibits 126 and 127—were handed to the judges. They showed one bullet which had been fired through a human skull, another which had gone through a sheet of paper, and the actual bullet found in the royal mattress. The first was dented out of shape, but the second and third bullets were almost identical in their apparently pristine condition. The prosecution also called a police expert to say that in his experience bullets fired at a human skull were sometimes found much dented and sometimes slightly dented; but then he somewhat overplayed the prosecution's hand by adding that sometimes they were not dented at all. The prosecution's embarrassment was soothed, however, by the judges who expressed surprise, and asked if it wasn't common-sense to conclude that a bullet hitting a solid object twice—front and back of a skull—could not possibly do so with impunity.

The prosecution case, then, as the first year of the trial ended and the second began in September 1949, had received a powerful fillip from the experts. The nitrite tests proved, they maintained, that Ananda's ·45 had not fired the fatal shot, which ruled out suicide or accident. The undented condition of the bullet in the mattress proved that it had been 'planted' in substitution of the fatal bullet, creating a strong possibility that the spent cartridge which Nai Chit said he had found was also a substitute. These substitutions could scarcely have been effected without inside assistance. Whose but the two pages of the bedchamber, Nai Chit and Butr, or one of them? And when the murder plot was considered in the elaborate detail that sought to hide the crime by creating an appearance of suicide, the presence of a master mind became self-evident. Everyone knew that Pridi had such a mind. But he had not reckoned on Detective Phinich, nor the marvels of science—and these were far from exhausted.

The most eloquent witness in a homicide case may be the victim. His body often lives after him. 'Poor poor dumb mouths,' cried Mark Antony over Caesar's wounds. But at a murder trial wounds are rarely dumb. The difficulty is to decide precisely what they are saying.

THE TRIAL

As the heat of the hot season summoned the clouds for the monsoon, and the Emerald Buddha changed his lighter harness of jewels for the treasures of his rainy season garb, a succession of doctors was called to give evidence. One had trained in Germany and the US; another had studied forensic medicine at Scotland Yard; all were impressively qualified. From them was now heard a phrase which they constantly used, explaining it in detail ample enough to fill a text book. It was new to Thailand's courts; and its novelty and repetition gave it almost the quality of an incantation, spell-binding the layman: *cadaveric spasm.*

When a person dies his muscles usually go slack for some hours until the stiffening effect of rigor mortis sets in. But sometimes a particular kind of brain injury causes an instant stiffening, a spasm. A woman knocked dead by a car may be found still holding her shopping basket; the corpse of a soldier in battle may mime the instant of death when he lunged forward with fixed bayonet. This phenomenon, long confused with rigor mortis, was distinguished early in the century by the name cadaveric spasm, which grips *muscles being used at the moment of death.*

Now Ananda was found on his back, his head on the pillow, his legs stretched out straight, his arms beside him outside the coverlet which extended from chest to feet; his features were impassive, his eyes and mouth closed. The defence raised the question of whether in the confusion, and with the Princess Mother flinging herself upon him and the Royal Nanny taking hold of his wrist, his original position might have been altered. But descriptions of how he was seen by Nai Chit, the Princess Mother, the Royal Nanny, Bhoomipol, the lady-in-waiting, and Dr Nit agree: he lay in an attitude of sleep.

Moreover, when the doctor and the Royal Nanny washed the body it was limp, indicating that no spasm had occurred.

The prosecution maintained that no spasm occurred because Ananda was not using any muscles at the moment of death. That is, he was lying as found, and he could not therefore have been handling a pistol, making the conclusion irresistible that an assassin crept up upon him unseen and unheard.

But there was one other explanation of the lack of cadaveric spasm. The particular kind of brain injury which causes it is this: the cerebral cortex, the upper part of the head and usually the controlling centre for the contraction of muscles, is destroyed while another part of the

149

brain, the basal ganglia, is left intact to take over from the cerebral cortex and continue contracting the muscles being used at the moment of death. If both parts are destroyed no spasm occurs, and if this happened in Ananda's case he might have been in another position when the shot was fired and then flopped into the sleeping posture he was found in. Therefore to establish its point the prosecution had to show that Ananda's cerebral cortex had been destroyed but not his basal ganglia, so that the spasm would inevitably have occurred had he not been lying supine at the actual moment of his death.

The prosecution's proof depended on the exact path taken by the bullet through Ananda's head. X-ray photographs and other methods traced it in the straight downward-tending line from his forehead to near the nape of his neck as already described. It passed through the cerebral cortex and narrowly missed another part of the brain, the cerebellum, immediately beneath it. Since the ganglia adjoins the cerebellum, had the ganglia been missed too?

At the autopsy the passage left by the bullet could not be measured because the wound had closed up. So the court was treated to the grisly spectacle of a human brain through which a glass tube six millimetres in diameter was inserted to follow the direction which had been taken by the bullet through Ananda's head—that is, through the cortex but narrowly missing the cerebellum. The tube narrowly missed the ganglia too.

Conclusive though this seemed, the defence had still a glimmer of hope. Even if the ganglia had not been destroyed, was there not still the possibility that the King was using his muscles but the spasm which would consequently have occurred was prevented by the violence of the pistol's recoil? This might have thrown his arm—or arms, if he used both hands—to the position found, and the pistol likewise (it lay close to his outstretched hand).

The prosecution had two answers. The ordnance colonel, expert on small arms, produced much technical data about pressure and forces. The long and short of it was that the recoil of a ·45 could not possibly have hurled the pistol nearly three feet from the vicinity of Ananda's forehead to his outstretched hand. And the medical evidence on muscular action was that the recoil would have thrown Ananda's arms away from his body, not drawn them to the sides of it.

After all the technicalities from the experts, the prosecution produced evidence more readily understandable by the layman. If Ananda shot himelf, one would have expected to find his hand—or hands—and the pistol in the vicinity of his chest, head, or neck. Common-sense told one this, even without the medical evidence that at death if there is no spasm every part of the body not already prone tends to flop inertly into the nearest position dictated by gravity. A senior police official was called to recite instances from his own cases: in none had a person who shot himself while lying down been found with his arms outstretched by his sides and the pistol where Ananda's was. Here may conveniently be recorded a passage in the evidence given much later by another police witness. He had made the experiment of firing a ·45 at close range into the corpse of a man about Ananda's age, and he found that blood and fragments of the skull and brain splattered on to his wrist and pistol. No such souvenir had been found on Ananda's wrist or pistol, the inference being that he could not therefore have shot himself—whereas the evidence of Lt Vacharachai's laundress had been that she washed blood off *his* sleeve.

It was some relief to the public if not the accused when the long excursion into ballistics and forensic medicine was substantially completed by the end of 1949—and with it the essentials of the prosecution case, which nevertheless was not to finish for another whole year.

It is difficult to resist pity for Chaleo and the two pages, however black the case against them. After all the bewildering scientific evidence, and with eighty witnesses still to follow the sixty who had already been heard, they had the impression that every resource of the State, every possible witness alive or dead, was marshalled against them. The leisurely proceedings, often adjourned, had already meant imprisonment of two years. It is easily said but less easy to calculate in minutes and hours. Time had become a rack upon which nerve and mind and hope itself were endlessly stretched. The knowledge that their wives and children suffered for them scarcely made it more supportable. There was not only the looming terror of the executioner, but the realization of the shame that would surround their memory if they were found guilty. Nor were these mental anguishes relieved by the physical conditions of imprisonment. For long periods they were kept in heavy chains over an inch and a half thick, and the police used every device to extract a confession. Their existence was a nightmare of two alternating scenes—the packed court with its intent faces, droning voices, and the still image of the Buddha; and the prison, eating away lives which only tight-drawn courage could not acknowledge forfeit. Once—it was a morning in December 1949— a sudden series of small explosions outside Room 24 roused wild hope of some great eruption which would miraculously rescue them. But the guards rushing along with cocked tommy-guns found only that schoolboys were putting fire-crackers on some near by tram-tracks.

Often during the proceedings the three men's gaze had wandered up to the portrait of King Bhoomipol above the judges; and as 1950, the Year of the Tiger, advanced so did their hopes of at least temporary release centre on him. For the first time since his departure soon after Ananda's death, he was coming back. In March, when his ship was nearing Thailand and the three accused had been in gaol for two and a half years, their families petitioned the court for bail during His Majesty's visit. The petition was rejected—but how few of the populace could care when all was given over to ceremonial that brought together in unique conjunction a nation's wild rejoicing and its sorrowful reverence. For Ananda was at last to be cremated, and his brother both crowned and wed.

IV

WHILE the full glare of public attention was on the trial of Ananda's alleged murderers, the royal family had retired into Switzerland and the shadows. But early the previous September King Bhoomipol's betrothal was announced to a seventeen-year-old girl named Sirikit.

Reports of her were enthusiastic: 'She has an abundance of shiny black hair beautifully arranged and falling just below her neck-line, nice eyes, a charming little nose, a fine mouth which is almost constantly smiling, revealing a perfect row of white teeth worthy of a film star. She is rather tall for a Thai girl and seems very fit and healthy.'

Bhoomipol had first met her a year before while visiting London where her father was the Siamese Ambassador. A few months later he had a serious road accident: the Chakri weakness for motor-cars was a constant source of danger to the family. Sirikit, summoned to the Villa Watana in Lausanne, helped nurse him. Operations on an injury to his right eye failed to save it from permanent impairment, accounting for its fixity and his use of tinted spectacles; and on medical advice he suspended his law studies, which remain unfinished. But with the tonic of love he rapidly recovered. Sirikit returned to her father who was presently summoned to the Villa Watana for the discussions which mark even an ordinary Thai betrothal, until the latter was ceremoniously concluded; though not until after her birthday party, attended by Bhoomipol who brought her a diamond ring, was the official announcement made to his Regent in Bangkok.

The news had the nation delightedly agog. No one was reminded that Sirikit's father was a friend of Pridi. They had been fellow-students, and Pridi gave him his chance in the diplomatic service—a fact acknowledged by the grateful inscription on a portrait of himself which he gave Pridi.

Astrologers were soon reported to be prognosticating next March as suitable for the wedding. A hint that Bhoomipol might intend acting upon their advice was given by the delivery in Bangkok of a superb new Daimler for his use. Costing £6,400 and equipped with air-conditioning and a telephone, it was solemnly anointed at a religious ceremony attended by the Regent and the Privy Council.

Orders for vehicles of a different kind excited rather more apprehensive attention. The already well-armed police were to get sixty new armoured cars weighing twelve tons each, and an enlarged flotilla of armed vessels. The total manpower of the force was to provide one policeman for every hundred and fifty people in Bangkok.

Had you lived in Thailand at this period you might have thought such prodigious concern for law-enforcement not excessive. The smuggling-out of opium, and of jewels, and of foodstuffs like rice; the illegal re-export of petrol, the secret manufacture of cigarettes and morphine and fake pharmaceutical drugs; and the waves of robberies—typewriters one day, gold bullion another, antique Buddha images a third—all this was conducted on a huge scale. Prevailing villainy was exemplified by the superintendent and staff of a penal island who ganged together with the convicts to use the Government launch and prey on small cargo boats, whose crews they bound hand-and-foot and drowned, over fifty of them.

But the fact is that the strengthening of the police was to enforce not the law of the land but the power of its political masters. A police state was in process of creation. Its creator was FM Pibul's henchman, thirty-nine-year-old Police-General Pao, one of the *coup* leaders who had restored him to power. The complete record of this man, the Butcher of Bangkok, will never be known. His activities ranged from murder to participation in opium smuggling and the ownership of brothels.

Through the Ministry of the Interior which controlled the police he could not only act corruptly himself but increase the corruption of the whole administration. Thus, of sixty criminal cases reported in a certain province only one came to trial. Or, to quote another example, the responsible minister smoothly instructed the State tobacco monopoly to issue free shares to favoured deputies. Politicians, policemen, army officers and businessmen were drawn into the happy hug of the 'squeeze' or imbibed from the gushing wells of 'lubrication'.

As head of the Government and himself the Minister of Finance, FM Pibul genially and generously distributed largesse in various forms. Where this was not expedient to maintain his power he always had Police-General Pao whose authorized gangsters shot or imprisoned at his nod. FM Pibul's political morality is illustrated by his cool admission that putting down Pridi's abortive *coup* attempt of February 1949 cost three million baht (£50,000), for which the State was plundered that bribes and rewards should not be lacking. (This was cheap: the *coup* that brought FM Pibul back to power cost £250,000, which the nation also had to pay.) After that February affair Police-General Pao rewarded many police officers with gold rings: 'I've never cheated or swindled during my whole life,' he cried as he presented them, 'and I urge you to follow my example.' When FM Pibul was questioned in the Assembly about how General Pao financed this practice, he replied, 'I believe he has his own way of raising money for the purpose.'

Questions in the Assembly were the only check on the increasing tyranny of the régime, for newspapers were constantly banned or their editors intimidated. One had a hand grenade (standard feature of the police arsenal) thrown at him. Another, daring to criticize Police-General Pao, had to take refuge in a monastery. Mom Seni's journalist brother Kukrit Pramoj was notable among editors for bravely using his satire against the régime, but for him and his fellows in the Democrat Party the hour was five past twelve. The promise of democracy, instead of being salvaged by their acceptance of FM Pibul's comeback, had become obliterated.

FM Pibul permitted the existence of the Assembly in order to give the appearance of a parliamentary régime, though he took care to control a docile majority and clamped down a State of Emergency when it suited him. Always he paid lip-service to the ideal of democracy, partly because his idealism was only second to his self-interest and partly because he needed friends at home and abroad. He wooed the royalists inside and out of the Democrat Party and tried to make people forget that like Pridi he had been one of the Promoters of the 1932 Revolution. His manners, dress and moderately luxurious way of life made him naturally closer than Pridi to many royalists and conservatives who, ever suspicious of Pridi's radicalism and daily made more convinced by the evidence in the regicide trial of his guilt, gravitated towards the man who not only overthrew him and was keeping him out but stood in undisputed command of the nation.

FM Pibul returned to his old game of gaining support by whipping up nationalist fervour. Having replaced 'Siam' by 'Thailand', new legislation was directed against the local Chinese. That he felt no shame for the Pibul who collaborated with the wartime invader he made clear by his greeting to a visiting party of Japanese businessmen: 'This is the first time since the war that I've heard Japanese and I'm very happy.' The West could hardly take exception, for as he consolidated his control it saw him a strong-man against the threat looming over South-East Asia with Chiang Kai-shek's final defeat on the mainland and Russia's recognition of the People's Republic of China. To present himself as a champion and Thailand a bastion against communism was henceforward his trump ploy. He needed it for getting economic help: a buoyant agriculture and the return of forty-four million dollars of gold by Japan were not enough to finance an economy bled white by corruption. A mission to London got a loan of five million pounds 'for financing development to discourage communism'.

He did of course discourage communism and everything else that might weaken his own power. However much he tried to give the appearance of governing through a parliament, the special force of one thousand riot police formed by Police-General Pao in Bangkok plainly told otherwise. So did two major trials which were going on besides the regicide trial in Room 24. These were of men charged in connection with treason plots, especially Pridi's attempted counter-*coup* of February 1949, though how many political prisoners never came to trial is unlikely ever to be known.

But six who did not *are* known of. These were former pro-Pridi cabinet ministers and deputies, and they never came to trial because Police-General Pao had them murdered in March 1949. Two of them were in fact among the defence counsel in the regicide trial. Replacements were found with difficulty and then they too were arrested, on October 30 1949—for alleged treason and distributing an anti-Pibul pamphlet. Nobody could be persuaded to take their place, and of the remaining two counsel one resigned—and who can blame him? Only the man who first volunteered to defend the accused, doughty Fak Nasongkhla, remained. Then a girl of twenty-three, just graduated in law, stepped forward to his side. She was Chaleo's daughter. With Fak she henceforward helped fight for her father and the two pages to the end of the trial.

However, pity for the accused or distaste for the terrorism and evil of FM Pibul's régime should not be allowed to prejudice our judgement. In spite of everything, the regicide trial was being conducted in more or less proper form, and at least in its accumulation of information could provide a valuable guide to the truth. By the end of 1949 when all the ballistics and medical witnesses had finished, upwards of sixty witnesses had been heard. The prosecution proposed still to call about another eighty in the ensuing year, and these were to include no less than the King himself and the Princess Mother.

They were not together when Bhoomipol made his long-awaited return to his country. He came with his beautiful fiancée, but his mother had herself been in a motor-car accident. At least her injuries saved her the distress of returning to scenes of tragic memory. The imprint of that memory was still strong upon Bhoomipol, showing clearly in his face, unsmiling from first to last. There was plenty to remind him: the journey up-river in a warship, the presentation of the gold sword of the realm, the addresses of loyalty, the chanting monks and the assembled diplomats at the royal landing place, the vast crowd watching him enter the Grand Palace—all was much as it had been that time, before the war, when he first came back on a visit. But then Ananda had been at the centre of the ceremonial while he had been but a little boy with a face like a bespectacled marmoset; and now Ananda was in the gold urn in front of which Bhoomipol, grown to handsome manhood, paid his respects before doing likewise to all his Chakri ancestors in the royal mausoleum, and lighting candles that were carried to every principal temple in the city. Before leaving the Grand Palace he worshipped in the Temple of the Emerald Buddha, and bowed low in that secret part of the Inside where lives the spirit of the nation, called by the pious the Guardian Angel of the Realm and by sophisticates 'the old gentleman at the Palace'. He was not to reside in the Barompiman Hall but in a newer palace a couple of miles distant. On the way, the Rajdamnoen Avenue was lined with decorations and the ever-enthusiastic multitude. The police had earlier checked that no washing would be hanging out to disturb the royal eye, nor anybody so disrespectful as to be above the King's head by watching from a rooftop.

Early the following morning Bhoomipol presented sixty-four priests with food as part of a ceremony to make his new palace auspicious. It was the start of a complicated series of rituals mined from the lode of Siam's long history. One day he sat in the glittering Amarindr Throne Hall of the Grand Palace, its walls lined in red and gold, while monks with lighted candles circled about him. Another day he attended a ceremony at the river to appease the Goddess of Water. But unscheduled was the drive he took in plain clothes to the Pramane Ground in front of the Grand Palace. There the great temporary pavilion had been built for his brother's cremation; and when the crowd recognized him he quickly drove off. A hundred yards away in Room 24 the trial continued of the three men charged with murdering his brother.

On 30 March, 1950, nearly four years since Ananda's swaddled corpse was immured in the silver urn, the funeral started. The great golden urn containing the silver urn was hoisted by pulley and tackle on to the royal catafalque nearly forty feet high. This was a spired pavilion upon a boat-shaped structure on wheels, drawn by a hundred marines. Its sides were built up in red and gold ornamented tiers inlaid with green glass mosaic, and so richly carved was it with scarlet-tongued dragons and praying angels and geometric designs that slowly though it moved spectators could take in little detail. At the Pramane Ground, the crematorium was another but vaster spired pavilion high above the plain and reached by four long flights of steps. Rails had been laid up the centre of one flight, and the urn, first transferred to an artillery carriage to be borne round the ground three times, was hauled up and deposited in the pavilion.

At 4.30 p.m. King Bhoomipol, wearing the uniform of Marshal of the Royal Guards, slowly mounted the steps and lit a candle in front of the urn. He then descended to listen to a sermon by the Prince Patriarch. Once more he went up the stairs to the platform of the pavilion. The urn and his own slow-moving figure seemed quite alone despite the vast crowd which had been arriving by road and water since 4 a.m. and turned the plain into a dark panoply of heads. Bhoomipol stood before the urn and there was a great silence under the rich blue sky. Then he took his leave of Ananda's remains, not merely bowing but prostrating himself, which was an act so humble that a soft murmur of awe and grief rose from the crowd. Presently he symbolically lit the pyre with a taper, soldiers fired three volleys, and buglers sounded the Last Post. Then dignitaries and members of the royal family followed slowly up the steps to pay their last respects; one bore a golden bowl of paper flowers from the Princess Mother.

That night the pyre was actually lit. When Bhoomipol attended the extinguishing of the flames at eight o'clock in the morning only ash remained of Ananda's body. But his spirit—not as Westerners think of spirit which carries the personality, the identity, of the dead person into eternity; but as Buddhists think of spirit, a profusion of qualities held back from eternity until after many earthly lives these reach perfection and merge into the universe—his spirit entered the body of some person or creature born at that moment, and by the laws of Karma this new body would prosper or suffer according to the true merit of Ananda's life.

The cremation was followed by rites which continued for weeks. And then, at the prospect of the royal wedding and coronation, all was suddenly joy. The Siamese divest themselves of nothing quicker than sadness.

On a morning a month later Bhoomipol attended the house of his grandmother, mother of Prince Mahidol, and there met his bride. They signed the marriage register. The royal grandmother entered the room to bless them by pouring lustral water over their hands. So they were married. In the afternoon at the Grand Palace the King declared before his royal relatives and the Government that he was married. The more important members of the audience poured lustral water over the royal couple's hands. The senior prince offered humble congratulations from them all. As simply as this was were the nuptials of a king concluded.

Very different was the coronation which followed after only a few days' honeymoon at Hua Hin. Since it provides the most exacting and curious day in Siamese state ceremonials, I must condense.

At 9.30 a.m. in a special part of the Grand Palace, Bhoomipol dressed in a white robe and facing east, had a sacramental bath while the Royal Astrologer sounded the Victory Gong. Then dressed in his golden coronation robes Bhoomipol took his seat on a throne sealed off from the gaze of any foreigner. Eight deputies of the Assembly, clad as the Gods of the Eight Directions and bringing lustral water gathered from river-sources in the eight directions of the compass, filled a golden conch held by the King. The Chief Brahmin handed

him the nine-tiered umbrella of majesty while the band played the
national anthem and soldiers presented arms. There were more
formalities before he walked to the adjoining Amarindr Throne Hall
where distinguished foreigners awaited. He sat on another throne
under the nine-tiered umbrella, facing east. The Chief Brahmin
chanted an invocation to the gods to be present, though it is hardly
credible that they would have absented themselves from a scene of
such flashing splendour and ancient pomp. Then came the crux.
Twenty-five pieces of regalia were presented to Bhoomipol, including
the diamond-studded golden crown weighing seven kilograms, which
he himself placed on his head. Each article of regalia represented a
quality or possession of his kingship, for by this ceremony the land,
water and sky of Siam, and the life of every person and creature, were
given in trust to him. All the while priests chanted blessings, traditional
music was played, a salute of one hundred-and-one guns thundered
out, and every monastery in the kingdom sounded gongs. The
Prince Patriarch blew out the Victory Candle, the King distributed
gold and silver flowers to leading monks, and with many more
ceremonies, addresses, vows, and the offering of silver trees to the
image of the Emerald Buddha; with processions, a declaration by the
Chief of the Royal Scriptures Division that Bhoomipol's wife was
Queen, and with audiences private and public, the day only ended at
past ten that night. Save for next day's traditional royal appearance
before the populace from a balcony in the wall of the Grand Palace,
the ceremonial was over. It had cost £35,000, of which the festivity-
loving Thais regretted not a tical. To mark the occasion, princes were
elevated in rank and convicted prisoners had their sentences reduced.
But for the three accused in the regicide trial, relief there was none.
Ananda had been cremated, the new King crowned, yet the past
remained remorselessly present while the mysterious tragedy which
was responsible for these events continued to be disinterred in
Room 24.

V

FROM all the officials, police, servants, politicians, and their wives and their friends who entered the witness-stand during the year (1950), the evidence proved if nothing else the thoroughness of the police investigators and the zeal of their chief, Detective Phinich. But while no scrap of evidence which could possibly be grist to the prosecution mill was neglected, the bulk of it merely corroborated or extended details already known.

Thus, the atmosphere of fearfulness among the royal family after Ananda's death; and the gloomy forebodings of Senior Page Chan who predeceased Ananda; and Pridi's efforts to steer inquiry from anything likely to upset the official explanation of accident; and much else—all were enlarged on. One or two points were of note—an alleged statement by Chan that Nai Chit's treacherous function had been to act as Secretary Chaleo's spy, and another by Pridi that Ananda had committed suicide through grief over family affairs—but little new was revealed. That little, however, was sometimes startling.

In this category falls a disclosure made by the infamous Police-General Pao. He had earlier told the court that a month before Ananda died a prominent supporter of Pridi was saying that Ananda planned to abdicate in favour of Bhoomipol so that Ananda himself could 'play politics'. But the real surprise in Pao's evidence was that Ananda was due to have met FM Pibul the day after he died. FM Pibul had at that time been but recently released from his trial on war crime charges. According to Pao, a brother-in-law whose wife was in the Princess Mother's entourage gave him a message that Ananda wished to see FM Pibul. Pao duly conveyed the message to FM Pibul and eventually arrangements were made for the meeting, not at the Barompiman Hall but in the secrecy of the Mahidol family residence, Sraptatum Palace. If the implications in all this were various, the common denominator was that whether or not Pridi had quarrelled with the King

THE DEVIL'S DISCUS

as the prosecution alleged, he could not have enjoyed Ananda's confidence. It was a strange and, to Pridi's cause, damaging tale. That Police-General Pao, the Butcher of Bangkok, should have told it might have imposed too great a strain on all but extreme royalist credulity, but no less a witness than FM Pibul gave evidence confirming it. At least, he confirmed getting messages from Ananda requesting the meeting.

Speculation on the subject, however, was quickly swept aside by equally new evidence that sprang upon the public in great press headlines. According to it, Lt Vacharachai undertook the assassination of Ananda at Pridi's behest only after a gunman hired for the purpose had withdrawn at the last moment.

The revelation came from a certain junior army officer. He had been, he told the court, in prison for his part in the 1933 royalist insurrection. There he met a man called See, convicted of robbery. The years passed; and then, four days before Ananda's death, this See came to see him in a considerable state of excitement, saying he had been hired to kill 'an important person'. The details See gave him were that the man who had hired him was a former member of the Free Thai Movement and a henchman of Pridi, that he had given See two US Army pistols together with ammunition and a hand-grenade, and that the price for the job was to be £6,500. The army officer next described how See called again the day after Ananda's death. The gunman told him that the day before the tragedy he had been taken to the Grand Palace where Nai Chit and Butr pointed out 'the important person'. It was no other than the King. At this, See told his friend, he had refused to continue, with the result that Lt Vacharachai did the shooting. See begged the witness to take him in because he was terrified of the police. After some days' hiding in the house, See announced that he was resolved to go after Lt Vacharachai and kill him. He wished first to speak to a certain general to ask him to look after his family if he died wreaking the vengeance he was bent on. On this point the army officer's account was confirmed by the general himself, who testified that See was brought to him by the officer and told the same story the court heard except that he could not recall the names of Nai Chit and Butr. He dissuaded See from his hot-headed proposal, and See returned to stay with the officer for a month. After that he is known to have worked for a police captain whose Number 2

162

King Bhoomipol at his coronation

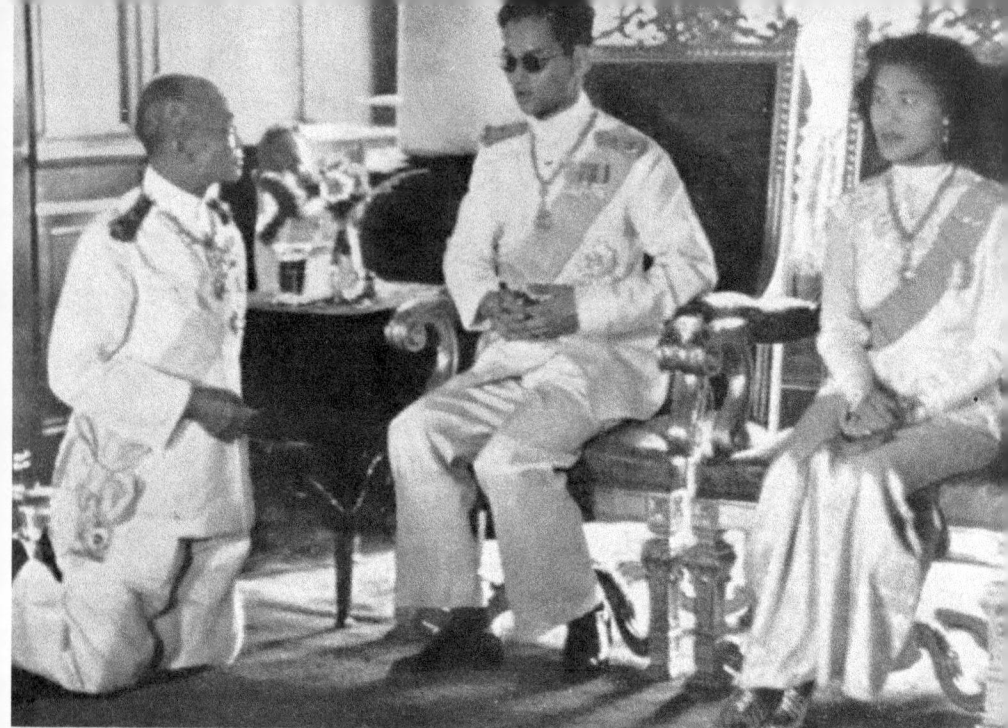

The marriage of Bhoomipol and Sirikit. Kneeling is Prince Rang-sit, former Political Prisoner and ex-Regent

Saffron-robed, and with head shaven, King Bhoomipol during his term as a monk. FM Pibul fills his begging bowl while Mrs Pibul looks on

wife wanted a chauffeur, but his further adventures can only be guessed at. There is a strongly held belief that he was murdered by the police captain, who could not be found to face a charge of murdering someone else. Certainly See had apparently died a violent death at the end of 1947 and Detective Phinich's investigators failed to produce him in court.

His character and career scarcely gave anything he said the stamp of credibility yet two details provoked thought. Being quite unconnected with the Palace he named Nai Chit and Butr within a day of the King's death. And if his story had been tailored to fit public rumours at the time, or concocted with somebody else's help, Chaleo rather than the named ex-FTM member (who was scornfully to deny his alleged part in the story) would more likely have been chosen as the gunman's hirer.

While all men are level in the grave, the great leveller of the living is a court of law. The evidence to rivet public attention after that of the lowly See came from the loftiest being in the land. The ninety-second witness for the prosecution was King Bhoomipol himself.

Few murder trials could ever have had a king give evidence; for him to have been a Siamese king, Lord of Life, made the event unique. The public was thwarted of its full drama, however, because Bhoomipol did not appear in Room 24. Judges, counsel, and the accused went to his palace, where five members of the Privy Council were present to preserve the royal dignity.

In his evidence, lasting a day and a half, he added nothing to the details of his movements on the morning of Ananda's death which are set out on pages 94 and 95-6. His description of the exact position of Ananda's body tallied with everyone else's except that he could not remember seeing Ananda's right arm, which by general agreement was outside the coverlet like his left arm and stretched out by his side. Bhoomipol continued (the royal 'we' and 'us' are here normalized):

King Ananda shot with guns at fairs in foreign countries and with toy guns. When he returned to Bangkok he used to shoot with guns given him by people at Cholburi in December when Pridi arranged the FTM demonstration . . . the person who showed him how to use the weapons was Lt Vacharachai. People who had given the King the guns said Lt Vacharachai should teach him and it was the King's own wish to learn. The shooting took place in the garden

163

behind the Barompiman Hall and I went too. The King shot with both short and long guns. They included the US Army ·45. When he shot with that some of the pages used to keep some of the spent cartridges. I saw both Nai Chit and Butr pick up spent cartridges. After shooting we'd let Lt Vacharachai take charge of the guns. The King had to wear glasses but I can't remember if he wore them every time he shot . . . Nai Chit could not point out where he had picked up the spent cartridge in the King's bedroom.

I'd heard that Chaleo let his car be driven right up to the door of the Barompiman Hall: whether my brother was displeased or not I don't know, but I do remember once when my mother wanted a car it couldn't be got because one was being repaired and Chaleo had sent the other to Pridi, so Kuang [Great Comedian, then Prime Minister] had to lend his car. The King never told me anything about Chaleo being disrespectful but I assumed he left because the King was displeased.

When the King went to Hua Hin on holiday, Pridi went too. There Pridi used the royal jeep, the King's personal property, without permission. He also did not get permission for a party of ex-members of the FTM. It turned out a very noisy party.

Pridi once arranged to get the King a piano to play at, I don't know where from, but when it arrived he was led to believe it was Pridi's own, until later he learnt it came from the Royal Household. I don't know if Pridi and my brother had any disagreement over the appointment of the Regency Council, but regarding the replacement of Chaleo, Pridi took so long that the man chosen by the King had not yet been appointed when he died.

It was my brother's own wish to visit the US and Britain on the way to Switzerland. He wished to leave in a hurry as the date was set for the thirteenth. . . . Between the King, myself and the Princess Mother there was never any trouble or misunderstanding. The King never told me that anything troubled him. The only complaint he ever made was about the heat. If anything was annoying him in his work he didn't tell me of it, but in his private life there was nothing seriously worrying him. He was a very calm person, and when he used guns he was very careful in every way and even warned me that when playing with a pistol I should make sure that the breach was empty. The King never discussed politics with me. I never heard that he wanted to meet FM Pibul. Chan [the senior page who pre-deceased Ananda] was very loyal and used to worry about our welfare and safety. He never said much to me but he used to tell me to be careful and I understood this to mean careful of myself. He'd told me this ever since we'd returned to Thailand.

Under further and cross-examination, Bhoomipol was taken back to the immediate events surrounding Ananda's death. The first he knew that anything was amiss was hearing the sound of running footsteps. He continued:

I did not hear anything abnormal before I heard someone running. While I was walking back and forth between my bedroom and playroom I didn't notice if anyone else was about. I paid no attention when I heard someone running. I heard both a shout of astonishment and weeping—it sounded like the same person. Apart from encountering the lady-in-waiting near the front porch I saw no one. I didn't notice if the door of the writing room was open. It was usually closed if the King was sleeping.

He recalled too that when he went into the bedroom the mosquito net was open. As to who gave the ·45 he thought it was Chan, at the time of Ananda's arrival in Bangkok. Ananda had stopped shooting with any weapons at all several days before his death.

This concluded His Majesty's evidence. Much of it was not new, but I have reported it almost in its entirety because of its importance.

With Bhoomipol's departure, not only from the trial proceedings but from Thailand—soon afterwards he returned to Switzerland with his Queen—only three more of the prosecution's witnesses need detain us. One was Detective Phinich's deputy on the police investigating committee. He admitted that Nai Chit and Butr had been injected with the so-called 'truth' drug and a recording made of what they said under its influence. But both had simply repeated their previous story of complete innocence. The witness nevertheless insisted that Nai Chit was withholding something, and that Butr had 'forgotten' vital details.

In August (1950) the court adjourned to Switzerland to take the evidence of the Princess Mother. Fak Nasongkhla decided against his or Chaleo's barrister daughter making the journey with the judges, prosecuting counsel and police, partly because funds were low enough already but chiefly because of the impossibility of submitting a royal personage to a really penetrating cross-examination. For security reasons the accused were not present either. The hearing took place with the consent of the Swiss Government at the Thai Embassy in Berne. The Princess Mother drove there each day accompanied by the faithful Anek.

There was no public release of her evidence until the court returned to Bangkok and assembled in Room 24 again. Because of a visit to

England by two of the judges this was not until late September. By then public anticipation was thoroughly titillated but in fact the Princess Mother's testimony contained nothing sensational.

With fair lucidity it recited events up to the moment of Nai Chit's cry, 'The King has shot himself.' But then, as if her anguish took hold even after all this time, an incoherence blurred her narrative, though her own explanation was that three motor-car accidents had affected her memory. She could remember, however, that the mosquito net round the bed was closed when she first entered after the shooting. She could remember that nothing in the room was disturbed. Later, she said, she had Ananda's desk searched, for if he had committed suicide he would have left a note. She said that he had played with air guns abroad. She recalled a private audience Pridi had of the King after dinner on 7 June, the night but one before Ananda's death. At that audience Pridi had wanted Prajadhipok's widow to be appointed to the Regency Council, while Ananda wanted his uncle Prince Rangsit. Ananda told her that under the constitution he had the power of appointment. She confirmed the Buddhist tutor's reporting to her Pridi's threat after this audience that he would not support the throne again. She continued:

> There was no trouble between the King and me. He always came into my room to see if I was all right if the electric current failed. He was always cool and calm. The only time he was angry was when I called for a car and the only one available had been taken by Pridi. Chaleo was discharged because he was not suitable for the post. A doctor and some ADCs were also discharged. They were Pridi's men. The King gave Chaleo a cigarette case after he had been told that this was customary for officials who were discharged for no specific offence. A few days before Ananda's death he ordered his attendants to clean his decorations: these were in a cupboard close to the bed, but it could be opened without noise.

This ended the Princess Mother's testimony. Its very meagreness may be found richly significant.

The last witness to appear for the prosecution, keeping himself to the end like a music-hall star at the head of the bill, was chief investigator Detective Phinich, who entered the witness-stand in October 1950. He described how he had risen from the rank of a non-commissioned officer in the police force to major-general by the time he retired in 1947. He came out of retirement because, he declared, he was not satisfied with the Pridi Government's investigations into the King's death. So he had offered his services to the Democrat Party régime installed by FM Pibul after the *coup d'état*, and the case presented by the prosecution these past two years in Room 24 was largely the result of his labours. Under cross-examination he denied having made a fortune dealing with the Japanese during the war. Before he ended his testimony he spoke of the meeting which Prince Subha Svasti (Tahn Chin) had brought about between Pridi and leaders of the Democrat Party in an attempt to restore political unity after the war (see page 85): the Prince had told Kuang that he should co-operate with Pridi 'because while he did not the throne was in danger.' (The remark, if made—Tahn Chin was himself never called by the prosecution to confirm Detective Phinich's evidence—was equally capable of meaning that national disunity necessarily imperilled national stability; in any event, the evidence being hearsay would not have been admitted in most Western courts of law.)

Detective Phinich was the one hundred and twenty-fourth witness. When he left the witness-stand the prosecution closed its case.

In November the defence case opened; and half in dread and half with relief the three accused were able at last to be heard.

VI

FAK NASONGKHLA's tactics throughout had been simply to exonerate
the accused from complicity in the assassination. That is, apart from
challenging the scientific evidence he had not tried nor did he try now
to blame others or to disprove the assassination itself—*could* that be
disproved? and could any loyal subject dare the attempt when disproof
of assassination might imply proof of suicide?

Whether he wished to or not he stood before the court as counsel
not only for the three accused but the two exiles as well, pre-eminently
for Pridi, because Pridi's alleged guilt and the accused's association
with him was the foundation of the prosecution's case. Fak denounced
this from the start, declaring that the allegation of Pridi's animosity
towards the late King was absurd.

Then he called his witnesses. He began with accused number one,
Chaleo. As the former secretary entered the witness-stand the sight
of the empty dock which he had so long occupied, made suddenly and
unambiguously clear that a crucial stage of the proceedings had
arrived.

Chaleo's answer to the prosecution case was a flat contradiction.
He denied that he was more than a mere political follower of Pridi,
denied close association with Nai Chit, denied using him as a spy,
denied knowledge of any conspiracy and denied all knowledge of or
any part in murder.

He denied also that he had been dismissed from the royal service.
There was not, he said, the slightest cause for dismissal. The allegations
of disrespect (page 141) were fabrications: he admitted only that he
drove into the inner courtyard two or three times, but this was
because of injuries he sustained when the jeep overturned during
Ananda's visit to the FTM demonstration. The first he had ever heard
of the King's decision to dismiss him was here in Room 24. He had
left of his own wish, because of his ill-health arising from the jeep

accident. He believed he had resigned while still enjoying the royal favour, which the silver cigarette case betokened.

He emphatically affirmed his loyalty to the throne. He was deeply distressed when he heard of the King's death on 9 June. He heard the news, he said, late in the afternoon and at first refused to believe it. In his capacity of Senator he went to the Assembly that evening and there voted for the accession of Bhoomipol. Earlier, the chief of the Palace Guard told him that the King had committed suicide for reasons which other palace officials repeated to him next day, when all agreed on the King's 'decisiveness' of temperament.

'What,' Fak Nasongkhla asked him, 'were those reasons?'

Chaleo hesitated. 'Can I tell the court in camera? It might be harmful to royal prestige.'

His request was granted and Room 24 presently cleared of the public and press. He told the judges that the palace officials said there had been bitter quarrels between the King and his mother. These, weighing upon Ananda's mind, moved him in his grief to take his own life. But Chaleo himself had never heard any quarrel.

The court then resumed in open session. Continuing his evidence Chaleo said that the day after Ananda's death he began to hear rumours of assassination. These rumours involved himself: he was said to have stolen one of the royal cars and already escaped abroad. Later rumours linked Lt Vacharachai's name with Pridi's, so disgusting him that he dropped out of politics. He believed that the rumours were worked up by the Democrat Party, of which he was an opponent. After he had been arrested he was kept in the heaviest chains and often injured when manacles were hammered on, for which he was given no medical attention. He had been driven to a state of nervous exhaustion by his gaolers who shone a light in his face every ten minutes through the night. But he had never deviated from the particulars he gave the police at the outset. Nor, he added, had Nai Chit or Butr, even after receiving the 'truth' drug which kept them unconscious for twenty-four hours.

With this, Fak Nasongkhla completed Chaleo's evidence-in-chief. It had lasted six days, but there was still the cross-examination to face.

'You have been quite clear,' the Chief Prosecutor said, 'that the post of private secretary to the King was a high honour, a cause of pride and satisfaction. Besides, you were at the same time a director of many companies so that you were financially secure. You must have had a very strong reason for leaving the royal service as you allege?'

'I told the court the reason: my health was getting bad.'

'Yet you immediately accepted Pridi's offer of a seat in the Senate?'

'That wasn't so tiring—not such long hours—and I wanted to follow a political career.'

'You kept your company directorships and you went into the Senate. There's also evidence that you intended putting yourself up for election as a deputy. That doesn't sound like the story of a man in poor health.' He waved aside Chaleo's demur. 'Now then, how do you explain your denial that you were at the Rear-Admiral's house when Tee the timberman, who never knew you before, picked you out at an identification parade?'

'The police dressed me in a distinctive green uniform for the identification parade. That's how Tee picked me out.'

'Let's leave out Tee, then. You deny you were ever at the house, yet both the Rear-Admiral and his maid say you were there.'

'I was not.'

'The colonel you spoke to at ex-Regent Aditya's cremation—he was lying when he said you told him the King wouldn't leave on the 13th?'

'I never heard anyone say that about the King.'

'The colonel was an old friend. He'd been to your house to bless it. Why should he lie? It's bad enough that you should have said the King wouldn't leave on the 13th, but when you deny saying it, that sounds like the denial of a guilty man.'

'I told you, I never heard anyone say the King wouldn't leave on the 13th.'

'Since you keep refusing to give a direct answer, let me turn to something else. Not only was there yourself in a position to influence Nai Chit but there's a family connection between him and Prince Subha Svasti [Tahn Chin] who made a political deal with Pridi. What can you tell us about that deal?'

'I never heard of any deal. I only heard that the Prince tried to bring the political leaders together.'

Much of Chaleo's evidence concerned Pridi. It may be précised thus. 'Though I deny being Pridi's confidant I admit to admiring him. I knew him from boyhood. We went to the same school in Ayudhya. I took part as a civilian in the 1932 Revolution. I respected Pridi for his devotion to his country in risking his life leading the resistance movement against the Japanese. I had no cause to doubt his loyalty. In fact he was conspicuously loyal to the royal family: he had arranged for the liberation of the Political Prisoners including Prince Rangsit, he had King Prajadhipok's property and honours restored after these had been spoliated following his abdication, and he removed the political disabilities of members of the royal family. During the Hua Hin visit Pridi's relations with the King were nothing but cordial. As to Lt Vacharachai, I scarcely knew the man. I declare again my absolute innocence and my absolute abhorrence of regicide.'

But how deep an impression this made on his judges no one could tell from their impassive faces. And then, his plea made, his last solemn oath of loyalty uttered, Chaleo returned to the temporary sanctuary of the dock.

Shortly before Christmas, Nai Chit's turn came.

As tall as Chaleo, but slenderer, with finer features, he spoke in the accents of the palace, while Chaleo's had smacked of the tougher world of business. But now birth, habit, appearance were of no concern. Himself as a person, like Chaleo and Butr as persons, counted nothing: all that mattered were facts—those abstractions plucked from concrete reality; the translation of past action into present description.

In the first place the case against Nai Chit was that his membership of a criminal conspiracy was not only implicit in his association with Chaleo but directly proved by the discussion Tee the timberman overheard. More: he had pointed out the intended victim to See the gunman; and he had told the lady-in-waiting and another page on separate occasions that the King would not leave on the 13th.

Nai Chit's answer to this aspect of the prosecution case was a denial from first to last. He protested his devotion to the King. He had played with Ananda when a boy. All his life he had been in royal service like his father and his grandfather before him. What had he to gain from such a dreadful crime as killing the King?

'You were bought,' the prosecution retorted.

Nai Chit scorned the accusation. As vehemently did he deny helping the assassin arrive and depart unhindered: it was the absolute truth that he saw no one, even though he rushed into the room only moments after the shot rang out. If he gave contradictory versions of where he found the (allegedly false) spent cartridge, the reason was his confusion and shock. And even if it was a full three days later before he led the police to the (allegedly false) bullet in the mattress, he was not aware of any earlier enquiry about it.

But Nai Chit still had much to explain. Neither confusion nor denials sufficed for the prosecution's two bull points—his presence at the palace when he was off duty; and his cry to the Princess Mother, 'The King has shot himself!' when he knew only that the King had been shot, not that he had shot himself.

The accused's explanation of his presence when off duty was lengthy. Shortly before eight o'clock on the morning of the King's death, he said, he went to a firm of jewellers near the Giant Swing (a structure like an enormous narrow pair of red goal-posts used at certain religious festivals in the central area of the city). He was introduced to them by a senior palace official who went with him. The object was to have a travelling box made, on the Princess Mother's instructions, for all the decorations belonging to the royal family. He took with him as a specimen a box of Bhoomipol's, of a smaller size than the one required. The senior official left the jewellers' before he himself departed for the Barompiman Hall to check the exact measurements of the decorations which were kept in a cupboard in the royal dressing-room. Encountering Butr outside the dressing-room at about nine o'clock, he heard that the King had been to the bathroom but returned to bed. He therefore decided to wait rather than risk disturbing him. That was why he sat down with Butr.

Now the fact that a man should work at his job when he is off duty will seem insignificant only to the Westerner unfamiliar with the Thai's extreme indifference to the virtue of industry: he works no more than he must. Nai Chit's own explanation of his extraordinary behaviour was that he had to go to the jewellers' that morning because the palace official had made the appointment to accompany him, and anyway time was short in view of the family's imminent departure. The prosecution questioned his reason for wanting measurements when Bhoomipol's box already had indentations of the correct size. And his reason for waiting with Butr was likewise questionable considering that he was accustomed to moving quietly in the royal quarters and could have reached the decorations without disturbing the King.

The critical point, however, in the prosecution's grilling cross-examination was Nai Chit's cry to the Princess Mother. For, in describing the tragic morning's events he had made the damning admission that *he never saw the pistol*. How then could he explain crying out that the King had shot himself?

He repeated what he had said so many times. When he heard the shot, a moment or two passed before he was certain the sound came from the King's bedroom. He went into the dressing-room from which he saw, through the open doorway, the King in bed within the closed mosquito net and apparently asleep. Puzzled, he tiptoed into the bedroom, saw blood on the King's head, shoulder and pillow, and at once ran to the Princess Mother.

'You heard a shot, and you saw the King lying in bed with blood on him. That was all you saw.'

'Yes.'

'Have you ever heard of a king committing suicide?'

'No.'

'Then why should you jump to the conclusion that the King had shot himself when you saw no pistol? Isn't the only explanation that you knew in advance that this was the story you were going to tell?'

'I was very frightened. I'd just heard the shot with my own ears, I knew the King had many weapons including the pistol in his bedside cabinet, and I saw the blood with my own eyes. There was no one else in the room. The thought that anyone would dare commit treason against His Majesty's person never came into my head. I could only think he must have shot himself.'

However plausible this may have sounded it remained to be submitted to the refined and subtle reasoning of the judges. To them Nai Chit, stepping down exhausted from the witness-stand, now entrusted his fate.

Butr took his place early in the New Year of 1951. Such a sad, anxious but somehow eager little face to belie the slowness of the mind behind it!

He spoke first of his birth in the Grand Palace, where his mother had been a maidservant in the Inside. He described his attendance on

Ananda as a small boy, and how during the royal visit of 1938 he went on fishing expeditions and motor-car drives with him. He had been selected to accompany Ananda back to Switzerland, and the Princess Mother had kindly given him money to equip himself for the trip. During the period of Ananda's visit of 1938 and when he came back to Bangkok for the last time he, Butr, grew to love him. As he said this he broke down in the witness-stand and wept.

Fak Nasongkhla asked him about his experiences in gaol. He had been beaten, kicked, chained and drugged. The police had repeatedly asked him who had gone into the royal bedroom—that is, the identity of the assassin—and each time when he replied no one they beat and kicked him more. Like Nai Chit he described how he was rendered unconscious by drugs. He had no idea what he said under their influence but he was told that everything had been registered on the tape recorder.

However this may have touched the heart of the listener it did not of course go to the heart of the matter—the immediate events surrounding the shooting. He related the events I have described on pages 92–4, in particular that he came on duty at 7 a.m., saw Ananda standing silent in the dressing-room at 8.30, and then when he tried to take in the orange juice, he was waved away. When the shot rang out, Butr now told the court, he was too dumbfounded to move and he watched Nai Chit put his head into the dressing-room—note that Nai Chit said he stepped right into the room—before going into the bedroom. Butr next saw Nai Chit rushing out and he asked him, 'What's happened?' Receiving no reply he followed Nai Chit after an interval, failed to catch up with him, and on returning towards the dressing-room along the back corridor he encountered Bhoomipol who sent him for a doctor.

The prosecution's case against Butr hung almost entirely on its case against Nai Chit. The two pages were sitting together and therefore if Nai Chit was guilty, so must Butr have been. Moreover, there was some evidence that the other door from Ananda's quarters, the one from his study to the front corridor, was afterwards found unlocked, and as Butr should have locked it when on duty the previous night he could deliberately have left it to give the assassin access.

Butr's defence was a complete denial of any treasonable act, thought, or knowledge. And he came up with two very curious statements.

The day before he died Ananda burnt about half a dozen sheets of paper in his bathroom: Butr understood that these were personal letters and that their destruction was part of the general preparations for the King's departure. Then on the morning he died, while the doctor was washing the body and Butr was in attendance, Butr heard a noise in the adjoining study where the grief-stricken Princess Mother sat on a sofa. She was stamping her feet and holding some sheets of paper while Bhoomipol paced the room; and Butr heard her exclaim, 'Whatever you want to do, do it.'

He had not told this to the Commission of Inquiry. Asked why not, he replied that the burning of the letters and the King's odd behaviour in seeming to avoid him by giving no greeting when he saw him in the dressing-room and then waving away the orange juice, had suggested suicide, which he wished to keep quiet about in order not to harm royal prestige or Ananda's memory. But was not the true explanation, the prosecution asked, that this additional evidence was a later fabrication to support the notion of suicide? Was not Butr's very silence on these matters proof of his complicity? Finally, there was the admission Butr made that having taken 'the holy bath for good fortune' shortly before the King's death, he took another holy bath to wash away misfortune after his evidence before the Commission of Inquiry. Was this not an attempt to expiate his guilt?

At the conclusion of Butr's evidence the defence proceeded to call some thirty-three men and women.

Most could give only negative evidence—about what they had not seen, not heard, did not know—like Pridi's wife, who for all the intensity of public attention which followed her into the witness-stand, could testify only to her ignorance of anything in her husband's deeds or words except unalloyed devotion to the monarchy. And if she had a vested interest in clearing his name there were many others who hazarded their careers, their social position and their safety by speaking up for his staunchness of character, his help to the royal family, his labours night and day for the welfare of his country. He was not perfect: one witness conceded that under stress he sometimes lost his temper. The Director of the Privy Purse, closely associated with him in his dealings with the Palace, declared he had never heard Pridi complain of Ananda interfering or proposing to interfere in politics. Another witness, who had been a pro-Pridi deputy, conveyed something of the immediate and sudden anti-Pridi feeling generated in political circles from the very day of Ananda's death, for on going to the Assembly that day the witness had his throat seized by a Democrat Party deputy.

While Pridi, though absent, never ceased to dominate the trial and the three accused were plainly there for all to see, the other leading player was but a figure lost in the mists of exile—the alleged assassin, the actual executant of the brutal crime. The public knew scarcely anything of Lt Vacharachai other than his later career as ADC and secretary. The group of witnesses who testified (page 136) to his being near the scene at the time of the tragedy had only briefly summoned him into existence, and that for the most part as someone seen at a distance. But in March a delicate-featured young woman called Cha-oom communicated to the intent spectators in Room 24 her own undimmed consciousness of his being, presenting him to them as her husband and the father of her three children.

In gentle accents—she was intelligent and educated—she explained that her husband had wished to leave the post of royal ADC. He had therefore played sick in the hope that the regulations which automatically brought dismissal after an absence of more than three months would gracefully release him from a job in which his pay was too low. Between eight and eight-thirty on the morning of the shooting he had been with her at their home in the suburb of Bangkapi, waiting on the doctor who was to call because she had been threatened with a miscarriage in the night. At nearly nine her husband's car came for him and he had then gone to her parents to report on her condition. Afterwards, at about 10 a.m., he went shopping before returning home, which he did at 11 a.m. He arrived in great distress because he had heard of the King's death, and she herself wept.

The prosecution made clear that it was not impressed. It was quick to seize on the fact that her parents' home was conveniently close to the Grand Palace. Also that her account of his movements, in any event disputed by his driver who said he took him to a point outside the palace wall at 9 a.m., had only the surface corroboration of her own family. In any event he could have entered and left the Barompiman Hall before calling on his in-laws. And how was the blood on his sleeve to be explained?

The defence called the former Police Chief who led the investigations immediately after the shooting. He firmly adhered to the opinion he had expressed then, that he ruled out assassination; and he rejected any suggestion that he was trying to cover-up for or had been hood-winked by Pridi who he admitted had appointed him to his post. One of the team of officers that he had brought in with him also gave evidence: he was present when Nai Chit produced the ·45, and to him it seemed there was still smoke in the barrel. But under cross-examination he admitted that he did not handle the weapon and so could not refute the other police officer who had declared that the ·45 looked and smelt as if it had not been fired for some time.

Two other defence witnesses may briefly be noted. One was the wife of the Rear-Admiral at whose house Pridi, Lt Vacharachai, Chaleo and Nai Chit were alleged to have been overheard: she disputed Tee the timberman's account of where he was when he overheard them, since this was in her mother's quarters where no men were ever permitted; she also added to the evidence concerning Tee's doubtful character. Then there was the ex-FTM member who See the gunman said had tried to hire him: he hotly denied any such transaction with the man.

On 9 May 1951 the defence closed its case. In all, the court had listened to one hundred and sixty-one witnesses in the space of two and a half years.

The following month both sides summed up. The prosecution asked for a verdict of guilty not only against the three accused but Pridi and Lt Vacharachai; and for the sentence of death. The defence asked for a complete acquittal, and here Fak Nasongkhla sprang a surprise. He suddenly entered a plea of *nolle prosequi*—a technical device for putting an end to the proceedings altogether. The prosecution protested with some justice that such a move should have been made at the beginning of the trial, not the end. The judges nevertheless allowed Fak to develop his argument. It turned on interpretations of Thai law, and amounted to this, that the Government was illegal because it had illegally overthrown the Pridi–Dhamrong Government by the November 1947 *coup d'état*, wherefore all actions flowing from this illegal government were illegal—the appointment of Detective Phinich and his investigating police committee, the investigations themselves (which, moreover, were often illegally attended by politicians as well as the police), the detention of the accused, and the initiation of proceedings. All these were unlawful and therefore the trial should be stopped immediately and the accused released.

Upon this legal argument the court reserved judgement, as it did on the merits of the case. For almost four months the judges were night and day to analyse and ponder upon the huge conglomerate of facts, opinions, deductions, surmises which had made Room 24 into a strange private world resurrected from the ashes of Ananda. How remote it seemed from the world outside, which cared nothing for the fate of a royal ex-secretary and two wretched pages in a far off oriental kingdom!

By chance the world outside was in fact at this time acquiring a fuller knowledge of Siam than its identity with a breed of cats and conjointed twins. But the Siam of a century ago. Since April a musical comedy called *The King and I* had been captivating Broadway, and presently its celluloid image would do likewise to cinema audiences everywhere. Not the dark mystery of Ananda's death, then, but the quainteries of Mongkut's never-never land beguiled a US still restive over Truman's dismissal of MacArthur, and stockpiling atomic bombs whose secret the Russians had not yet plumbed; an England disturbed by the weeping Mussadegh's grab of her Persian oil, the disappearance of Burgess and Maclean, the lung operation on George VI; and a world watching Tito hurl defiance at an ageing Stalin in Europe while the Korean War raged in Asia.

In Bangkok itself a new political drama suddenly jerked attention from the approaching climax of the regicide trial.

One of Pridi's favourite projects was ironically now coming to fruition under FM Pibul, the dredging of the mouth of the Menam to enable larger vessels to reach the capital from the sea. The US gave Thailand a dredger, the *Manhattan*, at a ceremony at the royal jetty near the Grand Palace on 29 June (1951). Diplomats, political leaders, service chiefs and other notables were present with their wives. Just as FM Pibul was graciously about to accept the presentation by the American Ambassador, he found himself at the wrong end of a pistol. It was held by a young naval officer who took him by the arm and politely hustled him to a waiting launch. A party of marines meanwhile covered the distinguished assembly, many of whom threw themselves flat so that not a few striped trousers and Parisian gowns came close to humiliating ruin. The incident was over too quickly for counter-action. The Field-Marshal was whisked to the battleship *Sri Ayudhya* moored in mid-stream and there locked in a cabin. The navy had been biding its time ever since Pridi's abortive *coup* of February 1949, and now with FM Pibul as a hostage they hoped they could bloodlessly effect a change of régime. But again they neglected the classic *coup* formula of arresting all effective leaders and controlling communications. Police-General Pao's para-military police, the army and the air force were quickly alerted. They closed the Chakri memorial bridge downstream of the *Sri Ayudhya*, barring it from the naval bases, the rest of the fleet and the sea. While heavy firing broke out along the riverbank and elsewhere in the city, the air force signalled that it would bomb the battleship regardless of FM Pibul's presence unless he was safely delivered up. Next day, to everyone's entire astonishment, this threat was acted on. A series of direct hits sank the pinioned battleship. But before the bombs fell, FM Pibul was unlocked and invited to swim for it, which he did, and so survived kidnapping as he had the three attempts to shoot or poison him.

A royal historian comments that 'it looked as if he was desired by Providence to be the leader of our country at this period of our history,' but a less ambiguous saying about those whom the devil looks after may be more apposite. By evening FM Pibul was back in full command and the thirty-six hour revolt fizzled out. It had been remarkably bitter: civilian casualties were 603, of whom 103 were fatal; and the armed forces' casualties have never been revealed.

Rumour had it that Pridi again took part but reliable evidence is lacking. As an extensive purge of the navy went on and Pao's police strengthened their grip on the country, any immediate hope of FM Pibul's overthrow was dashed. But if the judges in the regicide trial exonerated Pridi, his cause would remain alive—heartening his supporters, convincing the waiverers, discrediting his enemies; and so might the shifting tides of the future bring him home in triumph. But if he were found guilty, then the condemnation of murdering a helpless young man in his charge would be ineradicable. Perhaps as he waited in far-off China for news of the judgement, he envied Chaleo and Nai Chit and Butr, that if they were found guilty their end would be swift and not the lingering death of impotent exile.

On Thursday, 27 September 1951 the court met to deliver judgement.

VII

FROM an early hour the roads leading to Room 24 were blocked by traffic: motor-cars, trishaws, bicycles, trams, buses, and a vast amount of humanity afoot. Inside and outside the court over fifty police stood guard. The room could take only a fraction of the crowd, who overflowed in every direction and listened to the loudspeaker relay. Despite the heat and the crush they stood listening for five continuous hours.

Within the court everyone stood too, from 9 a.m. when the judges started reading the judgement in turn, until they ended at 2 p.m. The three accused stood with their counsel, Chaleo almost shoulder to shoulder with his daughter, and they dared not hope as the tide of words rolled inexorably on. 'Judgement: in the name of His Majesty the King, Court of Criminal Causes, 27 September Buddhist Era 2492. . . .'

The text ran to fifty thousand words. The charges arose, it began, from 'the death of His late Majesty King Ananda Mahidol, the 8th of Thai monarchs in the Royal House of Chakri, who died of a bullet wound amidst the greatest shock and lamentation.' The court was 'faced with a case so unparalleled in its significance, and so complicated in its facts and circumstances, as to demand the utmost care in adjudication; and so historic as to make it as memorable in the annals of Thailand as the circumstances which brought it about.'

The charges were then read out in the full ponderous verbiage to which indictments are everywhere prone. The defence was summarized as a complete denial, coupled with the assertion that the charges were a political device to discredit Pridi, Lt Vacharachai and Chaleo, while Nai Chit and Butr 'being no politicians were likewise caught in the mesh of this political plot.'

The court began its review of the evidence by outlining Ananda's life, his return to Bangkok where 'the royal qualities which endeared the King to popular affection were his democratic spirit, calm dignity and grace', his illness, the hearing of the shot, and the broad sequence of events up to the final investigations led by Detective Phinich.

The political events were also traversed, in order for the court to make its first finding. This was on the defence's *nolle prosequi* plea for an end to the proceedings on the grounds that FM Pibul's government was illegal. The court rejected the plea. 'It is a principle of law that no country can be left without a government at any time. If after a successful *coup d'état* all administrations were to be held unlawful, when would a country ever be lawfully governed?'

That point disposed of, the court defined the issues of fact that had to be decided: whether death was due to assassination or suicide; and if the former, whether the accused were implicated. Although the prosecution had sought to put Pridi and Lt Vacharachai at the centre of conspiracy, the court ruled at the outset that since they were not being prosecuted and had not been able to defend themselves, it would only consider such evidence relating to them as was essential for decision on the facts at issue.

The justice of this ruling is indisputable even if it meant that the court baulked at coming to grips with the crucial question of Pridi's alleged guilt. But the findings would still be very relevant to that question. If suicide were found, or assassination in no way connected with him, he would clearly be innocent; while findings to the contrary would leave his name entirely uncleared.

First, then, was the question of how Ananda came to die. Having concluded that with inside knowledge and help anyone could easily have entered Ananda's quarters without much risk, the court reasoned that thus far the possibilities of suicide and of assassination were equal. Did the scientific evidence provide a conclusive answer?

The nitrite tests which purported to establish that the ·45 had been fired at least five days before Ananda's death were carefully summarized. The court acknowledged that these were open to criticism. But if for this reason, besides the very novelty of the experiment, it would not accept the scientists' conclusions as decisive, it considered them weighty enough to be reserved for further consideration.

As to the amount of rust found in the barrel of the ·45, the court accepted that it was abnormal. While some doubt arose because the

THE DEVIL'S DISCUS

pistol had not been used for months, and because of the possibilities of slipshod cleaning and/or moisture causing undue rust, the matter should not be dismissed but likewise reserved for further consideration.

This brought the court to the complications of the spent cartridge which Nai Chit said he picked up near the King's bed, and the bullet embedded in the mattress. The defence did not dispute the prosecution's contention that both belonged to the same round which had at some time been fired by the ·45. The question was whether these objects were a 'plant'. There had been ample opportunity, and the court was dissatisfied with the evidence of the police officer who had said that bullets were sometimes found undented after travelling through a human head. It preferred the doctor's evidence derived from conditions approximating those of Ananda's death. 'However much the human skull may vary,' intoned the judgement, 'the difference cannot be such as to make the result the same as firing at a piece of paper.' Therefore the bullet in the mattress, and hence the spent cartridge, did not belong to the round fired at the King. The significance of this too was reserved for further consideration.

The court found as a fact that Ananda had died instantaneously, even though his heart would have continued beating for half a minute or more. How, then, did he get into his final position, the composed attitude of sleep with his arms stretched down by his sides? The cadaveric spasm evidence was that at the moment of death he must have been in this position, since if he were moving any muscle it would have been made rigid by the spasm. But there would have been no spasm anyway if the basal ganglia had been destroyed, and on this point the court had doubts. The glass tube which a prosecution witness pushed through a brain to simulate the passage of the fatal bullet had missed the ganglia, but it had passed very close—and no one could be sure that the demonstration simulated the *exact* path of the bullet; besides, the tube was six millimetres in diameter while a ·45 bullet is equivalent to eleven millimetres.

However, even if the cadaveric spasm theory were of doubtful application, the judges had to have regard to common-sense which, confirmed by the medical, ballistics and police evidence, would lead one to expect that if a person shot himself while lying down he would be found with his arm(s) somewhere near his chest and the pistol somewhere near his neck.

182

All these considerations were then collectively weighed by the court. The nitrite tests, the collection of rust, and the undented state of the bullet allegedly found on the scene, were not separately conclusive in proving that Ananda was killed by another pistol, another bullet, but put together they became so. Any doubts—which the judges said they dwelt upon unduly anyway because of the care required in assessing circumstantial evidence—then fell away. 'To go by analogy,' they said, 'if three small threads each incapable of bearing the weight of a brick are entwined so as to form a bigger thread capable of bearing the weight of the same brick, can it be argued that the threads cannot bear the said weight?' And if this were not enough to negative suicide, there was the cadaveric spasm evidence which had at least a corroborative value. And if still not enough, the court professed itself entirely convinced by the position in which Ananda's body and his pistol were found. '*The court accordingly rules that the death of His late Majesty King Ananda Mahidol was brought about by assassination.*'

But was this likely against a king 'so gifted with graces and the highest of merits' and who had never harmed the prosperity or happiness of anyone? Undoubtedly the court was thinking of Pridi. It answered its own question in the affirmative because 'someone' could have formed the mistaken notion that the King had harmed him or might harm him, or stood in his way: 'this is a state of mind which neither the prospective victim nor anybody else can fathom.'

Though the finding of assassination completely rebutted any idea of suicide, the judges proposed dealing with that idea once and for all. Ananda, they said, was not only King: he had youth, health, wealth, loyal followers; 'there was no wish that could not be fulfilled.' If he had any cause for 'extreme displeasure' in Thailand he would have been leaving it behind in a few days when he went abroad where, the court hinted delicately, he was more at home than in Thailand. Even if something upset him which could not be left behind, he could always have abdicated later or even committed suicide later: gifted with great wisdom and judgement, usually in good health, of a deliberate nature, a devout Buddhist, he would scarcely have made so unwise and irrevocable a choice as immediate suicide. Nor was the suggestion of a violent family quarrel convincing when everything appeared happy and normal up to the day of his death, and in any event the Princess Mother and Bhoomipol denied any quarrel. The Princess Mother's loving care and affection throughout the twenty years of her widowhood, and the family's long residence abroad alone among themselves, made any violent misunderstanding out of the question, especially since the Princess Mother told the court that Ananda 'had never, on any occasion, displayed a violent temper, and if he were displeased he would quietly seek understanding rather than give way to anger.' Ananda had made three appointments for the day of his death and was perfectly normal the night before; in the morning he took his castor oil at six o'clock and waited for it to take effect: none of this bore the slightest indication of a suicidal intention.

The judges took the opportunity also to dispose of the possibility of accident. In view of the position of Ananda's body, and nature of the wound, and the safety mechanism of the pistol, it was so remote as to be ruled out entirely.

Every path therefore led them to the conclusion of assassination. As this became clear, the atmosphere within and outside the court perceptibly tautened. There could now be no automatic dismissal of the case. The question of the accused's complicity rose stark, fearsome, inescapable before the judges; and they had to answer it. As if themselves unaware of the heightened emotion around them, they lingered over a side issue, the defence allegation of a political frame-up. But having disposed of that with a forthright finding that public agitation had been spontaneous and genuine and not artificially ignited by Pridi's opponents, they put each of the accused under scrutiny.

They had already been steadily reading for over three hours. The strain on the accused and their waiting families was intense, unrelieved by the slightest hint of which way the verdicts would go.

The first gleam of hope came when the judges weighed Tee the timberman's evidence of the conspiracy he alleged overhearing at the Rear-Admiral's house. They accepted the defence description of him as a 'gas-bag', a boaster and a liar: his story, which had implicated Chaleo and Nai Chit [also Pridi and Lt Vacharachai] could not be credited. But this did not entirely let Chaleo out, since the Rear-Admiral and the maidservant agreed that he had certainly been at the house. Did his denial of this fact betray guilt? The court held not: it was 'only a matter of conducting a criminal defence, quite usual in all criminal proceedings.'

184

Concentrating on Chaleo first in deference to his status as Accused No. 1, the court then summed-up the other evidence against him. In a nutshell, it found his close association with Pridi proved, likewise his statement to a friend that the King would not leave on the 13th, and it refused to believe that he had voluntarily resigned from the royal service. These were ominous findings. But then—wild hope for the ex-Secretary—the court went on to hold that without proof of conspiracy between him and Pridi the fact of close association was not enough. And the possibility that treasonable knowledge inspired his remark to his friend was no greater than the possibility that having a grudge because of his dismissal he merely 'said something meaningless though unholy to fit in with Western superstition', or that he was showing off or something of the kind. As to his dismissal, the court was not persuaded that this was likely to have turned him into a traitor, especially since the salary and prestige he lost were mostly regained by his appointment to the Senate.

What melodious, enchanting, almost incredible words these were to Chaleo, and his daughter standing next to him. With what emotion they heard them can scarcely be imagined. If they dared not leap to the logical conclusion, it was immediately uttered in words that seemed fantastically few after so many words, so many years, and so much anguish: 'The case against Nai Chaleo Patoomros must therefore be dismissed.'

Leaving Chaleo to stand half stunned by a vision of life reborn, the judges at once went on to the case against the two pages. They accepted that neither was the assassin; but if either or both had been party to the crime the penalty of guilt would be no lighter.

There was some immediate encouragement in the court's rejection of the story which the missing gunman See had told witnesses, about his being hired to kill a personage whom the two pages had allegedly pointed out. Nevertheless, that personage had been killed and some-one had done the killing, and the pages' proximity to this event placed them, the court said bluntly, in a precarious position. To begin with, they were sitting in the back corridor outside the dressing-room, and the court deduced that the assassin entered this way while the King slept or was in the bathroom. But possibly Butr had not yet come on duty or was busy about his tasks. The assassin could then have stayed concealed in the study or the Buddha-room before emerging to shoot the King—from behind, by leaning over the bed-head—and escaping down the front corridor via the study. Again the accused might not have seen him, and there was no convincing evidence that Butr had left the study door unlocked the previous night.

However, if this reconstruction of the crime thus far did not necessarily incriminate them, there was still the suicide-faking to be considered. The faking would have been simplest for the assassin had he used the King's ·45, but then in order to avoid fingerprints he would have had to wear a glove, which 'does not facilitate a true aim', and obtaining the ·45 in advance would have risked arousing suspicion if it were missed, so the assassin used his own weapon. This might have been a revolver, which does not eject the spent cartridges, or a pistol whose own spent cartridge was removed from the scene of the crime: in either event a spent cartridge ejected from the King's ·45 at a previous firing had to be 'planted'; likewise the bullet. To complete the fake the King's ·45 had to be placed near his hand either by an accomplice or by the assassin to whom the accomplice would have given the pistol or told where it was kept. Now both pages had an exact knowledge of the King's routine and where the pistol was kept; they were ideally placed as potential accomplices.

Of the two, the court addressed itself first to Nai Chit. His contra-dictory explanations of where he picked up the spent cartridge brought him glaringly under suspicion, especially since it was proved not to have been fired by the assassin's pistol but on some previous occasion by the King's ·45. The judges concluded that he must deliberately have been trying to create a false impression by producing the cartridge in the drawer. From this it followed that he had done the same with the bullet, to which he himself guided the police, in the mattress he himself had charge of. There were two other points they found significant: by entering the room first, he was conveniently placed to 'plant' the King's ·45 on the bed if the assassin had not already done so; and since he himself brought the pistol downstairs, he could easily have put it in the cocked (ready for firing) position in which it was then seen to be.

Nor was this all. The judges were unconvinced by his explanation of why he was outside the royal dressing-room: Bhoomipol's decora-tions box sufficed as a pattern, but even if he wanted exact dimensions he could have got them without disturbing the King. Then they

THE TRIAL

analysed his explanation of why he cried, 'The King has shot himself!' to the Princess Mother when he had not seen the pistol. If, as he explained, he said it because he could not imagine that anyone would kill the King, why should his imagination have embraced suicide when he knew of no convincing reason for it—had never indeed heard of a king killing himself—and saw no suicide weapon? The conclusion must be that there was treasonable knowledge behind his cry to the Princess Mother. Coupled with this was his remark repeated to two people about the King not leaving on the 13th: it was far more damaging than Chaleo's similar remark, which was less affirmative and less surrounded by suspicious circumstances.

But had Nai Chit any motive? The judges quoted a Thai proverb: *Unlike the deepest sea or the highest mountain the human mind remains immeasurable.* The accused's service in the Palace since King Prajadhipok's reign should have given him a 'natural gratitude and loyalty' far outweighing 'any dark and seditious motive', yet the offer of some overwhelming benefit could have made him forget himself. Though there was no evidence of an improvement in his material position since the crime, wealth could be concealed; or his 'unsurpassing reward' might have depended on the successful outcome of the conspiracy. Another possibility was that Butr's selection to accompany Ananda abroad roused his jealous anger: he was 'so blinded to reason and loyalty as to mistake the devil's lethal discus for the Buddha's lotus.' In any event, once guilt was established motive became of secondary importance.

What remained to be said of Nai Chit scarcely needed words. Neither pity nor hatred, nor any of the feelings by which men know they are alive were in the curt judicial pronouncement: 'The court therefore finds a conviction beyond doubt against Nai Chit Singhaseni, the 2nd Accused.'

But not against little Butr. Given that the conspiracy would have been restricted to as few people as possible and that the assassin could have entered without Butr's knowledge, and given that it was customary to take holy baths for good fortune or 'to set at rest some ennui', the evidence against him was insufficient. He was keen on going abroad with the royal family and not only did this deprive him of motive, but the conspirators would hardly have risked his giving them away when he was in a 'state of blissful gratitude'. The court

187

THE DEVIL'S DISCUS

observed that Butr was less bright than Nai Chit: 'in fact, Butr appeared to be rather dull'. Hence his slower reaction to the shot. Hence also Nai Chit's presence outside the dressing-room with him, for by timing the assassination so that Nai Chit was not alone on duty, the conspirators had hoped 'to reduce the weight of evidence against Nai Chit by the presence as well as the dull innocence of Butr, thus creating the confounding confusion required to be unravelled in this case.'

But now the unravelling was done. And at least there was no confounding confusion about sentencing the one accused found guilty: the Penal Code allowed no choice. 'The death sentence is hereby passed by this court on Nai Chit, the 2nd Accused, that he be done to death by authority of law.'

He was taken away, dazed by his fate like his erstwhile fellow prisoners were by theirs as they emerged into the sunlight sucking in the freedom with which the judges' last words had imbued the very air: 'The charges against Chaleo and Butr are dismissed and the two accused hereby ordered to be released.'

Five years, the court had said earlier in its monumental judgement, five years of investigation and trial, and evidence in 'unprecedented detail', had brought this moment of, as it seemed, finality. But it was not final.

It was not final by another three years and five months.

Nai Chit appealed against his conviction and the prosecution appealed against the acquittal of the others. The evidence given in the trial was again winnowed and threshed. Long written argument by either side preceded oral argument before the Appeal Court. The scene of the shooting was again visited; the legality of the proceedings again questioned. Not until six months after the lower court's verdicts was the Appeal Court even in a position to consider its judgement, and this was not expected for another three months. But it was not to be handed down for a whole *fifteen* months, which is to say not until December 1953.

The prolongation of the accused's agony was not the least offence of the FM Pibul régime. The regicide trial served as a Nero's circus for a nation in the grip of the creeping, ruthless and largely secret control exercised by FM Pibul through his henchman Police-General Pao. But prior to the first court's judgement in September 1951 even the docility of the Assembly was changing to restive protest. So in a bloodless *coup* Pibul reorganized the Assembly and reshuffled his government. This was in November 1951, timed to receive the formal approval of King Bhoomipol himself who the following month finally returned to Bangkok.

He returned with his beautiful Queen; but not, publicly at least, with his smile. His mask-like expression seemed unchanged by marriage, the birth of the first of his four children, or all the years since Ananda's death. A little ironically he had composed a jazz tune called *Smiles*, for besides photography his passions were composing or playing jazz on the saxophone, trumpet or clarinet. His preference for jazz, royalists explained to me, was due to a commendably royal dislike of the discipline of classical music. He shared his enthusiasm with his people by arranging for his collection of jazz records and his own recordings to be publicly broadcast daily for the hour before noon from the 150-watt transmitter in his palace. On Friday evenings transmissions were 'live' broadcasts by his own ensemble of friends, a notable member being Mom Seni Pramoj, Kuang's deputy leader of the Democrat Party. These 'jam-sessions' often went on until four or five in the morning. The Queen once good-humouredly greeted the ensemble with the words, 'I envy you. You're the King's concubines. He only smiles on Fridays, even for hours before you're due to meet.' The Siamese like a dash of eccentricity in their monarch. And when he had Bhoomipol's well-equipped, intelligent mind, so much the better. Better still that he was a man of feeling and compassion.

All these qualities of mind and heart were, however, of little consequence to events outside his control which the tragedy of his brother's death continued to enshroud.

The judicial process, inordinately long, came at last to the point of judgement by the Appeal Court. The event had a ghastly repetitive quality. Again the scene was in Room 24; again the great crowds, the police, the loud-speaker relay. Again five judges sat on the bench reading in turn.

They started at 9 a.m., and with a two-hour break at noon and another in the late afternoon they read until 1.55 a.m. next day, a total reading time of fourteen hours. One judge, tending to favour the accident theory, dissented from his four colleagues who agreed with the findings of the court below—except that they found Butr guilty along with Nai Chit. They reasoned that once assassination and Nai Chit's complicity were proved, it followed inescapably that since Butr was present with him he must have been privy to the plot: without such privity the plotters could not have hoped to succeed. So Chaleo returned to freedom and Butr to gaol, this time to await with Nai Chit the summons of the executioner.

A final appeal, however, lay to the Dikka, the highest court in the kingdom. Defence and prosecution both lodged appeals. After argument the court adjourned to consider its verdict. Nothing was heard for ten months after the conclusion of the previous appeal. Then, on the morning of 13 October 1954, a brief statement over Radio Bangkok gave out that judgement would be delivered that day. This last-minute announcement was calculated to prevent too great a crowd, and only about three hundred people went to Room 24.

Two judges in turn read the judgement on behalf of the Dikka, starting at 1.05 p.m. Butr seemed vaguely staring at the ceiling but Nai Chit was following intently as they heard the verdicts against them confirmed. The judges turned to Chaleo. All the while, he held locked in his gaze his wife and the daughter who had helped defend him. He had been taken into custody two days before, which was sign enough of what was to happen, but when he heard himself found guilty too he slumped into his chair. It is unlikely that a judicial tribunal had ever in history sentenced a man to death for sitting with his legs crossed, but in essence this was the fate of Chaleo, for the judges accepted the prosecution evidence of his conduct in the royal service, and they deemed it so disrespectful as to have betrayed a treasonable attitude towards the throne. Proof of this, they said, was clinched by his statement about the King's intended departure on the 13th.

The Dikka judgement had at least the merit of brevity. The court rose within less than an hour, having sentenced all three of the accused to death.

It seems in retrospect to have been a grisly variation on the nursery-room fate of the little nigger boys. First there were three; then two; then none.

Though not quite yet. Four months of anguished life remained to them while the Government considered, and rejected, their plea for mercy.

The doomed men awaited their final hour at the main Bangkok penitentiary, the Bang-Kwang Central Prison, about twelve miles north of the city. Five thousand prisoners occupy this model institution which has playing fields and a recreation hall and neatly laid-out paths and gardens between low buildings. The latter contain machine-shops as well as cells; and there are also vegetable plots and sties where the best pigs in Thailand are bred. Gazing down from the high watch tower in the centre, I was impressed by the well-ordered and humane atmosphere of the place, though from the information given me along with a cool drink by the thoughtful Head Warden was excluded the fact that the penal reform represented by Bang-Kwang was largely the pre-war work of Pridi. From this tower a small open space may be seen far off in a further corner, immediately before the high boundary walls give way to the characteristic pagodas and contours of a monastery. Here in the first instance are taken the remains of an executed man, and the gate to it is said to be dominated by a headless image of the Buddha. Except inside a temple an imperfection in the Buddha's image is an ill omen; and this image is not only truncated but painted red as a dreadful warning to the doer of evil.

At 5 p.m. on 16 February 1955, all prisoners were ordered back to their cells an hour earlier than usual because, they were told, there was to be a meeting of officials. In the middle of the night Chaleo, Nai Chit and Butr were taken to a small building by the place of execution. They were heavily chained. The ex-Secretary and Butr, realizing what was about to happen, felt too weak to walk and had to be supported. In a short religious ceremony the priest delivered a sermon. His subject was Karma, the Buddhist belief in a divine law of retribution: if the condemned men were as innocent as they protested, there was some previous wrong, perhaps in a previous life, for which they now had to pay. During the sermon Chaleo recovered his composure. Butr could not. He was obsessed by the fact that he was unable to cremate his mother. Nai Chit, calm throughout, comforted him: 'Make a good heart,' he said in the idiom of their language. As the priest was leaving in the still but warm hours of darkness Police-General Pao arrived. He had dressed himself for the occasion in a white lounge suit and a red beret. Red became him. It was the colour traditionally worn by the executioner, though discontinued in recent years.

The executioner himself was now present too, ready to set to work for which his payment would be twenty-seven shillings per person despatched. Tradition required him to make obeisance before his intended victims and beg their forgiveness. He was denied the opportunity on this occasion; but he nevertheless did so, he afterwards related, in his heart.

The clock showed a few minutes past 4 a.m. Chaleo was brought out. The pale electric lights showed before him a wooden cross set in the ground in front of a mound of earth. He was blindfolded. Facing the cross, pressed against it, he had his ankles tied to the foot of the upright and his wrists bound together behind the junction of the cross-bar. Into his hands were placed joss sticks and flowers, as if he prayed; which, if terror allowed, no doubt he did. In a wooden frame close behind him hung a dark blue curtain concealing him from the executioner who was summoned at the appropriate moment to a machine-gun mounted on a tripod. The curtain had a target marked on it in white, the bull's eye giving an exact guide to the position of Chaleo's heart. At four-twenty the governor of the prison signalled with a red flag. Five bullets streaked into Chaleo's back. The prison doctor, followed by Police-General Pao, stepped forward to examine him and pronounced him dead. The executioner retired then, to smoke and rest for twenty minutes before killing Nai Chit in the same fashion. But when little Butr's turn came he proved reluctant to die. He still groaned after the first burst of fire, which ripped out his stomach, and the executioner had to fire again.

It was still dark, a little after 5 a.m., seven years and three months since the day the three men were first arrested. At 9 a.m. their families, who had seen them four days before without knowing it would be the last time, were informed of their death and given permission to remove their remains from the monastery to which they had been taken, past the headless red image of the Buddha.

VIII

DETECTIVE PHINICH was proud of his work as head of the police investigating committee. He celebrated his triumph by having an account of the proceedings printed in a book which he distributed among his friends on his wife's birthday. Congratulations poured in from his royalist relatives and friends. None doubted the soundness of verdicts so painstakingly arrived at, so massively researched, so exhaustively argued.

Leaving Police-General Pao to plunder and tyrannize the nation at will, FM Pibul was off on a globe trot. He had cause for satisfaction. Whatever else the trial did, it did not exonerate Pridi. Pibul could therefore face the world with the righteous demeanour of a man vindicated in his resort to stealth and force in overthrowing a murderer. Moreover, Pridi (and Lt Vacharachai), having been denied asylum on British or American soil while the crime of regicide attached to his name made him liable to extradition, had taken refuge in the nearest country that would take him in, which happened to be China. This circumstance, too, eminently suited FM Pibul, busy as he was presenting himself to the West as its own true champion against communism. He played the rôle with increasing success to obtain foreign aid, enabling him to keep an economy afloat which corruption and excessive military expenditure would otherwise have sunk. 'The only way you can beat communism,' he told Los Angeles reporters, 'is by force.' To New York he said, 'The Third World War is inevitable, between communism and the free world.' It was a performance perfectly calculated to please the prevailing mood in the US, and President Eisenhower presented him with the Legion of Merit.

The irony is that the regicide trial, to which FM Pibul pointed as the vindication of his political morality, was in fact the complete vindication of the American and British Ambassadors' unorthodoxy in smuggling Pridi out of the country. In short, Pridi's belief that he

193

would not get his just deserts if he stayed to face the charge of regicide was sound. That, it seems to me, must be the inevitable conclusion of anyone who impartially considers the evidence and judgment given at the trial.

Say so to a Thai royalist, put a logically irrefutable argument to him, and no answer springs more easily to his lips than the bland, 'Ah, but you're a Westerner: you don't understand.' This fallacy of East and West never meeting endangers a world for whose future the twain *must* meet. The truth is that a study of the individual will show, in the words of a leading British psychiatrist

... that fundamentally man is one and indivisible; that whether he lives in a mud hut, an igloo, a prefab or a penthouse, whatever the political yoke under which he thrives or is oppressed, whatever his colour, race or creed, he is moved by essentially the same fundamental instincts and aspirations, hopes and fears, knows the same needs and contains in varying measure the same capacities.[5]

The particular *mores* of a society, historical conditioning, and so on, are relevant to any study of an individual's behaviour, but unless he is mentally sick he does not act contrary to what we broadly term human nature. He does not act in the teeth of reason, which we can understand whatever our race, save when he is overpowered by emotion, which also we can understand. For Pridi to have headed a murder conspiracy he must have had motives as comprehensible to an informed Westerner as to any Thai. Besides, if the regicide trial was conducted according to the juridical procedures of the West, if many of the judges were trained (like Pridi and Ananda themselves) in the West, if the law under which the indictments were framed was codified upon Western models, if much of the condemnatory evidence lay in the Western sciences of ballistics and forensic medicine, and if the final judgements were held up to the West as mirrors of truth and justice as these words are understood in the West, then mystical incantations of oriental impenetrability should not be expected to bemuse the Western inquirer.

Unbemused, let us examine the facts.

In arguing their case before the Appeal Court, the prosecution summarized the causes of Pridi's alleged hostility towards Ananda. According to it there were clashes between them over the desirability of Ananda's visit to the Chinese quarter of Bangkok, and over the selection of Prince Rangsit as a Regent in preference to King Prajadhipok's widow. Then there was Ananda's alleged displeasure with Pridi for having a royal motor-car when the Princess Mother wanted it, and for driving the royal jeep without permission at Hua Hin, where also Pridi held a party—noisy at that—without permission. Finally, there was *Pridi's* alleged displeasure with Ananda for favouring the Democrat Party, whose leaders like Kuang the Great Comedian and the Pramoj brothers privately conferred with him. In this last connection we may add Ananda's alleged secret arrangement to see FM Pibul, which was as strongly indicative of royal lack of confidence in Pridi as the King's rumoured intention of abdicating in order to beat Pridi at his own political game.

To get at the truth in these matters is extremely difficult. Ananda returned from Switzerland a green youth, to find a man controlling Siam who was mature in the affairs of State and the hero of the resistance: this was a man to be admired and learnt from. He was a man, moreover, who however Left he might have been in his Economic Plan of twelve years before, had done nothing but good for members of the royal family. To the ample testimony given on all sides at the trial, I can add that each week during the war when he visited his own family who had been evacuated to Ayudhya, he called on evacuee members of the royal family and did everything he could to ease their situation. This was no man with hate for royalty in his heart when Ananda returned to Bangkok. So harsh a passion as hate has never been associated with him. Instead, here was a compassionate and patient man long called the Mentor, and here was a conscientious and thoughtful youth, a student of law as Pridi was brilliantly a graduate in the same subject, so that every circumstance combined to make their relationship cordial. So, the evidence clearly shows, it was for at least the first few months. Is there any further evidence really to convince one that in the final few months this cordiality turned on Pridi's part into murderous hate?

Of all the hundreds of items of state business transacted between them day after day for six months, only two could be found by Pridi's traducers to have caused, allegedly, any dispute—Ananda's visit to Chinatown and the Regency appointment. The evidence on both is so slight (or, if one thinks of the Buddhist tutor's story, so incredible) and so uncorroborated (the Princess Mother apparently knew nothing of the first matter and Bhoomipol of neither), that apart from the inherent unlikelihood of either issue being seriously contentious, I should not have been surprised in the course of my own investigations to find, as I did, evidence flatly contradicting it. My information is that Pridi himself proposed the royal visit to Chinatown; and that although he first suggested Prajadhipok's widowed Queen as Regent—this as part of the posthumous honours previously denied that King—he readily accepted royalist (not Ananda's) advice and himself sent a delegation to sound Prince Rangsit.

As to the incidents alleged to have displeased Ananda, they are not only made doubly trivial in their context of a continuing relationship, but they prove nothing of Pridi's murderous hostility unless there were any evidence, of which there is none, that he knew of Ananda's alleged displeasure.

Finally, the reasons put forward to explain Pridi's alleged displeasure with Ananda are impossible to accept. The idea that the Democrat Party leaders' visits to the palace, and the story of FM Pibul's intended meeting with Ananda, implied an intrigue of which, to Pridi's knowledge, Ananda was the author, is unsupported and improbable. So is the story, said to have been believed or concocted by Pridi, of an alleged plan by Ananda to abdicate as a ploy to oust him. On none of these allegations did the prosecution offer a tittle of credible evidence about anything either *Ananda* or *Pridi* themselves said or did to confirm its case.

The prosecution, in short, failed to prove a single substantial reason, or even a sufficiency of cumulative minor reasons which conceivably could have turned Pridi's hand against the throne. It failed despite the most thorough hunt for evidence that can be imagined. But even if it had succeeded in proving Pridi's hatred—why, Ananda was going away for nearly three years: would Pridi, who was in full command of the country, have hazarded his life, his lifework, and the welfare of his family upon immediate regicide? No answer makes sense, nor does any search of Pridi's record or character provide a clue. Most crucial point of all: even if the prosecution's allegation of Pridi's murderous intent were for one moment acceptable, where is the evidence that he *acted* upon it, in word or deed?

His opponents have produced an ingenious answer to that

one. They suggest that in the hearing of his faithful henchman Lt Vacharachai he let slip an echo of Henry II's famous outburst that cost Thomas à Becket's life, 'Who will rid me of this turbulent priest?' Whether Pridi intended the consequence or not—runs the argument—the lieutenant promptly did the deed which, rightly or wrongly, he thought would please him.

Now from first to last no other assassin than Lt Vacharachai, acting either in pursuance of a conspiracy or of his own accord, has ever been named; nor, in connection with Pridi, hinted at. Yet extraordinarily little is known about him. It seemed to me essential to learn something of his background and character for what light these might throw on his fitness to fill his alleged role. It was not easy. No one now will readily claim to have known him, his family has faded into the anonymity of Bangkok's back alleys, and peril attends the footsteps of inquirer and witness alike. But with luck and at some hazard to all concerned it was possible for me to compile a reasonably complete dossier.

Lt Vacharachai was about thirty-three when Ananda died, a tall bony-faced man giving an impression rather too Mongolian to be handsome by Western standards. His father had been a chief physician in the navy and his mother a nurse. He was the youngest of four children, all boys, and went to the same leading high school Ananda was briefly to attend after him. At first he neglected his studies in favour of sport, or he would drop everything to frequent billiard saloons with his friends, so he was packed off to board at the Bangkok Christian College, where he matriculated. He was to have read medicine, but instead chose the Naval College. He did this to make up for the family disgrace of an elder brother who had failed there, and to impress the mother of a girl he had fallen in love with. He was usually top of his class at the Naval College, emerging a sub-lieutenant shortly before the war. He gained steady promotion in the navy, which he served in the war with French Indo-China, until he reached the rank of Senior Lieutenant (Flag Officer). Meanwhile he had married the sweetheart of his schooldays after a courtship of nine years. Her name was Cha-oom: I noted her appearance in court—a fragile-seeming graceful woman with a frank good-looking face, reminiscent of the Princess Mother's. She was the fourth of her father's twenty children by two wives. He was a senior civil servant of sufficient means to educate his children well. Cha-oom herself became a teacher at one of Bangkok's better private schools before marrying Vacharachai. They lived first in his father-in-law's compound, then he built their own house in the fashionable Bangkapi district. He was fond of outdoor activity and worked hard to lay out the garden; when abroad he bought furniture and other household articles for the new home. Cha-oom bore his four children, of whom the eldest was six and the youngest newly born in the year Ananda died. He tended to be as lenient with them as with his subordinates and servants, often passing them tit-bits from the special meals served to guests. The Japanese occupation brought a major change. Inflation on top of the demands of the new house and increasing family were more than his naval pay could bear. He left the navy to set up a shop in partnership with Cha-oom. It was a general store selling cloth, groceries and so forth. He lived quietly, not caring for social activity, though at cards and horse-racing he shared in a modest way the national vice of gambling. He did not go hunting or shooting. He regularly went to church, less from piety than because he enjoyed discussing religion and literature with the monks. After a while his friends wooed him back into the navy in order to serve the Free Thai Movement. Thus he took part in patrolling the river when the Regents locked themselves up in Pridi's house to escape FM Pibul's wrath (page 66). He was already an admirer of Pridi, who came to like his bluntness of speech as a refreshing change from the pretty superficialities which Siamese good manners encourage; Vacharachai responded with devotion to his lack of affection, his political ideas, and his brilliance. When Pridi became sole Regent after FM Pibul's fall, Vacharachai became one of his ADCs. Offered the same post in the royal entourage when Ananda arrived, he was reluctant because he could not speak the special language of royalty, but Ananda assured him that this did not matter.

I have earlier mentioned how he taught the royal brothers to shoot, drove Ananda about on private trips of exploration, and departed from the royal service; but this last episode warrants a word more. His pay at the Palace was two pounds ten a month, which scarcely paid for cleaning his uniform. To have made any representation on the subject involved loss of face. He therefore got a doctor friend to write a certificate of sickness—few Thai doctors would be so ill-bred as to refuse such a request from a friend—and stayed away from the

Palace, since three months' absence would automatically release him from service. He did not want to resume his naval career with its long separations from his wife and children. During his pretended illness he helped increase the profitableness of his and Cha-oom's shop by buying wholesale in Chinatown. They both also frequently visited Pridi, whose younger sisters-in-law had been at school with Cha-oom. The latter, an excellent pastry cook, helped Pridi's wife while Vacharachai joined in the discussions between Pridi and his visitors or went on errands for him to naval people. Pridi's attitude towards Vacharachai's desertion from the Palace is unknown; in any event Thais turn a tolerant eye on such matters. When the doctor sent by the Princess Mother discovered him playing cards, Vacharachai wrote to the King's secretary making a clean breast, and he was waiting to be formally retired from the royal service when Ananda died. He then became a secretary-aide (salary, £23 per month) to Pridi, and after Pridi to Admiral Dhamrong, Pridi's nominee to the premiership. There was in fact very little rumour linking him with Ananda's death until towards the end of 1947 when a political news-paper printed a verse obliquely naming him Ananda's assassin. Early in the morning following the November *coup* which restored FM Pibul, Pridi's chauffeur called to take him off to safety with him. And to exile where he remains to this day.

Many people who knew him did not particularly like him. But that is scarcely relevant. What is, is that this brief account does not suggest an impulsive killer, a rootless fanatic, or a desperado.

Nor does the actual evidence (page 136) brought against him alter this impression. My private investigations led me strongly to doubt the accuracy of the laundress and the chauffeur, a State employee; but this apart, the identification of Vacharachai as the person seen behind the Barompiman Hall at the time of the tragedy was rightly attacked by defence counsel as wholly unsatisfactory. Further, though the evidence of Cha-oom and her relatives (page 176) does not make a watertight alibi, it scarcely suggests a man waiting to commit and then returning from committing a terrible crime. The suggestion is the more unlikely when the time of his alleged arrival and departure means that the crime was dependent not only on split-second timing, but either a supernatural foreknowledge or the extraordinarily conve-nient circumstance of Ananda's being still in bed and dozing. Finally, even if the prosecution evidence were acceptable, the case against Lt Vacharachai still has this fatal flaw: there is nothing whatever to connect a man seen outside the Barompiman Hall with a dire event inside that building. Had he been seen at this time covered with blood or holding a reeking pistol; had he been implicated in a plot (the only evidence submitted was Tee the timberman's and See the gunman's, both rejected by the court); above all, had anyone only glimpsed him *inside* the building, some doubt of his innocence might arise. As it stands, the evidence against Lt Vacharachai makes him no more guilty of Ananda's death than you or me.

Of incidental interest is the allegation of blood on his sleeve. The idea that if he shot Ananda he must necessarily have got blood on himself will not do. It was asserted by the police officer who experimented by shooting at a human head and said that he got his pistol, hand and cuff spattered with blood, etc. But high-speed photographs in any reliable ballistics text-book show something different. A bullet's sudden swift emergence from the barrel pushes the air in front of it like a bow-wave, pressing *inwards* the skin, flesh, bone and brain of the victim's head at the point and moment of the bullet's entry. Of course blood may have soaked into Lt Vacharachai's sleeve if he, rather than his accomplice, recovered the fatal bullet in order to replace it with a false one. This supposition depends on whether he was the assassin—which I hope I have made clear the evidence does not prove—and whether there was in fact a 'switching' of bullets, which may best be considered along with the case against the three accused.

That against Chaleo would not have taken a Western court longer to throw out than is needed to say that if he did show disrespect to the throne, if he was dismissed, if he did say that Ananda would not leave on the 13th, and if he was Pridi's confidant and Pridi was the chief conspirator, there is no evidence whatever that he conspired with Pridi or that he acted in furtherance of a conspiracy. Quite simply, there is no evidence to connect him with the crime. As with Lt Vacharachai we are asked to gyrate on the perimeter of a possibility and imagine we are at the hub of certainty.

The case against Butr depends entirely on the conviction of Nai Chit. There is some logic in this. If Nai Chit proposed helping in a monstrous crime at a moment when he knew that Butr would be about, he would scarcely have risked the possibility that Butr might chance on something incriminating—unless Butr were first squared. Alternatively, if Nai Chit was concealing anything, Butr must surely have known. Yet these arguments recoil against the prosecution and tend to show Nai Chit's innocence if the ruling of the first court is accepted—as I think it must be—that the selection of Butr for service abroad with the royal family made his participation in any conspiracy unlikely. But if it is established that the fake-suicide could not have been effected without Butr's help, no amount of logic can save him. Here again the case against him hinges on that against Nai Chit.

The latter was damned for, among other reasons, being at the Barompiman Hall when he was off duty. The idea that no Siamese ever exerts himself is legendary among the Siamese themselves and has some foundation in everyday experience; but that no Siamese on any occasion feels sufficient concern or zeal to work when off duty is nonsense. Nevertheless, Nai Chit's explanation of why he was at the Hall would be more acceptable if the coincidence of his presence there at the time of the King's death were not made sinister by other allegations. These included his mock-gloomy prognostications about the King's intended departure. But why should that have had any greater significance than Chaleo's identical statement which the first court dismissed as meaningless? (Indeed, my own inquiry revealed that Nai Chit was an inveterate if amiable tease.) However, the suspicious circumstances most dwelt on by the court were his cry to the Princess Mother, and the alleged 'planting'.

It was not disputed that he cried out, 'The King has shot himself!' without having seen the pistol. But the court's conclusion ignores another interpretation which is at least equally valid. While Nai Chit's horrified attention might have been concentrated on the blood on Ananda, his eyes must also have seen the pistol, for it was plainly there to be seen—registering itself in his subconscious mind which darted to a conclusion perfectly compatible both with his knowledge that the King often played with pistols including the ·45 in the cabinet beside him, and with the absence of any sign of another person in the room when the shot had rung out only moments before. Besides, if an essential part of the plot was the planting of the ·45 to suggest suicide, and if Nai Chit was in the plot, would he not have made a point of saying he saw the pistol rather than candidly admitting the exact opposite? (The failure of a person's conscious power of observation at a time of shock is well illustrated by King Bhoomipol's admission that he could not recall seeing his brother's right arm, when every other witness said it was plainly outside the coverlet for all to see.)

As to the alleged 'planting', the possibility that Nai Chit *could* have planted the ·45 on the bed, or *could* have cocked it before producing it at the Palace Meeting, is of course no proof at all, yet these mere possibilities were worked in to the skein of proof because, essentially, of two other circumstances. One was his conflicting explanations of where in the room he picked up the spent cartridge. But the recollection of a shocked and confused innocent man can be as contradictory and evasive as a guilty man's, and become even more so with realization of how he is prejudicing himself. Again the slightest of evidence is slurred over by being added to the other circumstance which the court deemed suspicious, that it was Nai Chit who not only led the police to the allegedly false bullet in the mattress but did so three days after the shooting. As the more assertive and alert of the two men in charge of the royal bedchamber, however, it seems hardly odd that Nai Chit should have guided the police. The three days mean nothing. If the bullet was to be planted, this had to be done at once, for how could the conspirators have foreseen that the Police Chief's immediate examination would be stopped by Prince Rangsit?

The possibility remains that without inside help the assassin might scarcely have risked the time required after shooting Ananda to find and 'plant' the ·45, find the 'real' spent cartridge (unless a revolver were used), 'plant' the false spent cartridge, recover the 'real' bullet from its embedded position in the mattress, substitute the false bullet, and then get himself off. The further possibility remains that even the active assistance of Nai Chit alone might not have enabled all this to happen so quickly that when the Royal Nanny arrived from the other end of the Hall Ananda's pulse was still beating. Some help from Butr —for example, while Nai Chit was fetching the Princess Mother— seems to have been very nearly essential. Clearly, then, the only point of substance we are left with against the two pages is that if the situation was faked it probably needed their co-operation. The court's acceptance of the 'planting' theory thus became the fuse for a chain reaction of proof which otherwise did not exist.

Three things persuaded it that the ·45 found by Ananda's hand had not been the instrument of his death—the nitrite tests, the rust in the barrel, and the undamaged bullet. It conceded a degree of doubt about the first two, less about the third: in rejecting the police evidence that bullets were sometimes found undamaged after going through a person's head it arrogated to itself a knowledge of the strength of skulls, incidentally ignoring the softness of living bone compared with dead. It proceeded to say that if each of the three points was not of itself conclusive, they were like weak threads which together could support a weight beyond the strength of the individual threads. This argument is specious because a thread, however weak, is a thread— you do not doubt whether it exists at all. Since the court found the evidence on each of the three points inconclusive (that is, unproven as a fact) no amount of adding them together could make them conclusive. In any event, in deciding that the ·45 had not been fired on the fatal morning the court ignored the quite categorical Western authorities on the subject. Major General Sir Gerald Barrard, for example, in *The Identification of Fire-Arms & Forensic Ballistics* states: 'The truth is that it is utterly impossible to fix the date of discharge [of a firearm] with any scientific accuracy after the lapse of a comparatively few hours.' The ·45 was first tested three *days* after Ananda's death.

In any event the improbabilities in the planting theory reduce it to absurdity. The conspirators had no means of knowing in advance whether the ejected spent cartridge would be discoverable immediately; and even if a revolver were used, less could they have foreseen where the *bullet* would go: it might indeed have lodged in Ananda's head. If the situation was to have been faked, the chances are that the assassin would have used Ananda's own ·45 but the court discounted these chances because, it said, the assassin would have had to wear a glove, thereby increasing the risk of error, which is an argument any thin cotton glove makes threadbare; also, that he would have preferred a weapon that he was accustomed to, although ·45s were easily procurable and required little practice by an experienced person like the alleged killer, Lt Vacharachai, who had himself taught Ananda to use one; finally, the court suggested that the conspirators did not want to risk arousing suspicion by getting the ·45 in advance, though in all the circumstances this was surely the least of the risks. From beginning to end the 'planting' theory is untenable. That being so, no case is left against Nai Chit, and hence Butr.

Like Chaleo the pages were innocent. Three innocent men were condemned to die.

Their conviction is a remarkable instance of how reasoning, which is the judiciary's principal glory and the very soul of Justice, may unconsciously become utterly distorted. By Siamese standards, the trial was fair, and judgement the result of conscientious reflection. How, then, could such distortion have occurred?

The power of appointment, promotion, and regulation of judges in Thailand is vested in a Board of Control consisting of nine judges, so that it appears to be independent of the Government. But salaries and pensions are paid by the Ministry of Justice, which also appoints the secretary to the Board and can, albeit with the formality of the Board's consent, transfer judges from one position or place to another. Even without the itching trigger finger of a Police-General Pao to make any obstinate individual think twice, the effect is a subtle—sometimes not so subtle—permeation of the Ministry's influence. The judges are civil servants employed by it, and indeed a man only becomes a judge after first joining the Ministry. Since the whole of the civil service is considered a superior form of employment the actual department one happens to be in does not mean much; and the aloofness, proud independence and awed public regard which attach to the office of judge in many Western countries, cannot exist where a man becomes a judge at twenty-five and leaves at a correspondingly early age, on an inadequate pension which often obliges him to enter the market place as a practising lawyer. Being thus unexalted, the average judge conforms to the Siamese characteristic of cheerfully going before whatever wind of power happens to be blowing. Hence the Appeal Court in the regicide case could express such a purely political dictum as, 'The Pridi-controlled Government proved itself incapable of governing the country.'

And hence it is unsurprising to find, not the deliberate abdication of reason, but the sustained subconscious distortion of reason. It is this which makes the regicide case unique. Not over days or weeks but over years, men sincerely reasoned their way to their conclusions which they placed on the altar of justice: but their reasoning was faulty, and the altar was adorned by a curtain with a white target to guide the executioner's aim.

A legend persists that the accused knew more than they ever revealed. This legend derives from another, that royal servants safeguard royal secrets even unto death. But the consistency of the three accused's stories despite their long incarceration, torture, subjection to truth drugs, and the straits of their families, made a demand on mind and body impossible for *all* of the accused to have resisted *all* of the time, minute after minute for two thousand six hundred and fifty days. I tracked down a certain person of honesty and intelligence, who was intimately involved in the case, and who was imprisoned by FM Pibul for a month during which he shared a cell with certain of the accused; the circumstances made the withholding of at least partial confidence highly unlikely: yet he confirms categorically that nothing was revealed which we do not know. It is significant that no preferment or wealth came the way of the accused in the whole year and a half between the time of Ananda's death and the FM Pibul *coup* which put them in gaol. No motive could be found then, and my investigations revealed none now. On the contrary, I was convinced beyond doubt of the utter purposelessness of the accused's alleged crime. And in the minds of those who knew them best nothing is more improbable than that they ever could have been party to it.

Today their bodies have still to be cremated. Their families believe that while they are unvindicated the flames will not release their elemental selves to continue through other lives the search for Nirvana, but will serve only to create ghosts wandering in tormenting and tormented anguish over the face of the earth. So their bodies putrefy in temporary coffins. But these, though of stone, cannot contain the ranker stench of injustice.

Who Killed Ananda?

I

How did Ananda come to die?

The rumours, conjectures and theories make in sum a mystery as baffling to the East as the West, but they do cover the whole gamut of possibilities; and if the regicide trial achieved nothing else it unearthed an immense accumulation of evidence which I have tried to report fairly and in all essentials. The result is that we are now equipped to reach the core of the mystery. Our method need only be the simple process of elimination.

The accident theory has been shown to be almost worthless, but this has been on the assumption that Ananda was alone when he died. However, the fact that the boys always played with their guns together, and the less well-known fact that the high-spirited Bhoomipol sometimes playfully pointed a gun at Ananda who sternly told him not to, has given rise to a far more persuasive theory, which continues to be held by most Westerners. It is that Bhoomipol visited the sick Ananda and while they were playing with the ·45 *he* accidentally fired it.

No one ever gave more authority to this idea than Bhoomipol himself, by his extraordinary change from gaiety throughout his seventeen years preceding Ananda's death to unsmiling gravity in the following fourteen. The resilience of youth, and the Siamese trait of quickly forgetting disagreeable events, appeared in him to have been overborne by an emotion which many interpret as remorse or guilt.

The evidence in the regicide case also gives ample scope for speculation. Before the fatal shot, the Royal Nanny and Bhoomipol were in and out of the playroom and Bhoomipol's bedroom at the same time. She was in the bedroom putting away movie films when she heard the shot and rushed out, while Bhoomipol said he heard not a shot but a shout which drew him from the playroom. This difference is as odd as their lack of reference to each other in their respective testimonies; indeed Bhoomipol even said he saw no one. Moreover he said the shout drew him out to the front porch where, directly along the front corridor to Ananda's study, he met the lady-in-waiting. If indeed the study door was for some reason left unlocked, it is theoretically possible for him to have gone this way to Ananda, and after the accident run out by the same door, unremarked by the two pages in the back corridor outside the dressing-room but encountering the lady-in-waiting.

Then there is the Princess Mother's agitated conversation with him which Butr allegedly overheard when the body was being washed, 'Whatever you wish to do, do it!' The explanation of this could be that Bhoomipol wished to confess to the Palace Meeting going on below. An equally incriminating interpretation can be placed on his *cri de coeur* to the Royal Physician that evening, 'You can't leave me in a situation like this.'

Strangely, no inquiry was made at the regicide trial whether Ananda was right- or left-handed. He was in fact right-handed. Yet the pistol was by his left hand. Note also that the cabinet containing the pistol was on his left side, and the fatal wound above his left eye. These facts may mean that Bhoomipol got the pistol out as he stood next to his brother's bed, playfully pointed it, accidentally fired it, and after an instant of stupefied horror let it drop and ran out: the pistol could then have been where it was found.

Now however unfavourable all this is to Bhoomipol, how much more so does it become if the theory were not one of accident but murder. The notion that he visited Ananda then tends to indicate sinister intent, else he would have used the dressing-room entrance where the two pages were stationed (to his knowledge, since he had spoken to them there). A clear motive can be presumed, the ambition to be King. He had the opportunity. No one saw him at the crucial moments. He knew where the ·45 was, and how to use it. Add to these circumstances his demeanour during the years following, which suggested an emotion outside ordinary grief. Add the alleged equivocal passage between himself and his mother. Add the unreliability of his testimony in that he said he never heard the shot though the Royal Nanny did, that he never saw anyone though he could hardly have missed seeing the Nanny if he was where he said he was, and that he never noticed where Ananda's right (that is, firing) arm was though everyone else did. Add, finally, his conversation that night with the Royal Physician, when besides asking him not to leave him he spoke in favour of the accident theory although he should have known that the ·45's safety device, if not Ananda's habitual caution, rendered the theory highly improbable.

The resulting tally of suspicion is such that had Prince Bhoomipol been charged with regicide, and precisely the same reasoning and attitude been applied by the judges as they adopted in convicting the three accused, he must certainly have been condemned. But strip it down and what are we left with but faint shadows and surmise. The same simple reason that makes the impartial observer reject the case against them must also acquit Bhoomipol: there is absolutely no evidential link between him and the shooting.

Had he and Ananda been known to have quarrelled, or if Bhoomipol had ever expressed hatred towards Ananda, or had he been seen in the proximity of Ananda's quarters just before or just after the shooting, or had the pistol been in his possession immediately before the shooting, or had the two pages heard him talking to Ananda or moving about in Ananda's room, or had there been any suggestion by the lady-in-waiting that Bhoomipol approached her not from the direction of his quarters but Ananda's, or had the conversations with his mother and the doctor not admitted of other explanations—had there been by any means whatever any such link between Bhoomipol and the shooting, suspicion might begin to take root. But there was none.

Nor do the surrounding factors indicate guilt. The two boys' 'club' in the grounds of the Villa Watana was scarcely behind them: the bond of fraternal intimacy was especially strong, and with their mother they had been a singularly united family. Bhoomipol was, besides, only seventeen years old, and nothing suggests a desire to occupy the throne. He had known from birth that it was not his, and he had seen enough to know that it was a very doubtful privilege. Even if he nevertheless wanted it at all costs, his intelligence would scarcely have let him choose a bright morning with people everywhere, including two pages at the very door. This jazz-loving, conspicuously gay youth never gave the slightest hint in his life or character to suggest the impulsive murderer or the possessor of a homicidal rage. And when his conduct in the hours after the shooting is examined, one gets no impression of a youth who had just been the perpetrator either of murder or of a most dreadful accident.

His conduct beyond that immediate time is understandable enough. The shock of seeing his brother suddenly dead; and then the hours with his prostrate mother by Ananda's corpse, the macabre rites culminating in the closing of the silver urn, the treachery which the royal family gradually became convinced lay behind Ananda's death, and the threat to his own life implicit in such treachery, were not the only experiences that broke upon him after the sheltered, safe and unselfconscious life which he had always known. To the traumatic effect of Ananda's death was added the fact that he was suddenly King, Lord of Life, Protector of a nation, and answerable to history for his conduct. Finally, he was less delicately perceptive in human relations than Ananda; and this meant a harder dynamic that responded hardly to so convulsive an event in his young life that previously had been insulated from the realities of either peace or war.

Bhoomipol, then, was as guiltless as rumour was false. But conjecture is no respecter of persons. It has not even excluded the Princess Mother herself. Her motive is said to have been a desire to see Bhoomipol crowned, both because he was her favourite and because he would be more compliant with her will. The theory gained wide credence among the British Army in India where the royal family spent a short time during the flight which brought Ananda back to Bangkok. Many people observed how clearly, if gracefully, she had command of her sons who entirely deferred to her. This provided most of the foundation for a theory which the facts demolish at a puff.

Since, then, the royal family did not provide the assassin, we have not far to look for other suspects. The political party in opposition to Pridi, hence the heir to his power if he were disgraced, was the Democrat Party. It therefore had a clear motive; and it attracts suspicion for other reasons also. If some of its members helped stir up, fewer attempted to quieten, the public outcry against Pridi; it included many royalists with a loathing of his liberalism; and its leaders were frequently in attendance at the Barompiman Hall, which they therefore knew well. From these circumstances many of Pridi's followers concluded that the Democrat Party must have provided the assassin. If they are right, the result was ironic: after Pridi's fall the Democrat Party did get into power but only for the few months in 1948 that it served FM Pibul's purpose, and it has ever since been out of office. But Pridi's followers were wrong. There is no evidence of any kind to implicate the Democrat Party.

I should have been surprised to find otherwise. Kuang's high-class origins and the Pramoj brothers' royal ancestry find expression in the ultra-royalism of palace courtiers. No more than Nai Chit or Butr would they have dreamt of killing their King. It was indeed their very concern for the throne that contributed to the public agitation against Pridi.

The genesis of that agitation, fostered as it was by many royalists' genuine suspicion of his part in Ananda's death, is fascinating to trace. The key figure was the senior page named Chan who pre-deceased Ananda. He alone of all the palace officials and servants conceived a dire foreboding about the royal family's safety. He did so from the very first hour of their arrival. Perhaps his ill-health mentally un-balanced him; or his dislike of the uncourtly Chaleo may have spread to Chaleo's patron Pridi and to Nai Chit when the latter seemed too friendly with Chaleo; perhaps he wanted to ingratiate himself with the royal family by conspicuously showing concern for their well-being. Whatever the reason or combination of reasons, he appointed himself Cassandra at the feast. If he did not arm Ananda with a ·45 as Bhoomipol said in evidence, he certainly whispered dolorous warnings in the ear of Prince Bhoomipol and the Royal Nanny. I also know that he kept running to royalists with complaints about inadequate palace security and dark intimations of treachery. The royalist Democrat Party was at that time first in process of breaking from Pridi and then of actively opposing him, fundamentally because of incorrigible suspicion of him, so that Chan's words were seeds upon fertile ground. They sprang into a forest when the very thing he had warned against appeared to happen: Ananda was shot.

It became difficult then to see the wood for the trees. The whole affair, including the trial, is a classic of the way in which suspicion can become confused with fact—even by men trained in the disciplines of science.

If now, in continuing our search for fact, we choose motive for a guide, none compels attention more than that of the man who above all others profited by Ananda's death. From the proud position of Siam's dictator, than whom not even the sun shone brighter, FM Pibul had fallen into the disgrace of lodgement in the common gaol, and he was released only a few months before Ananda's death. The sun now was his old rival, Pridi, and who would have given a tical for Pibul's chances of a comeback? But he did come back—over Ananda's dead body. Clarification of the mystery of the King's death was the declared first aim of the *coup d'état*: that 'clarification' comprised the disgracing of Pridi. Moreover, the acts of violence which marked FM Pibul's subsequent régime, and his highly flexible approach to matters of principle, cast him far more naturally in the role of villain than Pridi. Equally cogent is the argument that FM Pibul's attitude to royalty during his previous régime had been equivocal: he kept the Political Prisoners in gaol, continued to deny King Prajadhipok the posthumous honours traditionally due, and so forth. All this imposes no strain on the imagination when the theory is advanced that he plotted Ananda's death in order, at a stroke, to obtain revenge on Pridi and clear the way for his own return to power. Advocates of this theory even point to the small pension which he arranged for the widows of the two executed pages, patently being conscience money.

The fallacy in the theory is that it ignores the time lapse between Ananda's death and the *coup d'état*. There was no immediate, certain reward commensurate with the risk of killing Ananda: FM Pibul could not have reckoned on the precise course of events in the ensuing seventeen months—the sustained suspicion of Pridi, the permanence of the split with the Democrat Party, the clamorous parliamentary scene, and the speedy withdrawal of the British forces which left a military vacuum that his friends in the army chose to fill in support of himself. The business smacks of opportunity seized, not created. But the decisive point at which any case against him falls apart is exactly that which acquits all the suspects so far considered: no evidence links him with the shooting of Ananda.

This does not, of course, exclude persons whose interests were so wrapped up in his restoration to power as to give them, too, a clear motive. Obviously one of these was Police-General Pao, whose record scarcely places him above any crime. But—there is absolutely no evidence against him, not the slightest suspicion.

A number of suspects remain for consideration. Most of them are suspects merely because their names have cropped up in Ananda's biography. They include palace attendants, officials, princes; and the group of people in Lausanne. We may safely eliminate every one of them for the simple reason that no evidence of any kind has been adduced against any of them. This has not stopped the manufacture of false scents. For example, a mysterious person variously identified as 'the Greek' (M. Seraidaris) and the Princess Mother's private secretary (Nai Anek) is solemnly said to have been smuggled in with the family when Ananda returned to Bangkok, and to have stayed in a secret part of the Barompiman Hall. The only foundation of fact in this story is that Nai Anek visited Bangkok on a subsequent occasion in King Bhoomipol's entourage. It is a good example of the fictionalized facts with which the case abounds.

A far more serious line of inquiry is opened by another theory altogether. It is that the Communist Party carried out the killing in order that the confusion and upheaval thereby caused would enable it to seize power. But the party was at that time under a ban which was only lifted late in 1946 (among other measures to satisfy the major Powers who else refused Siam's application for membership of the United Nations). There had previously been some underground activity by the party but on a very limited scale. Civil war still raged in China, and communism had gained nothing like the adherents later years have known in south-east Asia. In any event, the party could scarcely have been so maladroit at a time of trying to survive and expand as to provoke the national revulsion of feeling which it knew that the killing of the King would cause. Nor could there have been any point in creating an upheaval when not only had the party no hope of armed support but the country was occupied by the British— whose intervention in Greece at this time gave clear notice of how they would react to any communist attempt to seize power. Some vestige of an argument could begin from the premise of a communist plan to exploit Pridi's following by setting him up as a dictator, but no evidence whatever—before, at the time, or after Ananda's death—gives any scope for developing the argument. Any idea that the communists, Pridi himself, or anyone else, planned to seize power by removing the monarchy—which was merely a constitutional cipher, with no effective power anyway—could only have meaning if there had been an attempt to wipe out the whole royal family. Yet not only was no such attempt made but Bhoomipol was offered the throne the very same day—by Pridi.

In absolving the Communist Party we reach the end of the catalogue of suspected assassins. What of the outside chance of someone not named, not known, X? There is no room for him; no blank in the evidence, in the sequence of events, in the lay-out of the Barompiman Hall, which allows for him: there is simply no sign, no hint, no reason to suppose he ever existed. The catalogue is complete. Our process of elimination is complete.

Let us check back on what it has done. It has finally disposed of any case against Pridi. Against Lt Vacharachai. Against Chaleo, Nai Chit and Butr. Against Prince Bhoomipol and his mother. Against the Democrat Party. Against FM Pibul and his friends. Against anyone in Lausanne. Against the communists.

Yet Ananda was killed. Since none of these killed him, only one other person could have. Himself.

II

WE are dealing with circumstantial evidence. No one saw the shooting, much less read Ananda's mind at the time.

It is *possible* that someone unknown and unguessed-at entered and departed unseen by unfathomable means, such that not all the years since have produced any hint or rumour of that person or that means. All this is possible, in the amplitude of the word possible. But when the probability is nil, and the odds against almost infinitely great, mere possibility has no practical meaning.

However, for the benefit of those minds for which bizarre chance has endless fascination, let us test this by following an imaginary assassin as he went about his crime. We must remember that he is none of the people we know and that the two pages have been completely cleared.

Eluding the sentries at the gates of the Grand Palace, and then the guards outside the Barompiman Hall, and then the night watch inside, he finally enters Ananda's quarters at some time in the night and hides, let us suppose, behind the curtains of the Buddha-room. He decides to wait and is behind the curtains at 6 a.m. when the Princess Mother visits Ananda. After her departure the assassin still makes no move, even though if he knows anything of Ananda's habits he knows that he usually rises at between eight and eight-thirty. Ananda does in fact get up, and goes to the bathroom. The assassin possibly takes this opportunity to take the ·45 out of the bedside cabinet though he risks any one of several people coming in. To his agreeable surprise Ananda gets back into bed and, dismissing Butr with the orange juice, dozes. Alternatively, it is between this time and 9.20 a.m. that the assassin, having eluded the sentries and staff previously described but with the addition of Nai Chit and Butr who are immediately outside the dressing-room, gets into the King's bedroom and finds him conveniently in bed and dozing. Towards 9.20 a.m. the assassin

approaches the mosquito net, which surrounds the bed at a distance
of about a pace and is weighted by rods along the bottom hems. He
wastes precious moments and adds to his difficulties by parting the
mosquito net instead of simply pressing his pistol against it (no hole
was found). Inside the net the assassin leans over the four-foot-high
bed-head (the reason for this deduction will appear later) and shoots.
He then fakes a suicide picture—not by putting the pistol into Ananda's
hand but near it; even more remarkably, the wrong hand, though
indeed the most remarkable thing about him up to now has been his
ice-steel coolness. In not putting the pistol into Ananda's hand he
risks putting his own prints on the pistol; or, if he wears gloves,
rubbing off Ananda's; or leaving prints that were on previously,
which for all he knows might be those of the servant who last cleaned
the weapon—in short he risks immediately negativing the presumption
of suicide if the pistol were to be properly examined. However, that
is what we must suppose he does before running out through the
study and along the front corridor. The page preparing the breakfast
table in the front porch hears the shot and looks out along the whole
front corridor, but he sees no one; and the study door is still closed so
he returns to his work until he sees the Princess Mother running from
her room. Not one of the people who appear catches a glimpse of the
assassin—the Princess Mother, Nai Chit, the Royal Nanny (these
three arrived so quickly that Ananda's pulse was still beating, which
the medical evidence held could only have gone on for half a minute
after his death), Prince Bhoomipol, Butr, the lady-in-waiting, or the
page in the porch. The pages on the main staircase see no one. The
servants and officials on the ground floor see no one there. The guards
see no one suspicious. The assassin vanishes as mysteriously not only
as he appeared by Ananda's bed, but as he has been unheard of in all
the years since.

It is a story of this kind which the proponents of the assassination
theory would have us believe!

The question arises whether the assassin might not have scaled the
walls of the building and entered and left by a window; or, as some
imaginative royalists have suggested, got into the ceiling the previous
day and descended by a hatchway. No such suggestion was ever made
at any of the trials, in the course of which the judges closely inspected
the scene. Furthermore, I was in Bangkok when alterations were

being made to the Barompiman Hall which enabled me conclusively to establish that for anyone to have entered Ananda's quarters by any means whatever, undetected, was impossible.

If, then, the assassination theory has no foundation in fact or even reasonable supposition, and if every suspect has been shown to be innocent, the presumption of suicide becomes irresistible. Of course if this presumption can be rebutted, the near miracle of accident has to be accepted. But I do not think it can be rebutted. On the contrary, the greater part of all the evidence concerning Ananda's death points not away from but towards suicide.

First of all we should look at the instant reaction of the people closest concerned, since in a sudden situation this often gives the clearest indication of the true nature of that situation.

The Princess Mother has never gone on record with any explanation of Ananda's death, but her actions are noteworthy. She ordered the bed linen and Ananda's night clothes to be replaced as soon as the doctor had announced his verdict, and she asked him to wash the body. Her distraught exclamation to the doctor, 'Who could ever have imagined such a thing happening?' lacked fear or the slightest hint of any thought of murder. She had a search made for a suicide note; her grief was intense and prolonged (today she still cannot speak about Ananda's death) beyond what one would have thought possible had it been turned outward by reflection on the insanity or malice of the murderer. As to Prince Bhoomipol, he acted with a quiet sad calm, quite inconsistent with the belief that a murderer might still be lurking about. He did not immediately tell anyone what he years later told the court, 'The senior page Chan warned me of danger': on the contrary, having spent the day comforting his mother he that evening said to the Royal Physician, 'In my opinion there is no explanation other than accident for my brother's death.' The remark suggests he was clutching at the straw held out by the afternoon communiqué—and for the same reason that prompted the communiqué's draftsmen to conceal suicide by pretending to an accident, which Bhoomipol's knowledge of the ·45 must have told him was highly unlikely; while his vastly changed bearing suggests a deeper emotion than an accident would have given rise to.

What is to be concluded from these reactions of the two people longest and most intimately acquainted with Ananda? Clearly, the

sum of their immediate impressions, conscious or subconscious, was
not one of murder. Presently, the evidence suggests, doubts crept in
as the evidence or supposed evidence accumulated, until the verdicts
reached after prolonged and searching trials proclaimed the finding
of murder. But in those first hours, clearly, the idea of suicide was not
absent: it was not rejected as impossible, out of the question: it burned
with bitter anguish into their minds.

After his mother and brother, the two people in at least closest
physical proximity with the King for the final six months, and the
companions of his childhood, were his two personal pages. Nai Chit—
to his cost—concluded instantly that the King had shot himself. Butr
expressed no opinion, but what he kept from the Commission of
Inquiry and was dragged from him after his arrest, is conspicuously
interesting. He was referring to Ananda's behaviour during the few
minutes which were to prove the last time anyone saw him alive: it
was so unusual, said Butr, that considered with his burning of letters
the previous day, anyone knowing about it might deduce that Ananda's
mind was upon suicide. Even if for the moment we dismiss the burning
of the letters as a usual part of preparations for a prolonged departure,
Ananda's behaviour within an hour of his death cannot be dismissed.
Butr was a simple, dullish, good fellow who knew Ananda when all
the guards were down: he helped dry him, often combed his hair for
him, assisted at his private devotions, saw him into bed, saw him up;
and so warm was their relationship that he was to go abroad with him
as his personal attendant. He was not given to strange imaginings: he
had not the wit for them. If the way Ananda looked at him without
greeting, then lay in bed with up-raised knees and wordlessly waved
him away when he approached with the orange juice—and this is to
mention only such details as Butr could actually get hold of when
trying to describe a general impression—seemed strange, how much
stranger does such behaviour seem within an hour of Ananda's death?

Two other people were concerned in the immediate moments after
Ananda's death. The Royal Nanny contributes nothing to our study,
since her belief in murder was expressed much later. The lady-in-
waiting, approached inquiringly by Bhoomipol, said Ananda had
shot himself. She did not say, 'Nai Chit says the King has shot himself,
but that is impossible, he must have had an accident': she accepted
what Nai Chit had said as the fact of the matter.

When we move downstairs to the Palace Meeting of royal princes, cabinet ministers and police, there is unanimous acceptance of that same fact. Most of these people were not gullible nonentities. Suspicion, as the aftermath was to show, grows in Bangkok even faster and richer than the fields sprout rice in the surrounding countryside. Yet these men had no suspicion. Nothing they knew, saw, heard, gave them the slightest impression that the appearance of suicide was illusory, however much one or two of them later tried to show wisdom after the event. An important figure at this meeting was the then Police Chief. He is now dead but according to reliable people who knew him he occupied his position on merit, and was an intelligent and upright man. He made an immediate investigation of the premises and staff and he was helped by a number of his leading officers. Though he had begun with the thought of assassination uppermost, his conclusion was that Ananda had committed suicide.

Thus, Ananda's mother and brother, his personal pages, his relations, his cabinet ministers including the most brilliant mind in modern Siam, and the police—in short, everyone in a position to judge on the spot, closest to the time, and knowing Ananda—all either positively concluded that Ananda had committed suicide or did not reject that conclusion. Yet the judges in the regicide trial said they were wrong. The reasons for this lofty pronouncement years after the event are summed up on pages 183-4 and amount essentially to two—Ananda's character including his apparent lack of motive for suicide; and the 'scientific' evidence which negatived suicide because of the 'planting' theory, and the position of the body-cum-pistol together with the absence of cadaveric spasm. We can put the first reason aside, at least for the present, since if the fact of suicide is proved considerations of character or motive are not material.

As to the 'scientific' evidence, the 'planting' theory has already been disposed of as a wondrous contribution to science fiction. On the question of cadaveric spasm, the court seems not to have been fully informed since the theory could have no application where the victim's pulse beat for half a minute after the shot. In any event, on its own admission, the proof was so inconclusive that at best this could only corroborate other evidence which the court held to be decisive proof that Ananda could not have shot himself, namely the position of the body and pistol.

221

Let us re-examine this last point, the crux of the whole judgement, with some care. Police experience confirmed, as the judges observed, what common-sense would expect to find if a person lay in bed and shot himself through the head: his arm(s) would be flopped across his chest, and the pistol would either be still in his grasp or lying somewhere near his neck. But, disregarding the freakish results in many shooting cases, the judges' argument depends solely on the assumption that if Ananda shot himself he did so *while lying down*. It seems never to have occurred to them or anyone else that the downward-tending direction of the bullet through Ananda's brain is quite against that assumption (and is one of the reasons for supposing that the assassin, if any, stood behind the bed-head). For the bullet to have taken the direction it did while Ananda was lying down, he would have had to hold the pistol not somewhat in front of his face, which is the natural position, but directly above or even somewhat backward of it. But if he shot himself while *sitting up* and holding the pistol where one would normally have expected him to hold it, the path of the bullet would probably have corresponded with what the autopsy revealed. Moreover, as the doctors said at the trial, the recoil of the pistol would most likely have thrown his arms away from his body, but had he been sitting up this tendency would have been counteracted by the movement of his body falling back, which would have drawn his arms in towards his sides where they were found. It is possible also that if he sat up he drew his knees up and rested his elbows on them to steady his hold of the pistol: if so, his legs would automatically have straightened out as he fell flat and inert in the position found. Whether he had his knees up or not, the falling movement would have tended to push his whole body somewhat towards the end of the bed, and in fact the Royal Physician found Ananda's feet against the foot of the bed. Significant too is the fact that the bullet missed the pillow, which is not anything one would have expected if Ananda had been lying down, whereas had he been sitting up the trajectory of the bullet could well have been along an angle short of the pillow, especially because of the jerk of Ananda's head at the moment of impact.

The ·45 is big and heavy. Ananda could more easily have shot himself through his mouth or temple, but this is not a matter to be quibbled about when the time was hardly conducive to reasoning, and in any event such methods have a margin of error which by nature he would instinctively have wished to avoid. Moreover, police experience is that many people choose to shoot themselves in the way Ananda did.

He is more likely to have used two hands than one, to avoid awkwardly twisting his wrist. A likely sequence is that he took the pistol in his right hand, began twisting his wrist, and then brought up his left hand: he slipped the thumb into the trigger-ring while the rest of this hand enclosed the back of his right hand, the fingers of which enfolded the back of the butt to press against the safety catch. All sorts of conjectures may be made but this has the merit of being logical and simple. Also the fact that the wound and pistol were on his left suggests that his left hand chiefly applied the trigger pressure. In any event, where the gun would fall could have been anybody's guess and where it did fall—escaping from his twin grasp as his arms separated—is quite consistent with this explanation.

Some people never will be convinced that Ananda committed suicide. For those, however, who confine themselves to the evidence and to reason, the conclusion may be unpalatable but is clear. All possible suspects have been eliminated, their innocence confirming and being confirmed by the thorough discrediting of the assassination theory. The resultant presumption of suicide cannot be rebutted by the position in which the body and pistol were found, and it cannot be rebutted but gains support from the behaviour and belief of everyone concerned in the immediate sequel to the shooting.

Since the presumption of suicide cannot be rebutted it becomes conclusive. Therefore no inquiry into character is required, no evidence of motive; and our search for Ananda's killer is ended. But few would be satisfied to leave it there while the final element is missing.

Why Ananda took his life provides in fact a study with revelations of its own.

III

It is a perverse fact that a finding of suicide tends to come as an anti-climax to a murder investigation. Most people, indeed, do not think of suicide as murder at all. But of course it is as much murder as any other deliberate act of killing. And the fact that killer and victim are the same person gives the subject a more, not a less, compelling claim to our attention. It calls for a vastly more subtle inquiry, striking far deeper to the springs of the human soul and human relationships alike.

Something like 4,500 works have been written on the problem of suicide. Few were written before 1800 and these mainly on the philosophical question of a man's right to shorten his own life. The nineteenth century started with the firm belief of psychiatrists and sociologists that all suicides were madmen. Today, they estimate that only about ten per cent of suicides are insane. But one's distress at another's suicide still owes something to the notion of madness. Distress is greater the closer one's relationship to the suicide—because of remorse, or the feeling that one could have prevented it, and so forth, on the one hand; and on the other, concern for the reputation of the suicide, who has apparently made so unambiguous a declaration of his failure to cope with life. In addition, even in countries where suicide is not a crime it has a flavour of moral, sometimes religious, turpitude. Our attitude has something of horror: it has also compassion, evoked by thought of the mental anguish which is assumed to have led to the suicide. But behind everything else is essentially a kind of mystic puzzlement. Our minds are bowed before the mystery of how life, whose very stuff is the instinct to continue so long as the body functions, can make itself living non-life by overpowering that primal instinct during the moments immediately prior to the act of death.

The 4,500 works have not explained the mystery. No single one can even explore its many facets. It abounds with contradictions: for example, more chronically sick people commit suicide than the incurably sick. Nor is such statistical information of the general a sure guide to the particular. Suicide is most likely in June: this does not rule out November. A Roman Catholic mother of ten living on a farm is statistically less likely to commit suicide than a Protestant bachelor working in an urban industry, but this does not make Mrs O'Flaherty immune to suicide. When indeed we come to the particular, our difficulties increase, for family shutters are put up—and the suicide has often taken his secrets to the grave with him. He may leave a note, and though statistics are scanty these suggest that about one-third leave notes; but even if the motive is explained by a note or other circumstances, the experts say that conscious motive is not always the same as cause, which the suicide may not himself know. One might imagine that those who fail in a suicide attempt would afford illumination of the problem, but it seems that the suicide and the attempted suicide are different, if overlapping, kinds of people.

We are therefore dealing in uncertainties. However, certain known factors can help us in a consideration of Ananda's death. No class, no race, no stage of civilization is immune to suicide, which today—in the West at least—ranks fifth of all the causes of death among the more educated section of the community. And though, statistically, the male is more likely to commit suicide than the female and the old than the young, the recorded case of a girl of six committing suicide shows that neither sex nor age produces any guarantee against suicide. As to youth, the only clear statement I have come by is in *Du suicide et de la folie suicide* by one of the greatest nineteenth-century authorities[6]: suicide by young people, he says, is almost always due to an instinctive and unprepared decision, the explanation of which must be searched for in the personality as a whole.

But—to echo an issue raised earlier in this book—is it permissible for us to apply Western ideas about suicide to an oriental, however 'Westernized'? The answer suggested by studies of oriental immigrants to the West is that when people of one society move to another, they exhibit the suicide pattern not of their native society but of the adopted one. Since Ananda spent the greater part of his life in the West, it would not seem necessary to apply oriental suicide criteria to him.

On the other hand, his awareness that his life was to be wrapped up in Siam, and that his position identified him with the heart and soul of Siam, tended to keep strong within him his 'Siamese-ness', however Westernized he appeared or even took himself to be. Among the acknowledged stress conditions conducive to suicide in a particular society is a process of profound change. The Westernization of Thailand is such a process, and a leading Thai practitioner in mental health told me that the principal cause of neuroses among his people is the individual's maladjustment to the impact of Westernization. With Ananda, however, stress was caused by the reverse impact. He had grown up in a Western environment when he arrived in Bangkok to be not merely Siamese but *the* Siamese—King, embodiment of his nation.

To this difficulty of adaptation, the greater because he was a sensitive and conscientious youth, was added the strain of kingship itself. His boyhood visit prepared him for the ceremonial, the fulsome attention of courtiers, the doting of the populace; but the final six months of his life brought the new experience of responsibility. He had now to *understand* and to exercise his judgement in a period of harassing internal and international complexity. He could have accepted Pridi with unqualified admiration, and as pupil and friend been content to fulfil his constitutional function of rubber-stamping Pridi's decrees, but this was unlikely in an atmosphere of political acrimony and while many of the royalists about him were hostile to Pridi. (The irony is that had Pridi been the monster the royalists painted him, they would have been too afraid to make these visits and to try to undermine him.)

It is relevant here to consider Police-General Pao and FM Pibul's story about an intended secret meeting with Ananda. At first glance it seems unlikely that Ananda wished on the eve of his departure to have anything to do with a man so apparently in political ruin. Yet the possibility remains that such a meeting was in fact mooted if not arranged. The alleged original message to FM Pibul was conveyed ostensibly on Ananda's behalf via the husband of a woman in the Princess Mother's entourage; and the venue was not to be the Barompiman Hall but the Princess Mother's former home, the Mahidols' Srapatum Palace. To my own recent inquiry the Princess Mother said she had no knowledge of any proposed meeting: was not FM Pibul in gaol? Since Pibul had been out of gaol for some months, this answer shows a fault in her memory, but an interesting fault, since her mind did not select the utter unlikelihood of Ananda's wishing to see him. The possibility cannot be excluded that she did indeed

want her son to meet, without fear or favour, all the political personalities as part of his educational duty, nothing more, but the importance
of the story is that it reflects the existence of such personalities representing passionately conflicting political forces at work on Ananda.
If these did not positively distress Ananda they were a disconcerting
lesson on how uneasy must sleep the head that wears a crown, whatever
the temporary relief his impending return to Switzerland was to have
brought.

Now Ananda had not been born a king but he had been born a
Chakri. A family tree so bristling with eccentricity produced by the
singular ability, absolute power, and inter-marrying of the dynasty,
could scarcely put out completely normal or perhaps completely
strong shoots. A jocular saying among the many branches of the family
has it that, 'All the Chakris are neurotic.' While this is an exaggeration,
many members of the family have been prone to sudden outrageous
petulance in the face of a trifling frustration, to a strong exhibition of
equally self-willed obstinacy, or to pronounced if fleeting moodiness.

Ananda's father, Prince Mahidol, was an exceptionally fine man yet
not without these frailties. For example, once when waiting to go out
with his sister in Bangkok he was suddenly so overcome by exaspera-
tion at her delay that he jumped fully clothed into the nearest canal.
He abruptly threw up his naval career because the King refused him an
active role at sea; and being later refused the internship he wanted
at the Siriraj Hospital he as abruptly and obstinately (in the eyes of
his peers) went up north where he contracted his fatal illness. Such
incidents show that when confronted by a frustrating situation he
reacted with an abrupt decisiveness—which is the very word, decisiveness, that palace officials used about Ananda after his death
(see page 169).

Ananda was certainly his father's son in being thoughtful, idealistic
and kind, so that one is not surprised to find the Chakri frailties in
him too. As a small boy at the Mater Dei convent in Bangkok he was
one day rude to a classmate, and the Irish nun in charge told him to
apologize; when he did not, she shook him, whereupon to the class's
intense admiration he smacked her. Another time, the Princess Mother
was entertaining a visitor to tea in her usual informal manner and the
boys were helping to wait, when Ananda suddenly refused point-
blank to fetch something his mother asked for, and he had to be

packed off to his room. Recollections like these are hard to wrest from the legend which had arisen of Ananda's saintliness. They are in fact trifling enough, did they not show that a notably gentle and obedient boy was perfectly capable of all-too Chakri-like outbursts.

That these were not left behind with boyhood is proved by an episode which provides a most significant pointer to his state of mind in the last weeks of his life. The decision to visit the US and Great Britain prompted his advisers to suggest a date far enough ahead for adequate preparation, but Ananda suddenly and 'decisively', even petulantly, insisted upon a much earlier date, and refused to listen to any objection. His advisers were very surprised by such uncharacteristic behaviour. The reason for it, whether it reflected an inward anxiety to get the ordeal over quickly, or whether it involved a dispute with his mother, or whatever it was, may be put aside: for the moment let the phenomenon of this self-willed insistence stand alone, except to relate it to the unwonted moodiness exhibited to Butr within an hour of his death.

These facts tend to show that Ananda was quite capable of getting into what psychologists call a state of affective irritability. The significance of this may be measured by the following conclusion (here somewhat compressed) of a leading modern authority, whose use of the word 'affective' may roughly be defined as mood or intensity of feeling:

It is difficult to answer whether a mentally sound and normal individual will commit suicide during the pressure of unendurable external circumstances, because of the difficulty of defining what we mean by normal in this connection. The majority of suicides are committed in an affective state. A disproportion between the insignificance of the motive and the degree of seriousness of the reaction is often found. This points to the presence of an abnormal affective irritability or an abnormal tendency to make an affect result in an act. Even if the motives are sufficiently serious such an abnormality is perhaps the necessary prerequisite for the development of the suicide-bid. Deliberate suicide by mentally sound individuals certainly happens.[7]

Here we have the answer to why we may be incredulous on hearing that someone had killed himself whom we knew well and would not have classed as a 'suicide type': his very normality had obscured his occasional decisive—even disproportionate—reactions when pushed far enough. Ananda had this 'affective irritability'. As to the 'unendurable external circumstances', though the specialists make clear that these might be relatively trivial compared with the seriousness of the reaction (i.e. suicide), the circumstances already mentioned—the strain of adaptation and of being King—take us in fact only part of the way.

A visitor invited to tea at the Barompiman Hall during Ananda's last months, has told me how touched and quietly surprised he was to hear the King ask his mother's permission before having another piece of cake. In his memoirs[4] the then British Ambassador recalls attending a luncheon given at the Palace 'by King Ananda and the Princess Mother, a remarkably intelligent and attractive Siamese lady'; a few days later came the shocking news of Ananda's death: 'We felt deeply for his mother, the Princess, who only so recently had presided with such charm and grace over the palace luncheon.' These phrases leave no doubt that luncheon with the King meant luncheon with the Princess Mother. Moreover, my private information is that the majority of people commanded to the Palace came at her behest, not his—though always, as she believed, in his interest. The fact is that King or not, twenty years old or not, elder son or not, and male or not, Ananda deferred to his mother with the complaisance of a small boy.

If the observations of the British Army in India are forgotten (see page 212), it may be argued that his complaisance owed something to concern for his diet because of his stomach upsets; but these are themselves significant. They are not explicable merely by the change in conditions from the Villa Watana to the Barompiman Hall. Neither his brother nor mother had any trouble and he was probably stronger than they. His healthy life in Switzerland had produced a youth remarkably robust despite his slender build, as those who experienced his handshake became ruefully aware. When the Princess Mother first settled in Switzerland she retained a children's doctor, but later on she did not even need a family GP. It is the view of unimpeachable medical opinion that Ananda's stomach upsets in Bangkok were psychosomatic.

The truth is that the Princess Mother watched over rather more than Ananda's diet. She watched over the whole of him, over the whole of his life. All his years, and especially since her husband's death, she had regulated his coming and his going. A mother's devotion never went further than that of this remarkable woman who rose from obscure origins to breed and nurture two kings, and who asked of life nothing more than that she should do this successfully. But if the result was that she became the dominant factor in Ananda's life, her very concern brought a danger. It was that in his desire to please her—for he was gentle, loving and dutiful—he might be caught in conflict by thoughts and feeling displeasing to her. Had she been domineering he could perhaps have articulated a clear opposition to her. But it was not a simple issue of opposition. He wanted not to oppose but to please, while yet having the thoughts and feelings which were not merely normal in a youth struggling for adult self-assertion, but essential in one who had to act the King.

Self-assertion as a semi-adult, self-assertion as King: but could these selves be asserted against one whom he loved and all his life had obeyed? In this connection I was struck by a passage in an authority[8] discussing the high suicide rate among young people in pre-revolutionary Peking:

These facts can be well understood in the light of the traditional conservative and patriarchal culture with its great emphasis on filial piety and respect for the aged; with such an *ethos*, suicide-producing stresses must fall with especial severity on younger people, particularly young women constrained by the rigid family organization.

If we substitute a young man subject to a matriarchal discipline, the analogy with Ananda's circumstances is arresting.

Nothing I have written about the Princess Mother should leave an impression of some kind of ogre or over-possessive mother. Ananda's death is a tragedy of classic proportion because both he and those closest to him were—are—good people, and if you distilled the entirety of malice or evil in them you would have less than a raindrop to show for it. The Princess Mother had to bring up three children without a father, one of them to rule their country, amid the great flux and reflux of a restless world. Undaunted by her physical frailty she was sustained by the memory of her husband and a passionate sense of duty in her vigilance over Ananda, of whom she was the trustee for a nation.

She was sustained also by love; though Bhoomipol was her favourite.

It is usual enough for the younger of two brothers to come first in their mother's affection. The painfulness of Ananda's birth no doubt left some mark. And because Bhoomipol had not to be groomed for the crown, she could unconsciously feel more relaxed with and about him than Ananda. To this extent only were Ananda and his mother apart; and for this reason if no other, grief at his death took on the prolonged and terrible aspect of remorse.

The closeness of the family group, including secretary Nai Anek and M. Seraidaris, brought a sealing-off of the outside world, and if Ananda ventured into it to visit a friend M. Seraidaris accompanied him as an extension of his mother. Consequently when he felt keenly about something which might upset her he acted in secret. This is a normal growing pain of youth, and only the tragic denouement obliged me to investigate further.

In their evidence at the regicide trial the Princess Mother and Prince Bhoomipol said that prior to his last visit to Bangkok Ananda's sole acquaintance with firearms had been with airguns at fairs. I nevertheless asked M. Seraidaris bluntly whether Ananda ever had a pistol as a schoolboy: he replied emphatically not. The truth may surprise him. While Ananda was at the Ecole Nouvelle another boy offered to sell him a pistol in poor condition but workable, and Ananda much wanted it; being brought up on thrifty principles he lacked the cash, so he parted with an old typewriter to a schoolfriend who then bought the pistol for him.

This interest in firearms had an obvious stimulus in the war—and the war-game the royal brothers constantly played with the Greek—but the family's ignorance of the transaction is significant. Nor can another origin of Ananda's interest, though he was probably unaware of it, be overlooked in the genesis of his suicide. When he came to the throne in 1935 at the age of ten, the Regency Council appointed during his minority included his father's cousin Prince Oscar, a kindly man of fifty-two. That same year the Prince, distressed by political events, committed suicide by shooting himself in the head with a pistol. His death was a severe shock to the royal family who were deeply fond of him. There is a heredity factor of over six per cent in suicide cases; certainly the event must have bitten deep into the mind of a boy so compassionate that he felt sorry for cart-horses because they were not free to play like himself.

To the secret episode of the pistol during Ananda's late boyhood must now be added, from the close of his life, a story which likewise has never been told—nor known about except by three or four people who have stood scrupulous guard over it. The telling of it is a necessary climax to the story of Ananda, and incidentally the refutation of rumours, which continue to get a hearing, that Ananda had inherited his uncle King Rama VI's addiction to exclusively male company.

IV

In the same year that Ananda was born in Heidelberg, not very far to the south a daughter was born to a doctor of theology named Eugene Ferrari, pastor of the village of Grandson on the shores of Lake Neuchâtel, about twenty-five miles west of Lausanne. The pastor and his wife already had a son who was to grow up to be a doctor of medicine. They called their daughter Marylene. When she was about five the family moved to Lausanne, to the Avenue Verdeil in a well-to-do quarter of that well-to-do city. The houses there are large and placid in a setting of trees and bushy gardens, and the Ferraris took a commodious apartment within such a house. The pastor rose to eminence: he is today one of the six presidents—in effect the archbishops—of the Swiss Calvinist Church. He is a tall well-built man with a somewhat olive complexion derived from his Italian ancestry, his features firmly moulded, his manner friendly but aloof. His homely and hospitable wife devoted herself to him and the two children who grew up in a happy and unrepressive atmosphere, for all that Calvin himself might have advocated strangling disobedient children.

When Ananda matriculated from the Ecole Nouvelle and went to the law school of the University of Lausanne in September 1943, the only girl in the class of about thirteen was Marylene Ferrari. Her attractiveness in the bloom of youth may be guessed from the mature woman: a well-shaped figure, hazel eyes, fine teeth, rich brown hair; her tanned skin and slight accent suggest the country, but she has also sophisticated qualities of toughness and control which suggest the city; she smiles joyfully, but not often; and she speaks honestly, but not often. In particular she rarely speaks about Ananda, and in this resembles the Princess Mother whom she met only a few times in Ananda's lifetime and never since.

For six months a friendship slowly grew between the King of Siam and the Swiss pastor's daughter. They tended to sit next to each other at lectures. They met at small afternoon gatherings in other students' houses to which M. Seraidaris also went, as he did when Ananda several times called at the Ferraris' house. When a group of students was once or twice invited to the Villa Watana, Marylene was included. They played tennis together with other students at the Club Montchoisi. Except that Ananda, sedulously kept from the public eye, never went to coffee-houses or bars or restaurants, and the visits of friends to his own house were rare, he appeared to be like any of his fellow students in enjoying the casual acquaintance of each other, including Marylene.

Nevertheless the Princess Mother's instinct prompted her to have a serious talk with Ananda. She reminded him of his duty towards his people, who would not accept his marrying a Westerner. No one needed less reminding of his duty than Ananda, and accustomed as the Princess Mother was to his implicit obedience she was not surprised by his assurance that he would obey her in this respect as in every other. On Marylene's side, there was equally a warning-off. The pastor, with a sturdy Calvinist and Swiss democratic indifference to the dazzlement of a throne, made clear that while liking Ananda personally he would oppose marriage to an oriental because of the inferior status of women in the East.

However, there seemed nothing in the situation to alarm the elders in either camp, no question of barring meetings, and the policy of both was to keep the relationship at its pleasant student-acquaintance level. But instead of staying there it took wing, however much Ananda and Marylene might have tried to will otherwise, and perhaps it could not have been otherwise willed when two young people in the liberating atmosphere of a university felt so drawn to each other. An observer at close quarters recalls the romance as a 'lyrical mystical relationship'. They exchanged vows to tell no one and held unswervingly to this pledge. The ubiquitous M. Seraidaris continued to be present at student gatherings; he accompanied Ananda once when he and Marylene went to a cinema and another time to a concert; the couple attended the university ball but—sweet anguish—in separate parties. They were models of discretion. But secretly they contrived to be alone with each other whenever they could make opportunity.

While this was often only a hurried encounter between lectures,

234

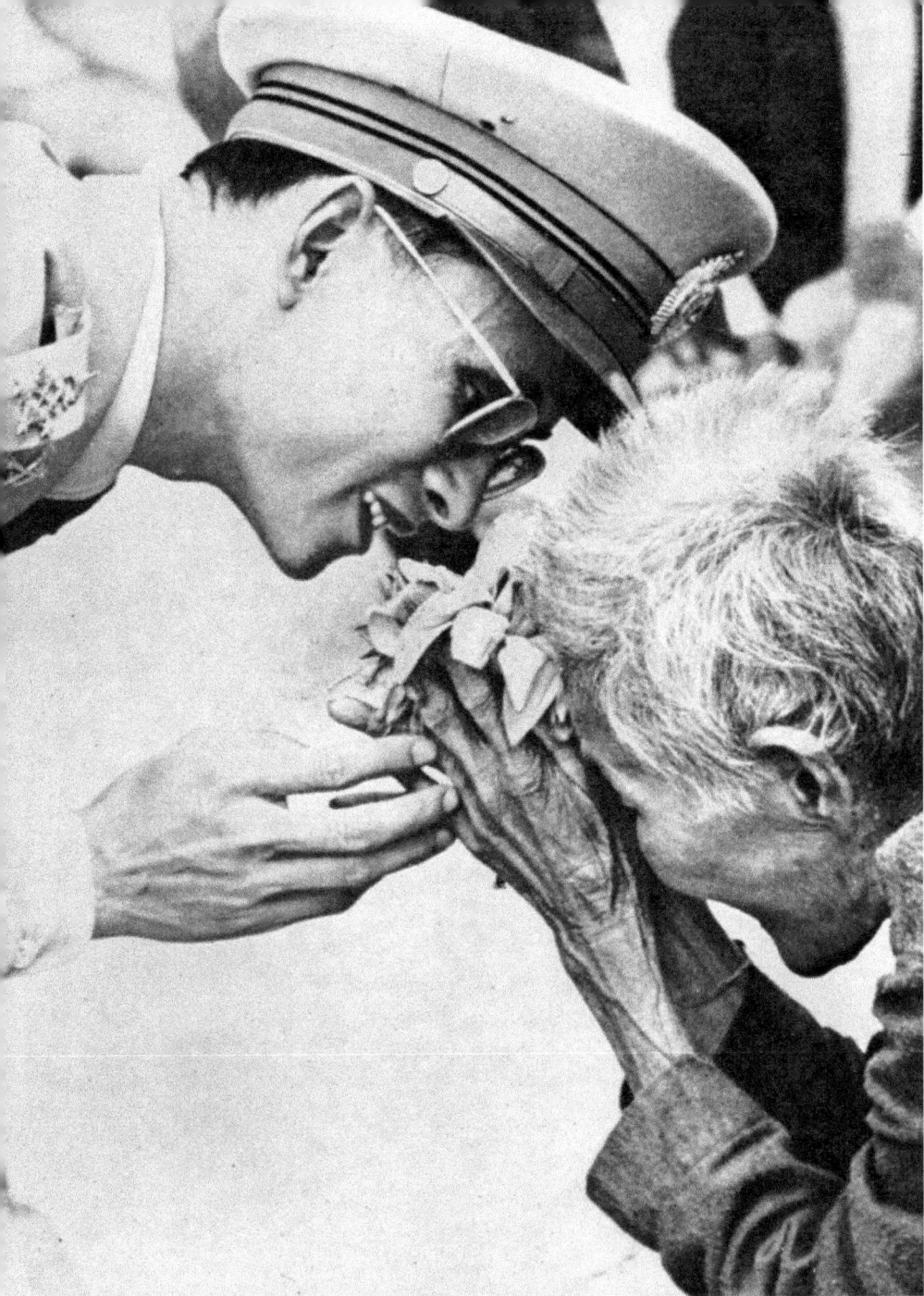

During a tour of the provinces King Bhoomipol, hearing that he had passed by an old woman who had been waiting for hours to present him with a lotus flower, turned back and sought her out. The flower had long since withered, but not the reverence and joy of the woman, who typifies the attitude of the great mass of Siamese people towards their monarch

Marylene Ferrari

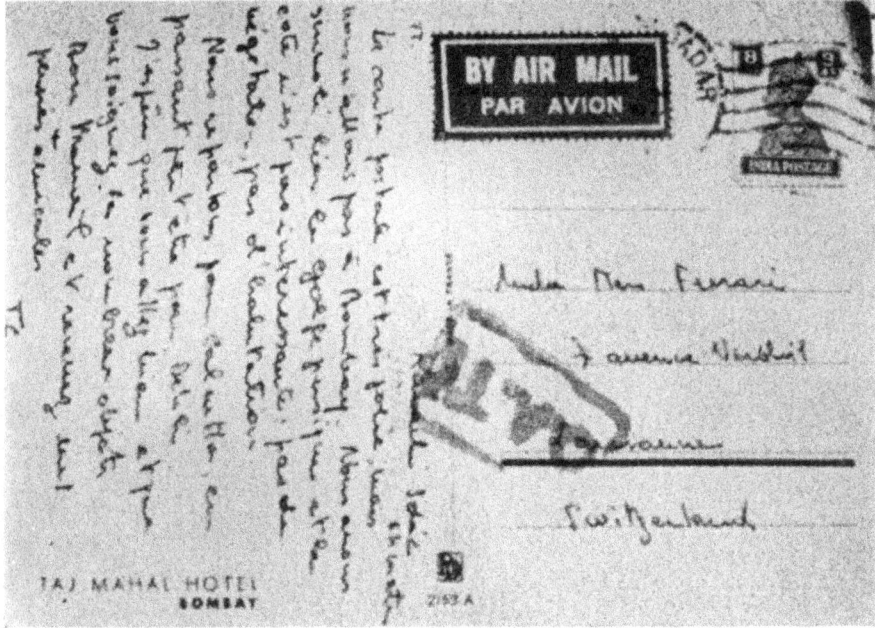

The Karachi postcard

Karachi 3 Dec. [1945]
6 in the morning

The postcard is very pretty, but we are not going to Bombay. Yesterday we flew over the Persian Gulf and the coast was not interesting: no vegetation, no habitation.
We leave again for Calcutta, perhaps Delhi in passing.
I hope you are well and that you are taking good care of the numerous objects.
Work hard and receive my friendly* thoughts.

T.C.

A broken FM Pibul speaking to reporters after his final interview with Field-Marshal Sarit

Field-Marshal Sarit Dhanaret, the dictator of Siam, September 1957–December 1963

every other week they cut lectures and cycled alone together: they rode five or six miles out of the city—southwards by the lake, eastwards to the vineyards, or among the woods in the north and west. At other times, first announcing himself by a telephone call which would send the Ferraris scurrying to tidy up, Ananda frequently visited the Avenue Verdeil. Mrs Ferrari took a mother's innocent pleasure in her daughter's obvious happiness with Ananda, whose modesty, beneficial influence and gentle good manners won her complete respect: she left them alone. Once, someone chanced to come in and found them chasing each other as if playing bears, but the frivolities of love had mostly to yield to the seriousness of their natures which could seldom throw off the awareness, acknowledged to each other, of the seeming impossibility of marriage.

More often they talked long and earnestly, taking all the world for their subject but most frequently Siam: Ananda taught her its alphabet and constantly spoke about its future progress. Often too, they worked together at their law books or she sang while he accompanied her on the Ferraris' upright. Impressed by her voice he suggested she learn singing; which, to please him, she did. In law, music, whatever she attempted, he urged her to strive to her utmost. He was disappointed when she failed in the first part of their law examinations which he passed, and he helped her prepare for a renewed attempt. The results came out while he was in Bangkok, so she sent him a cable announcing her success. The cable was signed OOLIRAM—the backwards spelling of Mariloo, her nickname. His was Bicot, a character in Swiss nursery tales.

Holidays enforced a separation but they contrived to correspond, and in the summer vacation of 1945 the Ferrari family by happy coincidence rented a house in the Valais at Champex where the Mahidol family stayed at an hotel, and as a chalet run by the Ecole Nouvelle was also in the vicinity the concourse of young people gave the lovers many chances of meeting.

For the greater part of eighteen months they had been living a secret idyll by shutting out the world. But when they arrived back from Champex the world came rushing in with Pridi's cable of 6 September inviting Ananda, upon achieving his majority later that month, to return to his capital. Even so, the visit was to be brief, and afterwards two years at least would remain for the idyll to continue:

at least two years: enough, for lovers, to push the frowning future out of sight and mind.

On 20 September, Ananda's twentieth birthday was celebrated at the Villa Watana to which only Siamese were invited. He and Mary-lene had their private festivity when she gave him a silver paper knife. On occasion he gave her small token gifts, for he had little spare cash, but his biggest gift could not be bought, a journal he had carefully compiled of all their activities together: time shared, treasured, and preserved. Before he left for Bangkok early in December he brought her all the letters, souvenirs and other tokens he had received from her, to be looked after and kept against his return. This was a pre-caution lest discovery was made during the packing-up to leave, or by the attendants who would have charge of his possessions in Bangkok; but he kept the silver paper knife. They also made careful arrangements for communicating with each other, using as code names their nicknames spelt backwards. On the day Ananda left he telephoned her twice. The second occasion was from the airport when for a moment he eluded the swarm of journalists who little guessed at the scoop they were missing. He had time only to say a hurried *au revoir*.

At Karachi, where the plane came down in the early hours of the morning, he scribbled her a discreet postcard. It concluded: *I hope you are well and that you are taking good care of the numerous objects. Work hard and receive my friendly thoughts.* He put a kiss sign over the word friendly, and signed the card *T.C.* (from Bicot in reverse).

From the time he arrived in Bangkok he wrote to her at least every other week. An occasional cable or letter went via his sister (kept in Lausanne by her new-born baby), and even M. Seraidaris—but no more than would sustain the pretence of mere student acquaintance-ship. The bulk of his letters went direct to the Avenue Verdeil. Her letters went direct to the Barompiman Hall where they were protected from prying eyes by Ananda's instruction that all correspondence from Switzerland should go to him personally. He complained to her that she was not writing to him enough; and in March when the prolongation of his visit was making him feel their separation more intensely, he cabled her: *Please write more intimately.*

By first post on Monday morning 10 June 1946, she had a letter from him which stated that a number of high-born women had been presented to him: *One of these*, he wrote, *might become my wife*. Ominous words, cold with outward reality from which he retreated to the warm inward reality of his idyll: *I can't wait to get back to Lausanne*. Such a cry at least would have struck sparks of joy from the girl's heart. But it was a shattered heart. On the radio the previous night the news had been given out that he was dead.

Journalists converged on the Villa Watana round which the Swiss Government threw a guard, and they nosed out Ananda's fellow students for background stories to the extraordinary happening in Bangkok. Inevitably they encountered the name of a woman student, Marylene Ferrari. Had she by any wild chance been his sweetheart? They besieged the mansion at the top of the Avenue Verdeil. M. Seraidaris had been quick on the draw: the royal family then maintained and to this day believes that Marylene was a mere acquaintance like any other student in Ananda's class; nevertheless the Greek urged her to keep quiet lest the newspapers made more of the acquaintance than he thought justified. Indeed, her mother kept her in her room for eight successive days until the journalists, gaining nothing from their vigil, went away. Rumour faded into silence where it has ever since been kept by the disbelief of the royal family and the rigorous discretion of the Ferraris.

The story of Ananda and Marylene adds a footnote to the regicide trial. So unsatisfactory in much else, the judgement, and especially the judges' assessment of the suicide possibilities, loses almost all meaning when one remembers that scarcely any evidence was led concerning Ananda's Lausanne background. Since they actually went to Switzerland the opportunity was not lacking. At the very least they might have been enabled to deduce whose letters Ananda burnt the day before he died.

Was there one letter he did not burn, that Butr said he saw in the Princess Mother's hand as she beat her foot on the floor while Bhoomipol walked up and down wanting to do something (tell the Palace Meeting?) which she opposed? Did she suspect the true extent of Ananda's feelings for the girl and urge him to curb them before returning to Lausanne, and was this the occasion of the rumoured quarrel between them?

But the testimonies of both the Princess Mother and Bhoomipol have no reference to such a letter or the girl, both insist that there were no quarrels, and really we have no need to speculate on the subject: the significant fact is that the Princess Mother has never subscribed, in public or private, before the Commission of Inquiry or the trial court, or for her intimates, to any theory whatever concerning her son's death.

At the Berne sittings of the court she merely replied, as she was obliged, to the prosecution's questions, which were all angled at drawing out every possible detail unfavourable to the accused and Pridi. There was no cross-examination to correct the balance. Police-General Pao and his men went on that trip to Switzerland, and they gave out all sorts of 'inside' information to convince even the former admirers of Pridi in the Princess Mother's circle that he had committed a diabolical crime. But she herself has never condemned him nor laid the blame on anyone. She is too brave and honest a woman to blame without certainty, and proof or disproof of anything—murder, suicide, accident—was so circumstantial that she never speculated on something so terrible and inexplicable. Shock and grief drove her into herself. The mills of politics and law ground slowly, at a great distance, for she was in Switzerland all the years of the trials and their upshot; and if, by the execution of the two pages and Chaleo, the Buddha's lotus was confused with the Devil's lethal discus, this was not for her to judge. She could not judge, any more than she could have altered the fate of these men which multiplied many times over the tragedy of her son's death.

Little more remains to be said of it.

A leading authority on suicide coined[9] not long ago the word hypereridism which has some currency among psychiatrists. He defined it as a state of morbid tension arising from a series of provocations which might result in 'explosive behaviour rather more aggressive than is appropriate to a given set of circumstances'. We are back upon the trail started in the last chapter. A hypereridic suicide has the following characteristics: Socially he is subordinate to another person, usually a parent, and is under provocation by the latter; he may have an aggressive nature but is also often unusually meek and yielding ('meek and obedient' were the Royal Nanny's words for Ananda); precipitating causes of the suicide include not only an acute quarrel but even a minor reprimand; inducive to suicide by a young person are circumstances strongly requiring family conformity and obedience.

238

These characteristics, like those I have mentioned as significant in the opinion of other authorities, apply with remarkable aptness to Ananda; though the allegation of a quarrel remains unproven, this authority's explanation does not exclude a tiff or motherly reprimand so minor that the Princess Mother thought nothing of it. But perhaps the most illuminating commentary of all is to be found in Freudian ideas. The able exposition of them by an American authority, Karl A. Menninger[10], may be summarized thus:

We have two primary instincts, the life-wish expressed by love or constructiveness and the death-wish expressed by hostility or destructiveness. As we develop we externalize these instincts, which keep in balance. But if our full development is prevented, or because of the behaviour of someone loved, the balance is upset. Our hostility then becomes paramount. It can erupt into the murder of the object of our hostility, or if we are intimidated by the consequences or if enough love remains to check us, it turns in upon itself. The result is suicide if we *wish to die*, which is the primary death-wish in command; if we *wish to be killed*, which is the product of a guilty conscience demanding punishment for thoughts as well as deeds; and if we *wish to kill*, identifying with ourselves the object of our hostility (like the Japanese who commits suicide on his creditor's doorstep).

This last process, like the other two wishes, is mostly or wholly unconscious though 'it may have been conscious once or occasionally but been repressed, disguised by a conscious attitude of love, protection, obedience.' Menninger's words stir one's memory of Ananda's conspicuous solicitude for his mother, and of his obedience. The crux of the theory is that although it posits a turning-in upon the self, the self actually treats its body as an external object or as if it included someone else's body. The capacity to do this is a commonplace of the unconscious; and it may even have been strengthened in Ananda if, having suddenly at the age of ten found himself King, he never quite fused the two beings of man and monarch.

Whether or not we accept these particular ideas, whichever way we consider the question, what are we inescapably left with but the certainty that Ananda took his own life? And when all is said by the wise men and their books, the mind's eye is informed by simple intuition to see the simple truth. A young man lies alone, his resistance lowered by illness, and brooding upon himself as lover, as son, as king, he is engulfed by hopelessness; he sits up and stretches out for a weapon whose kind has long fascinated him, a kind of familiar; he holds it up; perhaps there is no conscious cause and effect, merely instinct, release in decisiveness, and his hands close around the butt, harder, pressing trigger and safety spring: so simply, in a thousandth of one second, the thing is done.

In this a possibility remains, that Ananda held the pistol with the idle, unhappy but not homicidal thought, 'This is what I should do if I were to do it', and then the thought undeliberately stumbled into action. It is a possibility that cannot be disproved. Someone closely connected with the regicide case put it to me privately, and I pass it on for those who still cannot accept suicide plain and know the improbability of accident simple.

What can no longer be argued is that three innocent men were done to death by a corrupt régime illegally brought into being upon a false prospectus; and that of the two men wrongly exiled one is the most considerable in modern Siamese history, his absence a continuing loss to his homeland. And if either Siam or the fate of obscure individuals means little because Justice no longer sounds its ancient call to the conscience of the living, at least the peace of the world is cause enough to demand our awareness.

FM Pibul returned from his triumphant tour in 1955 intent on playing his new role of defender of the West's democratic faith. Inspired by Speakers' Corner at Hyde Park in London he designated a corner of the Pramane Ground for free speech, until he and Police-General Pao found this outlet for public criticism altogether too upsetting. He also announced that in a few years the nominated half of the Assembly, which always ensured his own majority, would be replaced by deputies elected on a popular franchise the same as the others, for whom he meanwhile held a general election (February 1957). His party gained a narrow win over the Democrat Party, but agitation at alleged vote-rigging in this so-called Dirty Election burst out for the first time into public demonstrations, and students massed on the lawns of FM Pibul's official palace.

Now ever since Pibul's restoration to power by the 1947 *coup d'état*, one of the *coup* leaders had been growing in importance. This was the then Bangkok garrison commander, a man of Laos extraction named Sarit, who had become head of the army and a growing rival to

Police-General Pao, whose villainies he resolved to end as soon as he could. The outcry at the Dirty Election gave him his opportunity. He threw down the gauntlet by sending for FM Pibul—a gesture eloquent enough to remind FM Pibul too late of the lesson he had once so well learnt, that who commands the army commands Siam. He returned from the interview to pack his bags.

In the years since, he has lived in California, in India where he entered a monastery for some months, and finally in Japan where he now has his home. Police-General Pao, whose last pathetic claim to importance was a lie that the condemned men in the regicide case had told him 'the true facts' on the morning of their execution, fled to Switzerland: he died there in 1960—in the agony of delirium tremens, or so popular fancy depicts the Butcher of Bangkok, his ill-gotten millions useless and a mockery. And Field-Marshal Sarit ruled Thailand as dictator until his death in December 1963.

Corruption continues on a huge scale. Siamese economists say (very quietly) that if it could be ended, foreign aid would not be required. Corruption has become a state of mind, as easily reconciled with patriotic qualms as the Thai lorry driver's habit, when he wants to go in by the OUT gate, of simply entering it backwards in the belief that thereby law and personal convenience have been happily reconciled. No branch of society is immune from corruption. The army, for example, is said to own a bank, radio station, television studio, newspaper, night club, bus company, factories and other lucrative sources of baht for the favoured. The truth or otherwise of such allegations* is of no consequence: what is, is that the prevailing state of mind among the public should be so ready to believe them.

But there have been gains. Sarit did more than rid the streets of flies and filth, more than shoot a few well-insured incendiarists as an example to others. He restored some measure of dignity to Siam's national life and international status by his personal bearing, his ready co-operation with United Nations' agencies, and his support of extensive schemes for economic and social progress.

But such personal dictatorships and the continuing corruption direly threaten the future. The West, and especially the US, can do better

---

* Sarit himself, though greatly respected, was not immune even in his lifetime: his alleged number of 'wives'—estimates varied between twenty and seventy—led rumour on to assume a vast discrepancy between the cost of maintaining them and his official salary.

than merely lavish arms and money on anyone who opposes communism. That policy did not work in China, or Vietnam, or Laos:
why should it work in Thailand, the next and worse potential source
of international crisis? As the headquarters of SEATO and at the centre
of the vast areas ranging from India through the Antipodes to the
Pacific, it is one of the chief fulcrums of the precariously balanced
see-saw of international power. The time has come when the West,
for its own sake if no one else's, should show impatience with the old
excuse of despotism that Siam is not ready for democracy. Even if the
price to be paid is Siam's withdrawal from SEATO and alignment
with the neutralist bloc, encouragement of true democracy may at least
avoid the anti-West revulsion the present policy threatens to promote.

Among young people in Thailand today, especially the products of
the universities, there is great and growing frustration at the lack of
democratic opportunity. Among them the name Pridi still sounds like
a clarion call to freedom and to social justice, despite ceaseless propaganda of his alleged communism. This propaganda is based on allegations that he broadcasts anti-West speeches from Peking and that he
is the creature of the Chinese communists among whom he lives.
The fact is that some years ago he wrote a letter to the press, urging
the King to use his wealth rather than American aid to help finance a
proposed canal between the Indian Ocean and the Gulf of Siam: this
letter was read in Peking news broadcasts. He has not made any
broadcasts himself; nor does he live anywhere near Peking, though he
lives in China true enough because until the Siamese Government or
the West acknowledge his complete innocence he cannot safely or
without fear of extradition go anywhere else. The Chinese hope that
when revolution breaks out in Siam he will lead the insurgents and
be bound by Chinese influence. Whether he will—if exile, the ebbing
of his life, pressure by his hosts, and concern for his country have not
already committed him—depends primarily on the Siamese Government.

During Sarit's régime I asked him whether he would agree to a
panel of international jurists examining all the evidence in the regicide
trial and whether, if this panel exonerated the three executed men and
the two exiles, he would permit Pridi to resume normal life in Siam.
Sarit made no reply. His successor, General Dhanom Kittikachorn, is
too recent to dare grasp the nettle.

The onus therefore passes largely to King Bhoomipol, now the happy father of four children. Over the years he has increased in stature, and he enjoys increasing respect among responsible observers of the Siamese scene. Previously powerless to affect the course of events, he may now, if the contents of this book are placed before him, be advised for the honour of his country and the survival of his throne to urge upon his Government the course I suggested to Field-Marshal Sarit. Even honour and survival are small objectives besides the greatness which the Siamese have it in them to achieve. Given the political framework of a true democratic-constitutional monarchy, and inspired to work for social progress, they could with their happy natures spread beneficence over a large segment of the world. But the need is for the purge of self-honesty that would obliterate the wrongs of the regicide case and cure the disease of corruption. And the West must help by insisting more than hitherto on the moralities and splendours of democracy.

The Chinese have a saying that no one keeps a chicken unless to lay an egg: certainly Pridi has laid no egg for them yet. He lives in modest comfort in a house they have lent him, with a secretary and chauffeur also provided by them. Whatever his political interests, he works at translations or at a philosophical work in which he seeks to interpret Buddhism in the context of the modern world. His hair is prematurely grey; he takes a little wine at meals, but he has had to give up smoking his Gauloises. Siamese refugees, communist and non-communist, come to him, the Mentor of old, and he tells them to take heart. One day the tragedy of Ananda will no longer send its repercussions into the world of power politics; and all the restless ghosts which that event sent forth in torment, including Ananda's own, may end their wanderings.

It will be a good day. Until then, I will not write finis to this curious tale.

SOME OF THE *DRAMATIS PERSONAE*

The Chakri dynasty:

Chulalongkorn, fifth of the line, King from 1868 to 1910.

Rama VI: King from 1910 to 1925 ⎱ Half-brothers of Prince Mahidol.
Prajadhipok: King, 1925–1935 ⎰ All sons of Chulalongkorn.

Ananda: King from 1935 to 1946
Bhoomipol: King since 1946

⎧ With their sister Galyani these were the children of Prince Mahidol and Princess Mahidol (Sangwalya; later the Princess Mother). ⎭

———

Aditya, Prince Regent ('Regent Aditya'): one-time Regent.

Anek ('Nai Anek') Subrabhaya: Secretary to the Princess Mother in Lausanne.

Bahol, Colonel: one of the 1932 'Promoters'; Prime Minister 1933–8.

Butr Paramasrin: a page of the royal bedchamber.

Chaleo ('Secretary Chaleo') Patoomros: businessman; politician; Secretary to Ananda in Bangkok; senator.

Chit ('Nai Chit') Singhaseni: a page of the royal bedchamber.

Cha-oom: wife of Lt Vacharachai.

Dennis, Captain Stratford Hercules: British Naval Attaché in Bangkok.

Dhamrong, Admiral: Pridi's successor as Prime Minister until the 1947 *coup d'état*.

Fak Nasongkhla: leading defence counsel in the regicide trial.

Ferrari, Marylene: a student in Lausanne.

Gardas, 'Skeats': US Naval Attaché in Bangkok.

Kuang ('Great Comedian') Abhaiwongse: one of the 'Promoters'; twice Prime Minister; leader of the Democrat Party.

Kukrit Pramoj, Mom: journalist and politician; brother of Mom Seni Pramoj.

Nitayavejvisidh ('Dr Nit'): former Royal Physician.

Mee: a page, witness in the regicide trial.

Pao Siyanon, Police-General: a leader in the 1947 *coup d'état*, called the 'Butcher of Bangkok'.

Phinich ('Detective Phinich') Chonkadi, Police-General Phra: chief investigator in preparation of prosecution case for the regicide trial.

Pibul ('FM Pibul') Songgram, Field-Marshal.

Pridi (the 'Mentor') Banamyong.

Rangsit, Prince: Ananda's uncle; imprisoned after FM Pibul's 1938 purge; Regent after Ananda's death.

Sarit Dhanaret, Field-Marshal: a leader in the 1947 *coup d'état*, dictator of Siam 1957-63.

Sawang, Queen: one of Chulalongkorn's wives and mother of Prince Mahidol.

See: a gunman.

Seni Pramoj, Mom: lawyer, formerly Ambassador to the US, founder of the Free Thai Movement, and Prime Minister; deputy leader of the Democrat Party; brother of Mom Kukrit Pramoj.

Seraidaris, Cleon O.: one of the royal brothers' tutors in Lausanne.

Sirikit, Queen: wife of King Bhoomipol.

Stanton, Edwin: US Ambassador in Bangkok.

Subha Svasti, Prince ('Tahn Chin'): soldier grandson of Mongkut and brother of Prajadhipok's Queen; head of British end of Free Thai Movement.

Thompson, Sir Geoffrey: British Ambassador in Bangkok.

Vacharachai, Lt: ADC to Pridi and Ananda; Secretary to Ananda and Admiral Dhamrong.

REFERENCES

1 Or so legend has it.
2 Prince Chula Chakrabongse in *The Twain Have Met*.
3 Aram Ratanakul.
4 Sir Geoffrey Thompson, *Front Line Diplomat*.
5 David Stafford-Clark, *Psychiatry Today*.
6 Brierre de Boismont.
7 Karl Gustav Dahlgren, *On Suicide & Attempted Suicide*.
8 P. M. Yap, *Suicide in Hong Kong*.
9 E. Lindemann, *Epidemiology of Mental Disorder*.
10 Karl A. Menninger, *Man Against Himself*.

In addition to the works mentioned above, other sources of information about Siam include the following, though the reader should be warned that some not called novels properly belong to that category:

Barnett, David: *The Mask of Siam*.

Blanchard, Wendell (and others): *Thailand*.

Busch, Noel: *Thailand*.

Chula Chakrabongse, Prince: *Lords of Life*.

Churchill, Winston S.: *The Second World War*.

Collis, Maurice: *Siamese White*.

Crosby, J.: *Siam: The Crossroads*.

Deignan, H. G.: *Siam—Land of Free Men*.

Gilbert, O. D. G.: *Men in Women's Clothes* (re Phaulkon).

Gunther, J.: *Inside Asia*.

Hammerstein, O.: *The King & I* (book of musical comedy).

Korwong, K., and Rangthong, J.: *A New Guide to Bangkok*.

Landon, K. P.: *Siam in Transition.*

Lederer, W. J., and Burdick, E.: *The Ugly American* (novel).

Lightwood, Teresa: *Teresa of Siam.*

MacDonald, Alexander: *Bangkok Editor.*

Maugham, Somerset: *The Gentleman in the Parlour.*

Polo, Marco: *Travels.*

Rangthong, J.: *A Week in Bangkok.*

Reynolds, Jack: *A Woman of Bangkok* (novel).

Sayre, F. B.: *Glad Adventure.*

Sivaram, M.: *The New Siam in the Making.*

Smith, Malcolm: *A Physician at the Court of Siam.*

Sparrow, Gerald: *Land of the Moonflower; Return Ticket; The Star Sapphires; Murder Parade.*

INDEX

Abhaiwongsi, Kuang ('The Great Comedian'), 78, 104, 119, 164, 167; as temporary Premier to bluff Japanese, 68–9; again Premier, 83, 84; resigns, 84, 85, 86, 87; monarchist sympathies, 84, 195, 213; Premier after 1947 *coup*, 115, 120; retires, 121

accident theory: official announcement, 98–9, 103–4, 219; Bhoomipol's acceptance of, 100, 209, 211; rejected by Commission of Inquiry, 109–10, 111; Dr Nit's belief in, 136–7, 143: alleged 'cover-up', 143, 144; believed ruled out by pistol tests, 148, 211; rejected by judges, 184; arguments for, 209–10

Adam, William, 118, 119

Aditya, Regent, 63, 66, 67, 78, 90, 170

America, 63; treaty with Siam, 12; Siam declares war on, 63, 64; Free Thai Movement in, 65; occupies Siam after Japanese defeat, 69; post-war discontent, 72; and Britain's treaty with Siam, 82; invites Ananda for state visit, 88, 89, 164; supports Pibul as anticommunist, 193

Ananda, King: ancestry, 8–17, 23, 32–5; birth at Heidelberg, 21, 23, 35; early years in Boston, 35–6; education in Bangkok, 38–9; in Lausanne after 1932 Revolution, 41, 42–3, 51, 53–4; accepts throne, 31, 41; education at Lausanne,

43–4, 52, 53, 54–5, 233–4; character, 44, 49, 54, 73, 86, 134, 137, 164, 169, 221, 227–30, 238–9; first official visit to Siam, 44, 48–50, 58, 59; relationship with brother, 53, 135, 137, 164, 209–12; relationship with mother, 53, 55, 86, 164, 166, 212, 229–31; at Lausanne Law School, 54–5, 70, 233–4; invited by Pridi to take up duties as king, 57–8, 70, 235; agrees to return for short visit, 70–1; arrival in Bangkok, 72–3, 74; domestic surroundings and household, 74–9; daily routine, 79–80; interest in firearms and shooting, 80, 163–4, 198, 209–10, 231; common interests with Pridi, 86; signs proclamation of Pridi's renewed premiership, 88, 90; prepares for return to Switzerland, 88–9, 132–3; invited to visit Britain and America, 88, 143, 228; last public visit, to Chinese quarter, 89, 195–6; disagrees with Pridi over Regency Council, 90, 105, 142, 166, 195–6; indisposition, 90–1, 136, 142; last hours of, 91–4, 172, 175, 184; found shot, 94–6, 149–50, 164–5, 173, 174, 202; death, discussed by Palace Meeting, 97–8; announced as accidental, 98–9, 100, 103–4, 136, 143, 219; body prepared for cremation, 100–2; assassination rumours, 103–5, 106, 169; alleged abdication plan, 105, 131,

Vacharachai,—*contd.*
 career, 197–8; case against, 197,
 199–200; author's belief in innocence, 200, 216
Vietnam, 143 *n*

white elephants, 7–8, 10, 15, 41
women, status of, 9–10

Youth Movement, 61

ABOUT THE AUTHOR

Charles Rayne Kruger was born in 1922 at Queenstown, South Africa, to the daughter of a British military officer, and died in 2002, at age 80, in the United Kingdom. The young Kruger studied at Witwatersrand University but was expelled for a schoolboy prank; thereafter he embarked on an eclectic list of endeavours including miner, law clerk, merchant mariner, lawyer, property developer, newspaper operator and restauranteur, the latter together with his wife, Prudence Leith, a much celebrated chef.

Throughout his early years, he pursued a successful writing career, as an author of both fiction and non-fiction, as well as occasional journalist and playwright. *The Devil's Discus* (1964) was a product of this phase of Kruger's multifaceted life, and its publication earned him a ban on ever returning to the Kingdom of Thailand.

Lightning Source UK Ltd.
Milton Keynes UK
UKHW011223180321
380575UK00002B/380